CRAZY STUPID SEX

DR. BARB'S GUIDE TO KEEPING IT SAFE

© 2018 Barbara Keesling
All rights reserved. This book or any portion thereof may not be reproduced or used in any manner whatsoever without the express written permission of the publisher except for the use of brief quotations in a book review.

ISBN 978-0-692-08661-2

Book design © John H. Matthews
www.BookConnectors.com

CRAZY STUPID SEX

DR. BARB'S GUIDE TO KEEPING IT SAFE

BARBARA KEESLING, PH.D.

ALSO BY BARBARA KEESLING

Sexual Healing

Sexual Pleasure

How to Make Love All Night

Rx Sex: Making Love is the Best Medicine

Talk Sexy to the One You Love

All Night Long

Getting Close

Super Sexual Orgasm

Sex So Great She Can't Get Enough

The Good Girl's Guide to Bad Girl Sex

Making Love Better Than Ever

Men in Bed

DISCLAIMER

This is a book for adults. It is sexually explicit. It is not intended to offend. Some sexual behaviors described in this book are illegal and/or dangerous. The author does not advocate any sexual behaviors that are dangerous or illegal. The author is not responsible or accountable for actions or feelings of future readers of this book.

CONTENTS

INTRODUCTION 1

CHAPTER 1 9
The Genius of the Penis

CHAPTER 2 29
The Perils of the Penis

CHAPTER 3 51
Vaginacology 101

CHAPTER 4 75
Advanced Vaginacology

CHAPTER 5 89
Who, How, What, Where ?

CHAPTER 6 119
Contraception

CHAPTER 7 — 137
Sexually Transmitted Infections

CHAPTER 8 — 151
Paraphilias

CHAPTER 9 — 179
Extreme Masochism

CHAPTER 10 — 191
Anal Eroticism

CHAPTER 11 — 205
Sexual Coercion

CHAPTER 12 — 235
Sex For Sale

CHAPTER 13 — 269
Making Sexual Decisions

AUTHOR BIOGRAPHY — 291

SELECTED REFERENCES — 293

INTRODUCTION

Every year, thousands of people in the United States seek medical help for conditions related to sexuality. Some of these people see their personal physician because they need contraception or because they have contracted a sexually transmitted infection. Some seek emergency room services because they have been the victim of a rape or sexual assault. Still others need emergency medical services because they were the victim of an accident while having sex, or they injured themselves while engaged in solitary sexual practices. All of these situations can result in lost wages and lost productivity.

The cornerstones of safe sex up to this point have been preventing unwanted pregnancy, preventing sexually transmitted infections, and avoiding being the victim of sexual coercion. Typical safe sex advice includes abstaining totally from sex, using a condom, and using effective contraceptive methods.

Crazy Stupid Sex takes this advice several steps farther. The book does include chapters on contraception, sexually transmitted infections, and sexual coercion. It also includes chapters on other dangers to the male and female genitals. It includes a chapter on accidents that can occur during sex. There are several chapters on the paraphilias—so-called "abnormal" sexual behaviors, some of which can be quite dangerous. Prostitution and use of sexually explicit materials are also included.

All of these chapters are written with an eye toward the physical safety and/or dangers related to these sexual practices. The final chapter is about emotional safety. Just because something does not involve physical risks doesn't mean it's necessarily a good idea.

Is *Crazy Stupid Sex* a sexuality textbook? Not really. It does contain material such as contraceptive information and facts about sexually transmitted infections. In addition, it contains my perspective on all of the topics, honed from several decades of teaching this material. Some of the content of this book occurs in any textbook on sex. The difference here is that I've added my own perspective from years of experience not only having sex myself, but talking to clients. I knew there was a reason I had all that sex!

Crazy Stupid Sex also includes historical anecdotes and information about cross-cultural diversity. That's a reflection on my education and training—the field of sexology is interdisciplinary.

There is information about accidents and/or medical conditions that can affect your sex life. There is material about negative consequences that can occur in sexual situations and material about physically dangerous practices. There are anecdotes about unintended consequences of sexual behavior. Some of these cases involve bad luck, and in some cases, people brought problems on themselves. Some of these stories are funny, some are tragic, some are disturbing, some are horrifying, and some are just plain stupid. Most chapters include "Safe Sex Rules", some of which are humorous. Some chapters don't contain specific safe sex rules, because the whole chapter is basically a safe sex rule; for example, "Protect yourself from being the victim of a sexual predator", or "Don't have sex without contraception."

Some of the events in *Crazy Stupid Sex* happened to me or my acquaintances—students, friends, clients. (Names have been changed). I got others from books, journal articles, newspapers, and the Internet. I have done my best to verify them in all cases. This book is kind of the combination of every weird story I ever heard about people having sex.

MY BACKGROUND

My interest in sexuality began when I was a young adult. After high school, I didn't go directly to college. Instead, I worked for the United States Postal Service for six years.

One day I was reading the newspaper and there was an article on sexual surrogate partners. Surrogate partners are trained people who work directly with therapy clients who have sexual dysfunctions such as erectile disorder or premature ejaculation. The use of surrogate partners to treat sexual dysfunctions was pioneered by the sex researchers Masters and Johnson in the 1960's and 1970's.

By the time I finished reading the article, I knew this was the job for me. I took a college course in Human Sexuality and connected with therapists who trained and used surrogates. I worked as a surrogate partner for many years while attending college, earning a doctorate in Health Psychology. Between the 1980's and the early 2000's, I wrote several books on sexuality. I appeared on many television and radio shows, including Howard Stern, Geraldo, and Montel. I was all set to become the next Dr. Ruth! But it didn't happen, so I had to get a job.

I've been teaching college now for over thirty years. For the past twenty-some years, I've been teaching Human Sexuality at California State University, Fullerton.

In addition to teaching, I'm also an independent sex educator with a private practice. In 2015 I joined the American Association of Sex Educators, Counselors, and Therapists (AASECT). I have thousands of hours of education and employment in the field of sexuality. I guess that means I'm a sexual intellectual—a fucking know-it-all. I also have a web page—www.masteryourjohnson.com—so that potential clients can contact me.

I've written other books in the past but they've all been written from the clinical perspective; that is, they were about treating clients or using sex therapy techniques to solve your sexual problems. *Crazy Stupid Sex* is the first of my books to be written from a sex educator perspective.

What does that mean? The basis of the sex educator perspective comes from Dr. Jack Annon, who was active as a sex researcher and therapist back in the 1970's. He realized that not everybody who has sexual problems needs intensive therapy. His treatment model is called the PLISSIT model, which stands for permission, limited information, specific suggestions, and intensive therapy. Sex educators provide the first three—permission, limited information, and specific suggestions. As sex educators, we don't deal with issues involving extreme trauma and deep personality problems related to sexuality.

SEX AND DRUGS
They just seem to go together, don't they, in more ways than you would think. In *Crazy Stupid Sex*, I'm taking some stuff from the playbook about drug addiction. Back in the 1980's, the thinking about drugs was "Just Say No". But it's not that easy. As we now know, the use of substances to change one's emotional state is a cultural universal. It's not going to go away. That's why the current thinking on substance abuse is harm reduction or risk reduction rather than expecting people to quit doing drugs completely.

That's my point of view in this book. People are going to have sex, whether you think they should or not. They are going to engage in risky practices. My aim in *Crazy Stupid Sex* is to show you how to minimize the risks from whatever sexual behaviors you choose to do.

WRITING
This book has some serious issues in it, but I have tried not to be too academic. I throw in some humor and I'm not afraid of four-letter words. I would describe the tone as intelligent, but graphic and down-to earth, with colloquial expressions. Think of reading this as taking a sexuality course from a knowledgeable but smartass instructor. There will be adult language. Hey, we're all adults here, even if most of us don't act like it. And yes, I know I can write better than this, but I have chosen not to.

You'll also find a fairly strong heterosexist bias in here, as you will in all my books. That reflects my client base rather than prejudice on my part.

WHO WILL LIKE THIS BOOK
If you enjoy Cosmo Confessions, Sex Sent Me to the ER, and Jackass, you will enjoy this book. If you liked the "Guide to Getting It On" by Paul Joannides, "Everything You Always

Wanted to Know About Sex" by David Reuben or any books by Dan Savage, I think you will like this book.

TIMELINESS
As I was putting the finishing touches on this manuscript, the whole Hollywood sexual harassment scandal is coming to light. Developments are emerging at an alarming rate. I won't be able to keep up with them in this book. Maybe that will be the subject for the next one.

SEX RESEARCH
I did a lot of research in order to write this book. It includes an extensive reference section. In addition to that, I wanted to be sure you know about the most famous sex researchers in history.

Alfred Kinsey and his colleagues in the 1940's and 1950's surveyed hundreds of people about their sex lives. I cite some of their findings in this book. In the 1950's, 1960's and 1970's, William Masters and Virginia Johnson observed people having sex in their laboratory and recorded the physiological changes they experienced during sex. They also invented the techniques that are used in sex therapy. I just wanted to make sure you knew who these people were before we got started.

WELCOME TO SEX ED 101
I wrote this book because I have taught sexuality at the college level for decades. It contains some of the same material I use in my class as well as anecdotes from all over. I have the ability to hold my students' attention as well as make them laugh and gross them out at the same time. That's the purpose of this book.

The main message is—have fun, but be careful out there. I'm not here to tell you that certain sexual behaviors are good or bad or right or wrong. I'm here to give you advice on relative risk and safety, not to judge. There doesn't have to be a trade-off between safety and pleasure.

This doesn't mean I'm neutral. I'm very opinionated when it comes to some aspects of sexual behavior. Throughout the course of the book, I'll do my best to tell you what's fact, what's unknown, and what's my own opinion.

CHAPTER 1
THE GENIUS OF THE PENIS

This first chapter is about male sexual anatomy and physiology. When I talk about this subject in my class I usually start with the penis. Does the human penis contain a bone? No, even though occasionally someone will say, "Hey, take a look at this boner", it does not contain a bone. Does the human penis contain a muscle? Again, no, it does not, even though some men refer to their penis as their love muscle.

What the human penis does contain is three cylinders of erectile tissue, plus the urethra. The penis is the organ for sexual intercourse, for conveying semen outside the body, and for urination. The two cylinders of erectile tissue in the penis that run along the sides are called the corpora cavernosa. The larger cylinder of erectile tissue that runs inside the base of the penis and extends into the head of the penis is called the corpus spongiosum. As the name implies, the tissue in the corpus spongiosum is spongier than the other tissue. The urethra runs through the middle of the penis and usually opens out of the body through the penile head.

If you look at a penis from the outside you can see that it is divided into two parts. The long part is called the shaft and the end is called the penile head, glans, or corona. Everybody's penis looks different, not just in size. The shape of the head and shaft differ in men.

One important but often neglected area of the penis is the frenulum. This is the area on the underside of the penis where the head meets the shaft. This area is significant because it's usually very sensitive.

When male infants are born the head of the penis is partially covered by a piece of skin that is called the foreskin. In some cultures the surgical removal of this piece of skin (called circumcision) is practiced. Circumcision has a long and controversial history so I'm going to go into quite a bit of detail on this. Do people hate penises? Why else would societies decide to lop off the end of an infant's penis for no reason? Here's the historical overview.

There's evidence that some ancient Egyptians practiced circumcision but the practice really did not become popular until it was done by the ancient Hebrews. If you know anything about ancient history, you know that the Hebrews were not terribly popular. Many of the tribes that surrounded them practiced human sacrifice, but the Hebrews couldn't afford to do this. They needed all the Hebrews they could get. So they substituted circumcision—the removal of the foreskin of the penis. In time this came to be known as the way Hebrews could be distinguished from members of other groups.

This practice continues into modern society. Orthodox Jews have their sons circumcised shortly after birth. Most of the time this is not done in a medical office. The accompanying ceremony is called a bris and may be performed in the home by a special rabbi called a mohel. I attended a bris once and almost had a heart attack. They needed to give the wine to me, not to the kid.

I understand that circumcision is part of Orthodox Jewish tradition. But how did it catch on with other cultural groups? Between the 1940's and the 1980's most male kids in the United States were circumcised. How did that start? Was there a legitimate reason for this?

Prior to World War II in the United States most kids were not circumcised. When the war came along a lot of men were drafted and many of these people had grown up without the benefit of indoor plumbing. These kids were not taught to pull their foreskin back and clean under it on a weekly or even a daily basis. Because of this, many of them developed foreskin adhesions—their foreskin literally got stuck onto their penis. The foreskin contains tiny glands that secrete a fluid. If this fluid is allowed to collect, it can result in adhesions. When these men showed up to be inducted into the military and the doctors realized they couldn't retract their foreskins, the military surgeons had to perform many adult circumcisions which took six to eight weeks to heal. So the military surgeons wrote articles recommending infant circumcision for everybody.

I had a friend who was a scrub nurse in World War II. He saw this firsthand. The first twenty operations he scrubbed in on were adult circumcisions due to foreskin adhesions. Interestingly, he himself was not circumcised, but his father was a physician who taught him how to keep the area under his foreskin clean.

Needing a circumcision during those days didn't keep you out of the service. It just delayed your active duty. Men with foreskin adhesions are also more susceptible to catching sexually transmitted infections (STI's) because they can't retract the foreskin to identify the discharge associated with gonorrhea, for example.

The rationale for recommending circumcision for all male babies was the following. Doctors believed that infants don't feel pain. We don't know that. We know they don't remember it. It's much easier to do circumcision on an infant than on a full-grown adult man. That's true—there are fewer complications and the recovery time is faster because the amount of tissue that is removed is so much smaller. Infant circumcision would prevent adult foreskin adhesions—also true. So doctors everywhere in the U. S. started doing infant circumcision without considering that it is genital mutilation without the patient's consent.

This point of view received support in the 1960's when it was found that female partners of uncircumcised men were more likely to develop cervical cancer than were female partners of circumcised men. This finding was not borne out over time and appears to have been related to hygiene issues with uncircumcised penises.

In the early 2000's, the American Academy of Pediatrics concluded there was no medical justification for the routine circumcision of newborn males. Lately that has been called into question. Current evidence suggests that possible benefits of circumcision may outweigh the risks. This finding is based on African studies which show decreased risk of HIV in circumcised men. Other research showed increased risk of HIV and other STI's in circumcised men. So it's hard to know what to do if you are the parent of a male infant.

Another issue with circumcision is decreased versus increased sensitivity. In theory the exposed head of a circumcised penis grows additional layers of skin which reduces sensitivity. Some men who were circumcised as infants are upset about this because they believe that their penises would have been more sensitive if they had not been circumcised. There's also some evidence that the foreskin may provide a lubrication function or even an immune system function.

Are circumcised men less sensitive than uncircumcised men? That's hard to say, and there really is no way to do meaningful research on this question. That's because if you asked men how much they enjoy sex on a 1 to 10 scale, everybody will put "10". There is no way to discriminate because everybody answers on the high end. In research this is called a ceiling effect.

There is research on whether women prefer circumcised versus uncircumcised penises, but results have been mixed. This can be hard to measure because many women have only had sex with one partner and so have no point of comparison. Generally women prefer the type of penis of their first sexual partner.

Sex with a man with a circumcised or uncircumcised penis feels the same, because when a man gets an erection his foreskin stretches out. So circumcised and uncircumcised penises look similar when they are erect. Also, most uncircumcised men don't just let their foreskin hang over the head of the penis. They usually pull the foreskin back and anchor it behind the head.

There is a medical condition that makes circumcision necessary. It's called phimosis. In this condition, which may occur in infants, teenagers, or adults, the foreskin is too tight and cannot be retracted behind the head of the penis. This can cause urinary problems as well as erection problems in teenagers and adults. Sometimes if the foreskin is not all that tight the condition can be corrected with frenuloplasty in which the foreskin is loosened. Sometimes a full circumcision is required.

When I was a surrogate partner I had a client who was a very young man, maybe twenty years old. He came to sex therapy because he claimed that when he got an erection it was extremely painful. In the first session in which I saw him naked, I recognized the problem immediately. He had such a bad case of phimosis that his penis could only get about half erect. He had so little sex education that he had no idea what was wrong with him. We referred him to a urologist for a circumcision, which was not pleasant, but it worked. That poor kid! Thank goodness he got something done about it before he got all psychologically freaked out after another ten or twenty years.

Some men become obsessed with the idea that they were genitally mutilated without their consent and are resentful because they believe that their penises are less sensitive as a result. Some men have gone so far as to try to have a piece of skin from some other part of their body grafted onto their penis to replace the missing foreskin.

One of the arguments for infant circumcision is that you should have your son circumcised if his father is circumcised. The logic behind this is when a boy reaches two or three years of age and starts to be interested in genitals, his penis should look like his father's to help him with his sense of masculine identity. In a Freudian sense there's probably some truth to this, because the penis is so important in establishing a masculine identity.

This argument goes a little further. Some parents want their son to be circumcised if all the other kids are. Their reasoning is that if your son is around other boys naked as in a school locker room, and your kid is the only one not circumcised, the other boys might make fun of him. I'm sure this is true, but let's face it, kids will make fun of other kids for just about anything. If it's not your penis it will be something else.

If you think circumcision is bad, there are penis mutilation practices done in other cultures that are even more dangerous. One of these is called subincision. In this practice, which is usually done as a rite of passage into manhood, the bottom of the penis is sliced lengthwise from the head to the base, all the way down to the urethra.

Circumcisions in Africa are generally not done in infancy. They are done at puberty as a rite of passage into manhood. Sometimes the people performing the circumcisions get overzealous and end up involuntarily sterilizing the boys.

Circumcision done in infancy is generally medically safe if performed correctly. But there can be complications. Here's a case of a benign complication.

I had a friend who had a weird looking penis. There were several pieces of skin connecting the head and the shaft. It looked like his penis had belt loops. This situation wasn't painful and didn't bother him. He claimed the doctor who performed the operation was drunk.

The following is the best-known circumcision accident true story. Unlike in the U. S., infant circumcisions were not routinely performed in other countries. In the mid-1960's, twin boys were born to a couple in Canada. When the twins were about sixteen months old, they were believed to have phimosis and circumcision was recommended. The first twin, whose name was David Reimer, was taken in for circumcision. For unknown reasons, the surgeon used a cauterizing knife instead of a scalpel and accidentally burned off David's penis.

This is horrifying enough. But what happened next is even worse. Naturally, the parents were distraught and didn't know where to turn. It was recommended that they consult with Dr. John Money at Johns Hopkins University in Maryland. At the time Dr. Money was known as the worldwide expert on gender.

His advice was to destroy any evidence that David had ever been a boy and to raise him as a girl from that point on.

The parents followed through on this advice but by the time David was a teenager he knew something was wrong with him. It took him several years to get his parents to admit what had happened. At that point at least he had an explanation for his feelings. As an adult he underwent phalloplasty (construction of an artificial penis) and married a woman who had children and lived as a man.

In 2001 he collaborated on an autobiography called "As Nature Made Him" with author John Colapinto. Unfortunately the tragedy of his life had taken its toll and David committed suicide in 2004.

We now know that there are male brains and female brains and you can't turn one into the other. Why would Dr. Money give the advice that he did? Back in the 1960's the state of the art in psychological theory was learning theory or behaviorism. Money and other psychologists genuinely believed that you would accept whatever gender you were raised as. That does not excuse Money, however, for falsifying data. He examined "Brenda" (as David was called then) once or twice a year and assured everyone that "she" was fitting nicely into her new identity and that was far from the case as we now know.

THE SCROTUM AND TESTES

The scrotum is the skin sack that hangs outside the body and contains the testes, the male reproductive organs. Hanging outside the body as it does the scrotum is subject to injury. Before you're born the testes are inside the body cavity and don't descend until shortly before birth. Sometimes one or both testes don't descend and have to be surgically moved, which is a fairly minor operation. Wouldn't it be easier if the testes just stayed inside the body? They'd be much safer in there, that's for sure. The problem is that the testes produce sperm and sperm must be produced at a lower temperature than 98.6.

The testes have two functions. They produce both sperm and male hormones. The sperm are produced in tubelike structures called the seminiferous tubules. Cells in between these tubes (called interstitial cells or Leydig's cells) produce male hormones called androgens. The main male hormone is testosterone. It's responsible for the development of the penis and also male secondary sex characteristics such as facial hair and pubic hair. It's also responsible for your sex drive. Women produce testosterone too but in smaller quantities than men do.

At the back of each testis is a structure called the epididymis. It's a storage area for sperm. It can become infected which causes extreme pain and swelling of the testicle. It's treated with antibiotics.

Sperm travel into the body cavity through the vas deferens which are tubes on each side of the scrotum. In the male sterilization operation, the vasectomy, these tubes are cut.

Sperm need a medium to swim in which is called semen. It's produced in structures called the seminal vesicles. Some part of semen is produced by the prostate gland also.

There are a couple of other structures that affect male sexual functioning. The two Cowper's glands secrete a clear fluid into the urethra when a man gets aroused. The official name for this is pre-seminal fluid or a pre-seminal emission, but most people know it by its porn name—pre-cum. Men secrete varying amounts of this fluid. While it is not of the same composition as semen, the pre-seminal fluid may contain live sperm. For that reason, if you are relying on condoms for contraception, it is important to put the condom on the penis before any of the pre-seminal fluid appears at the urethral opening.

Another structure that is important for both male and female sexual functioning is the pubococcygeus muscle or pubococcygeal muscle group. This is the muscle that runs from the pubic bone in the front to the tailbone in the rear. We call it the P. C. muscle for short. It's the muscle that spasms when you have an ejaculation. It's important to exercise this muscle to keep it in good shape because if it's out of shape this can lead to problems such as premature ejaculation, delayed ejaculation, or even erection issues.

MALE HEALTH CONDITIONS

A point I'll make throughout this book is that one aspect of safety is preventing illness by recognizing potentially dangerous symptoms. The male genitals are subject to a number of diseases. Testicular cancer is one of the more common forms of cancer in young men aged eighteen to thirty-four. Symptoms are pain in a testicle, swelling of a testicle, a lump on a testicle, or a sense of heaviness or dragging on one side of the scrotum.

Men should examine their testicles for lumps on a monthly basis the same way women examine their breasts. While in a warm shower, run your fingers over the surface of each testicle through the skin of your scrotum.

Testicular cancer is highly treatable with surgery. A testicular implant can be put in place of the missing testicle to normalize appearance. Usually if you have one testicle removed, the remaining one makes enough testosterone. If not additional testosterone can be prescribed.

The prostate gland is highly susceptible to cancer. In the area in which I live, about one in nine men will develop cancer of the prostate at some point in their lives. Prostate cancer tends to be a cancer of older men. The recommendation is that you get screened for prostate cancer regularly after age forty. Men with a family history should probably start getting screened earlier. Screening for prostate cancer includes a digital rectal exam in which a doctor physically feels the prostate for any enlargement. There is also a blood test called the prostate specific antigen (PSA) test.

Prostate cancer can spread to other areas of the body and be fatal. Treatment can include surgery to remove all or part of the prostate, radiation, or chemotherapy. There are many new treatments for prostate cancer and the prognosis is much better than it was years ago.

From a personal standpoint, I have known many men who had prostate cancer, with a variety of outcomes. In some men urination and erections were largely unaffected. In some cases men opted for a penile implant to restore functioning. Some unlucky men ended up with complications that resulted in major disabilities. It all depends on how fast-growing the cancer is and how soon it is caught and treated.

Men are notorious for not taking care of their health. The prostate exam is unpleasant so some men just don't get it done. They are often in denial that anything is wrong and often it is up to their partner to nag them to get a checkup.

The prostate can also become enlarged even if it's not cancer. This is called benign prostatic hypertrophy (BPH). It is an extremely common condition in older men. The main symptom is difficulty urinating. It is treated using a procedure called trans-urethral resection of the prostate (TURP) in which the physician goes in through the urethra and removes excess tissue. A lot of guys resist getting this surgery but putting it off too long can result in having to catheterize yourself on a frequent basis, which is not very pleasant either.

The prostate can develop a non-cancerous infection called prostatitis. Symptoms are chills, fever, and intense pain. Treatment is antibiotics.

Cancer of the penis does exist, but it is not common in the U. S. Any growth or unusual lump on the penis or scrotum should be investigated.

There's also a medical condition in which a man can develop varicose veins on his scrotum. This is called varicocele. It should be treated as it can affect blood flow to the area and possibly affect fertility.

MALE PHYSIOLOGY

Let's review. Sperm and male hormones are produced in the testes. The penis is the organ for sexual intercourse, ejaculation, and urination. Let's take a look at the male arousal process—the male sexual response cycle.

This was the work of the famous sex researchers William Masters and Virginia Johnson. In the 1960's they had single people and couples come into their lab and they hooked them up to devices to measure vital signs such as heart rate, respiration, and skin temperature. They were interested in the physiological changes that occur in men and women as they proceed from stimulation to arousal to orgasm.

Masters and Johnson used a device to measure erections. It's called a penile strain gauge. It's a flexible loop that fits around the base of the penis and it is connected to a computer lead. As a man gets an erection, the loop tightens and the device records how strong of an erection a man got and how long it lasted. Versions of these devices are still used to diagnose erection problems and for sex research.

Masters and Johnson's findings are called the Human Sexual

Response Cycle (HSRC). The cycle has four stages—excitement, plateau, orgasm, and resolution.

In the excitement phase a man starts getting an erection. Blood flows into the penis and fills the small blood vessels in the corpora cavernosa and corpus spongiosum. In this phase a man's testes and scrotum swell and move up closer to the body. At the plateau phase the man gets his hardest erection. Due to increased blood flow, the head of the penis may become quite dark. At orgasm a man usually ejaculates. Ejaculation occurs in two stages—emission and expulsion. In emission, the sperm and semen travel from the testes into the body cavity and collect in a swelling under the prostate gland called the urethral bulb. In expulsion, the P. C. muscle spasms and forces the semen out of the penis.

Some men experience a condition called retrograde (backwards) ejaculation. Instead of the semen coming out of the body, it goes backwards into the bladder due to a faulty valve. This is not harmful but can be a problem if a man is trying to get a woman pregnant.

An aside on pregnancy—remember how I said that sperm have to be manufactured at a lower temperature than 98.6? If you're trying to get a woman pregnant, avoid hot tubs, saunas or other venues that might cause the testicles to become too hot, as this could result in a loss of viable sperm.

There was a guy who used to be the player development director for the L. A. Dodgers baseball team. He told the players that if they wanted to be stronger, they should sunbathe their balls. I presume he meant their testicles and not their baseballs. I doubt this would increase testosterone production. In fact, it might actually kill sperm.

How frequently do men ejaculate, and how frequently should they ejaculate? There's some controversy about this. In terms of how frequently men ejaculate, the normal range goes from never to many times a day. The controversy is that in some Asian cultures it's considered bad for your health to ejaculate too often or even at all. The belief is that frequent ejaculation robs you of your vital fluid or energy. Sex practices in these cultures often involve lengthy periods of intercourse with the man experiencing orgasm but not ejaculating. These two experiences are not exactly the same and I have explained the difference in a previous book—*How To Make Love All Night*.

The opposing point of view is that frequent ejaculation is good for you especially as you get older, as it helps your prostate gland fully empty and keeps it healthier and keeps it from getting enlarged.

My opinion on this is that I will go with the science rather than the religion. I believe it's good to ejaculate as frequently as you feel like it as long as you can do so without straining or putting psychological pressure on yourself.

ERECTIONS

A lot of people have misunderstandings about erections. A lot of men expect to be able to get erections whenever they want to even under very adverse circumstances. They think they should be hard all the time or as hard as they were when they were twenty.

Erections can be initiated psychogenically (in the mind) or physiologically through direct stimulation of the pelvic area. The reality is that most men get turned on by both thoughts and touch in the genital area. Psychogenic erections are sometimes called spontaneous erections because they appear to start for no reason.

Some men get freaked out because as they get older, they find they need actual physical stimulation to get an erection, whereas when they were younger they could think about sex and get one. There are some men who have never had spontaneous erections. They have always needed touch, whether their own or that of a partner. This is important so I'm going to repeat it. It's normal to require touch to get an erection. That in itself is not a sign of a problem.

If you are concerned that your erection response is declining, there are ways to tell if there's a problem. The first is to look at medications you might be using. If you recently started taking medication for high blood pressure and all of a sudden you have erection problems that weren't there before, that would be a good indication to me that the medication might be to blame.

You also might want to look at medical conditions. Any cardiovascular condition can cause erection problems. So can diabetes as it gets progressively worse.

There is a simple test you can do at home to try to figure out if your erection issues might have a physical basis. It has to do with observing your sleep patterns. First let me explain a little bit about the sleep cycle.

Sleep proceeds in a series of stages from light sleep to deep sleep and back again. About every ninety minutes in a night's sleep, you go through a full cycle. During the rapid eye movement (REM) phase of your cycle, you dream, and men get erections. We don't know why this is. These are called nighttime erections or nocturnal penile tumescence. Women also have genital lubrication and swelling during this sleep stage.

Nocturnal erections or morning erections are a sign that your body has no disease processes (such as cardiovascular problems or diabetes) that are interfering with erections. So if you have morning or nighttime erections, if you are experiencing erection problems with a partner, the problems are probably psychological. If you don't know whether you have nighttime erections, vary your sleep schedule slightly (for example, wake up fifteen or thirty minutes earlier or later than usual) and see what happens. Track down those wily nocturnal erections! Your partner might notice if you get them also.

Another factor that can have a negative effect on erections is depression. If you are reasonably sure you are having no nocturnal erections, it's time to consult a urologist who specializes in erections (not all do). They can do much more sophisticated tests including scans to find out if there is something physical going on.

MEDICAL TREATMENTS FOR ERECTION PROBLEMS

We've all seen the TV ads, right? I still don't know what taking baths in two separate outdoor tubs has to do with erections. The purpose of this section is to tell you what treatments work for erection problems and which don't, so you don't panic and do something stupid like stick your penis in a vacuum cleaner (see the next chapter). I'll start with treatments from the cheapest, easiest, least invasive and least painful and move to other extremes.

Many health food stores sell so-called male enhancement products. They usually have a whole wall of them. Keep in mind if you choose to try these products, they have not been tested or shown to work. Best case scenario is they don't hurt you. Worst case scenario is these supplements may include herbs that are stimulants and may not be good for people who have anxiety or heart problems.

Some herbal products such as yohimbine are sold over the counter and may promote erections because they increase blood flow. They can also cause rapid heart rate which you don't want if you have a history of anxiety or heart palpitations.

There is a device to treat erection problems called a vacuum erection device (VED). It was satirized in the Austin Powers movies as the "Swedish penis enlarger". It's a real thing. It's usually used therapeutically by older men who have problems maintaining an erection. It's a clear plastic cylinder that fits over the penis. You pump air out of the cylinder, creating a vacuum and this draws blood into the penis. It's kind of like an artificial blow job. You place a thick rubber band at the base of the penis to hold the blood in. Possible danger—if you leave the rubber band on too long you risk damage to your erectile tissue. Plus, using this device interferes with the psychological flow of a sexual encounter. A lot of partners don't want to put up with this.

Viagra, Cialis, Levitra, and other drugs like them were first introduced in 1998. They have been an absolute godsend for many men with erection problems. Some prescriptions are taken as needed and some are designed to be used every day. They work at the cellular level to relax the smooth muscle (the P. C. muscle group) at the base of the penis so blood can flow into the erectile tissue.

Possible side effects include vision changes, indigestion, nasal congestion, and interactions with heart medications. I've seen a lot of men have great success with these medications. You have to be careful where you obtain them. Many men order them from sources outside the U. S. to get them cheaper and sometimes they find they get a bad batch that doesn't work. Viagra and other similar drugs are not miracle erection pills. You still need stimulation. I'm not sure what's really working here—the drugs work for men with psychological issues involving tension in the P. C. muscle, but I've also seen them work for some men with physical problems. These drugs may not work for men who are quite elderly and have a P. C. muscle group that is really out of shape.

Men unable to tolerate the side effects of Viagra could use a urethral suppository called MUSE. It's a drug called alprostadil that you insert in the tip of your penis. I haven't seen great success with this drug.

There are some substances such as papaverine that can be injected directly into the erectile tissue with a small-gauge needle. Personally, I can't imagine myself injecting something into my genitals just so I could have sex, but this doesn't bother some men. You have to be careful to inject into the erectile tissue and not some other area of the penis, plus you have to switch sides for the injection site so you don't develop scar tissue.

A penile implant is the last resort for men who can't get erections due to a medical condition. This would be used in cases of advanced diabetes or surgery for prostate cancer.

There are two types of implants—the semi-rigid rod and the inflatable. A semi-rigid rod is placed in the penis alongside the urethra. When a man wants to have an erection, he bends the penis upward and it stays there until he bends it back down. Possible complications include pain, urinary problems, scar tissue, and any problems associated with the surgery itself. Since the semi-rigid rod is very simple, it is unlikely to break or be defective.

The inflatable devices are more complicated. They consist of three parts—a hollow cylinder which is implanted alongside the urethra, a reservoir of fluid that is implanted in the lower abdomen, and a valve which is implanted under the skin of the scrotum. To use the device, you turn the valve and fluid moves from the reservoir into the cylinder in the penis, causing an erection.

Penile implant surgery is painful and expensive. A certain number of implants fail every year. They are only guaranteed for a specific amount of time (versus mileage, I guess). With men's lifespans increasing, we find that penile implants often have to be replaced.

Men who have implants can have orgasms but not ejaculations. When a man who has an implant gets an erection, the penis gets hard but does not increase in width or length so some men are unhappy with it because of that.

Depending on the medical problem you are experiencing, sometimes other surgery can be done. Men with blocked blood flow to the penis can have an arterial graft. Leaky valves at the base of your penis can be repaired. These surgeries are not common.

If you have been recommended for a penile implant, please get a second opinion, as these surgeries are major.

BE KIND TO YOUR PENIS

In the course of working as a surrogate partner for many years, I had occasion to watch many men masturbate. I can't believe how rough some men are with their penises. I think treating your penis a little better in a sensuous way is one way of preventing erection problems down the road. I've seen cases of men whose penises were literally numb. They couldn't feel anything and couldn't even tell if they had an erection without looking.

In the next chapter we'll look at some of the really bizarre things men have done to their penises. We'll also look at types of penile accidents and injuries.

CHAPTER 2
THE PERILS OF THE PENIS

In the previous chapter we looked at some basic facts about the penis. Now we turn our attention to some of the tragedies that can befall the penis when you don't practice safe sex. I'll start here with the safe sex rules also.

MINOR PENIS AND SCROTUM INJURIES
There have been cases in which the skin of the penis or scrotum gets caught in a zipper. Remember that scene from "There's Something About Mary"? Pubic hair or the skin of the penis or scrotum can be caught on orthodontic braces or jewelry, especially earrings. None of these situations should be life-threatening.

SAFE SEX RULE
Keep sharp objects away from the penis and scrotum.

The penis and especially the scrotum are subject to sports injuries and that's why men wear athletic supporters, right? A sport that you think wouldn't be dangerous to a man's genitals is cycling but it is. There is a lot of research showing how bad long-distance cycling can be for men, especially when men ride on those really skinny seats. This can cause pressure on the arteries that supply the penis and result in erectile dysfunction and other circulation problems.

Cycling accidents have also caused a number of penis injuries. In an accident, the skin of the penis could be sheared off by contact with the top bar of the bike. To prevent this, make sure the bike you are riding is the correct size for your body. Wear cycling clothes with padding.

Injury to the penis doesn't have to involve sports or fashion accessories. In one case a woman was with her boyfriend who had one of those long ropy penises that don't enlarge that much when you get an erection. She got the brilliant idea that when his penis was flaccid she should tie it in a knot and did. And then they couldn't get it untied. Fortunately cold water shrunk it up enough that they were eventually able to get it untied.

Dogs have also been responsible for injuries to the penis. There's a reason those guys wear protective gear on their crotch when they're training attack dogs. Any dog bite in the genital area should be evaluated because a dog's mouth can contain bacteria.

VIAGRA AND A COCK RING

A few years ago there was a headline on the front page of the local paper that serves my community that read "Man's Member Removed from Ring". Apparently, a man in his fifties took several hundred milligrams of Viagra. (The normal dose is between twenty-five and one hundred milligrams). He then got drunk and put a solid metal ring around the base of his penis and attempted to masturbate. He passed out for several hours and when he woke up, his penis had turned black and swelled up to the size of a football.

He called the paramedics but they couldn't figure out how to get the ring off, so they took him to the local hospital. The emergency room doctors were also stumped (probably the wrong choice of words). Finally a janitor found a small saw that was used to cut off the ring. But the man's penis had been trapped in the ring for over twenty-four hours at that point.

Of course, there was no follow-up article to indicate what kind of damage he suffered to his erectile tissue. (Inquiring minds want to know!) I'm guessing the damage was fairly severe and permanent, as this guy was no youngster. Several people complained to the newspaper that this article was on the front page. I wanted to complain because there was no picture.

The above example illustrates two safe sex rules—

SAFE SEX RULE
Don't use Viagra unless you need it.
Don't put anything around the base of your penis unless it has a quick release option.

(Incidentally, this same newspaper, which I will not name, sent a reporter to interview me, not about this story, but about my career as a sexuality author. The interview appeared on the front page on a Sunday. The previous week an interview with Dennis Rodman, another local resident, appeared in the same place. A woman wrote in to the paper and complained, "I can't believe you don't have anything better to write about than people like Barbara Keesling and Dennis Rodman. Why don't you write about something important, like the weekly cafeteria menus for the middle schools?"). True story.

There have also been cases of men sticking their penises into appliances and getting them stuck. More than one man has tried to solve his erection problems by sticking his penis in a vacuum cleaner hose and turning on the vacuum cleaner, and in more than one case, this has led to a fatal result. I also know of cases in which men stuck their penis in a bathtub faucet, the penis got stuck, and a plumber had to be called.

SAFE SEX RULE
Don't insert your penis into an appliance.

PRIAPISM
The man in the above newspaper example had an erection that wouldn't go down because of two factors—he took too much Viagra and put a solid metal ring around the base of his penis. I don't consider this to be a true case of priapism, which is an erection that won't go down, because he brought the problem on himself.

Priapism is named for the Greek god Priapus. He was a minor fertility god and was always shown with a huge erect penis. Priapism can occur without the use of a cock ring. It can be caused by certain medications (anti-depressants), brain injury, exposure to toxins, or excessive use of illegal stimulants such as cocaine and methamphetamine.

If an erection lasts for more than four hours and won't go down even if you want it to and run cold water on it, you might need to go to the emergency room. What happens is that the valves that close to allow the penis to stay hard experience a glitch. They stay in the "on" position and don't allow blood to flow out of the penis as it normally would after an ejaculation.

PENILE FRACTURE AND PEYRONIE'S DISEASE

Even though the human penis does not contain a bone, the erectile tissue can become so engorged with blood that it can fracture. Picture this scenario. You're kind of drunk and you're having intercourse with your girlfriend in a dark room. She's on her hands and knees and you're using the rear entry position. Because of intoxication, your movements aren't too coordinated and with every stroke you're pulling all the way out and re-entering. Suddenly, on an instroke, you miss the vaginal opening and slam your penis into your girlfriend's thigh instead, resulting in excruciating pain. You scream, turn on the light, and notice that your penis is now curved and the underside is turning black.

This one is a definite trip to the ER. You are experiencing bleeding in your erectile tissue. If this injury is not too severe, the curvature may straighten out on its own. If the injury is severe, you may need surgery to straighten out your penis. The bleeding will stop and the bruising will go away.

SAFE SEX RULE
Never operate heavy equipment while under the influence of alcohol.

Curvature of the penis is called Peyronie's Disease, named after the Frenchman who was first to write about it. It can result from injury to the penis or can occur on its own for no apparent reason especially in older men.

Nobody's penis is perfectly straight. Most men curve a little to the left or right or even up or down. This is no problem as long as you can get full blood flow when you have an erection. Peyronie's Disease occurs when the erectile tissue on one side of the penis forms a calcified plaque which causes the penis to lean to one side. In severe cases this is corrected by surgery to remove the plaque and straighten out the penis.

If you believe your penis is starting to take a U-turn, take pictures of it with your phone a few weeks apart and show them to your doctor.

I have seen some very severe advanced cases of Peyronie's Disease in which the penis resembled a corkscrew. This can prevent erection and interfere with urination, and in some cases may require a penile implant.

I researched Peyronie's Disease online and could not find when it was first identified. However, I did find a number of possible treatment options that seemed highly suspect (penis stretchers or extenders), so buyer beware.

INVOLUNTARY PENILE AMPUTATION

As opposed to voluntary penile amputation, right? Men have had their penises severed in accidents or assaults. The most famous United States case was that of John Wayne Bobbitt. In 1993, John Bobbitt and his wife Lorena were residents of Virginia. She claimed that he raped her and she got a knife and cut off his penis at the base. She took the penis, got in her car and drove around, and threw the penis in a field. It was retrieved and surgeons reattached it. Apparently, it was functional and Bobbitt went on to appear in porno movies and become something of a celebrity. I can think of easier ways to make it in Hollywood. The most recent information I found on Bobbitt was that he broke his neck in a vehicle accident in 2014.

In 1996 a friend and I took the redeye to Washington D. C. to visit my sister. We stopped at a 7-11 in Manassas, Virginia to get coffee and I called my sister to tell her that our flight had arrived. When I told her where we were, she started laughing like a maniac. What was so funny? Apparently the field next to that 7-11 was where Lorena Bobbitt threw her husband's penis. Thanks for the tip!

I read of a more recent case that apparently occurred in Arizona. A man and a woman were having sex and she was upset because the man wouldn't make eye contact with her so she got a knife and cut off the tip of his penis. The best part about this story was the woman's mug shot, which showed that she had some kind of eye problem in which her eyes pointed in different directions. No wonder he couldn't make eye contact with her—nobody could! I kind of wondered whether that story might be fake, but it referenced a legitimate newspaper article. There certainly have been verified cases in which women cut off their partners' penises.

SAFE SEX RULE
Remove all knives and other sharp objects from the home before you have sex.

Back in the late 1990's I was a member of the Society for the Scientific Study of Sexuality (known as Quad S). I attended one of their conferences in Southern California and went to a presentation given by a Beverly Hills physician who is certified in both plastic surgery and urology, specializing in surgery on both male and female genitals. His presentation was accompanied by slides, and before his talk he gave a disclaimer. "I know all of you are professionals, but if any of you have a weak stomach, leave now".

It was true—many of the slides were extremely graphic. Some of his slides depicted a case that happened in California's Central Valley. A young man had overdosed on methamphetamine and hallucinated that the devil was telling him to cut off his penis because it was the source of sin. He took a knife and severed his penis about halfway up the shaft. He was airlifted to UCLA and the doctor reattached his penis.

The doctor showed a slide of the amputated penis and the remaining stump. They were shown in cross section and the viewer could clearly see the three cylinders of erectile tissue. It was not difficult to imagine the challenge of reconnecting all of those tiny blood vessels, not to mention the nerve connections that allow you to get an erection.

SAFE SEX RULE
Don't listen to the devil when you're on drugs.

Surgical reattachment of an amputated penis can be successful in that the patient may be able to urinate and have at least a partial erection. However, the penis will be shorter than its original length. (Ya think?)

HISTORY LESSON

Here's another weird instance of penile amputation. In 1872 a retired American Civil War physician named William Minor was arrested in England for shooting a man to death in the street. Minor believed that people were breaking into his house and trying to kill him. Today his condition would be diagnosed as paranoid schizophrenia.

Minor was judged insane and sent to a famous British mental hospital called Broadmoor Asylum. During the day he seemed normal, reading and painting. At night he was tormented with delusions that people were breaking into his room and forcing him to commit unspeakable sexual acts.

While in the asylum he found out that researchers led by James Murray were beginning to compile the Oxford English

Dictionary (OED). The team was looking for scholars to read old books and submit dictionary entries. Minor became one of the two biggest contributors to the OED project.

What does this have to do with penises? In 1902 Minor became so disturbed by his sexual delusions that he cut off his penis and threw it into the fireplace. Being a doctor, he knew to tie a string around the base of the penis to minimize bleeding. He survived this and lived until 1920 without a penis. (Yep, he cut off his own dictionary).

As I was finishing this manuscript I read a newspaper article that said that Mel Gibson was making a movie about this story. He was to play Murray and Sean Penn was cast as Minor. Unfortunately this movie will probably never be completed because of disputes among the many production companies that were involved.

It's also possible to transplant a penis from a cadaver onto a man who lost his in an accident. A case reported several years ago in The Guardian, a British newspaper, described the world's first successful penis transplant. The recipient was a Chinese man who had his penis severed in an accident. The donor was a young man who had died in an accident. The donor penis was attached and several weeks later it was functioning, according to the patient's doctors. However, the recipient decided to have the penis removed, even though it was functioning, because his wife didn't like it.

I have no comment on this. Or, rather, I have several, but I don't know where to start. Ever hear the phrase, "I wouldn't fuck her with someone else's dick"? I guess this is the opposite.

LIFE WITHOUT A PENIS
In the United States, penises are rarely amputated for medical reasons such as penile cancer. However, there is a medical

condition called aphallia (or penile agenesis) in which a male fetus develops without a penis. Normally these fetuses are miscarried or the babies are stillborn or die shortly after birth because this condition is accompanied by other major abnormalities of the genito-reproductive system and the digestive system.

There have been cases of men who have survived with this condition. In one case, the man took on a female identity and had genital surgery to conform to that identity. In a second case, the man chose to keep a male gender identity and live without a penis.

I read about a case in which an uncircumcised man did not clean under his foreskin for decades. He developed a fungal infection and had to have his penis removed.

OTHER MEDICAL CONDITIONS

There are other medical conditions that can cause abnormalities of the penis. One of these is hypospadias. This is a condition in which the urethral opening is somewhere other than the head of the penis. In the least extreme version of this condition, the urethral opening is located on the underside of the penis at the juncture of the head and the shaft. Although this may cause the penis to be shortened or curved, it is usually not necessary to treat this condition. All that happens is that urine and semen come out in kind of a weird direction.

In more severe cases of hypospadias, the urethral opening may be halfway down the shaft or at the base of the penis, in which case the opening may resemble a small vagina. These more extreme conditions require surgery and may result in medical complications and even issues with gender identity.

A WEIRD PENIS ACCIDENT

One of the weirdest penis accidents I ever heard of happened to someone I knew back in the 1970's. I was working as a mail carrier and so was my friend. We'll call him Jim. One morning when we all came in to work the place was buzzing. "Did you hear what happened to Jim? The supervisor took him to the hospital."

What happened was—Jim got to work early and had to use the bathroom. Apparently he really had to make a run for it. The janitor had just cleaned and so the toilet seats were up. Jim attempted to pull down his shorts with one hand and push down the toilet seat behind him with the other hand. His penis swung (!) under the toilet seat and he sat on it with his full weight. Yow!

He was okay. He later went on to father children. (Some of us tried to recreate this incident but we couldn't find anybody whose penis was long enough to get caught under the toilet seat.)

Here's another one I heard from a friend. He and several male friends were driving to a baseball game and brought along a bunch of beer. Of course there was a traffic jam and they all had to pee. One of them tried to pee into the small hole of a beer can and all of a sudden there was blood all over the place. He started screaming, "Stop the car! I cut my dick off!" Of course this wasn't true—he had cut his hand on the opening of the beer can.

SAFE SEX RULE
Always carry a Red Solo Cup for this purpose.

Don't try to open the car door and hang your penis out the door and pee. I knew someone who did this and fell out of the car and ran over himself.

PENIS DELUSIONS
In some cultures, delusions about the penis are common. One

of these delusions is called koro. It usually occurs in Asian or African countries or among immigrants from those countries. It can affect one man at a time or several men.

In koro, a man believes that his penis is retracting into his body or disappearing. Further, he believes that if this process is allowed to continue, his penis will disappear completely and this will result in death. In order to prevent this, the man holds onto his penis. If he gets tired, he asks a friend or family member to hold onto it temporarily.

Could this really happen? Well…there is a medical condition called hidden penis or concealed penis. It usually occurs in older men but can occur congenitally. Here's what happens.

The penis is connected by ligaments onto the pubic bone. The ligaments are called the suspensory ligaments of the penis. The penis itself has a root about an inch long that extends into the body. You can feel this on the underside of your penis. If a man gains a lot of weight in the groin area, the fat literally engulfs his penis because it is still anchored to bone. When you see a man with this condition, it literally looks as if he has no penis. It's in there—you just can't see it unless he has an erection. This condition can cause urinary problems as the man has to reach into what looks like a hole and pull his penis out. Treatment for this condition includes weight loss, liposuction, or surgical removal of fatty tissue. There is also a surgical procedure to anchor the penis outside the body.

Another delusion involving the penis is called penis stealing and occurs in some countries in Africa. Here's the scenario. A man walks into the emergency room and tells the doctor that someone stole his penis. The doctor examines him and assures him that his penis is still there.

"No, that's a fake one. A witch put a spell on me and stole the real one. She told me that if I pay her a bunch of money, she'll reverse the spell and put my penis back."

At this point the doctor calls the police. I don't know if there should be a safe sex rule for this one—"Beware of penis-stealing witches." Actually, being a penis-stealing witch sounds like easy work if you can get it. Come to think of it, most people who know me probably think I've been one for several decades now.

MODIFYING THE PENIS

Some men have the urge to change the appearance of their penis even though there is nothing medically or functionally wrong with it. There are various ways to pierce the penis and wear jewelry on it. Some men do this because they like the way it looks, and some men do it because the piercing enhances their sensations during masturbation or partner sex. (This is not the same as masochistic sex practices that involve repeated piercing of the penis or scrotum for sexual pleasure. This will be covered in a future chapter.) Some of these piercing styles are safer than others. One style is called the "Prince Albert" which involves piercing through the head of the penis and the urethra. Chances of infection are high.

Some men insert small round objects along the shaft of their penis under the skin. They believe this makes sex feel better. Apparently this practice started in Japan during World War II.

I also heard about a man who bifurcated his penis—cut it in two. He claimed that both sides could get an erection. I don't know how this is possible, but I saw a picture of it (in the book "Modern Primitives") and it didn't look photoshopped.

SAFE SEX RULE
Don't pierce your penis with a kit you bought online. Use a professional.

Men often believe that their penis is too small. There is a medical condition called microphallus, which is defined as a penis that is less than one inch long when erect. Men with normal-size penises are usually satisfied with the way their penis looks when it is erect, but believe it looks too small when it is flaccid. They turn to so-called male enhancement surgery to enlarge the penis.

The following section has been greatly simplified from accounts that appeared in medical journals. There are two ways to enlarge a penis—one to make it longer and one to make it thicker. Penis-lengthening surgery involves loosening or cutting the suspensory ligaments that hold the penis onto the pubic bone. This makes the penis hang lower and therefore look longer. A problem with this surgery is when a man gets an erection, the penis may swivel from side to side. This procedure is often accompanied by surgical removal of fat from the area if that is contributing to short penis length.

The procedure to make the penis wider is potentially more problematic. In most procedures, fat is taken from a man's love handles and injected into the penile shaft at multiple points. Two problems may occur. Due to gravity, the fat may settle under the head of the penis and cause a lump. Or, the fat may gather in rings along the shaft, creating a sort of "Michelin Man" effect. Side effects of penile enlargement surgery also include pain, redness, scarring, inflammation, or redness at the injection sites.

When I was working as a surrogate partner, I had several clients who had male enhancement surgery. Some of them were unhappy with it, for the above reasons. In all cases, the penises looked unnatural, kind of lumpy like potatoes. I will say they were bigger.

If you really believe that your penis is too small, and you

don't want to have surgery, which I totally understand, there are other options. Using a vacuum erection device every day for fifteen minutes can make the penis look larger because you are training your penis to always be half-erect all the time. Creative shaving also works. Shaving all of your pubic hair off will make your penis look bigger. If you don't want to be that extreme, shave about a square inch right above the base of your penis. This will give the illusion of length.

When I attended the Quad S presentation by the urologist I described above, he discussed how he does not do male enhancement surgeries, as he is not satisfied with the outcome. Someone in the audience (not me, believe it or not) asked him if there really was any way to enlarge a penis. He stated that hanging weights on the penis over many years would lengthen it, but he did not recommend this. They advertise small weights online that you could use for this purpose, but the catch is, to show any real changes, you would have to start using the weights at puberty and use them every day.

I also saw a picture of a guy in the book "Modern Primitives". He claimed he had elongated his penis by putting metal rings around it in a graduated manner. It looked like it worked; however, recall the danger of putting solid rings around your penis.

In India, there is a group of holy men who are called sadhus. As part of their religious practice, they do things to their penises to prevent themselves from getting erections. Their belief is that sexual desire and behavior would interfere with their spiritual progress. They tie weights onto their penises or encase their penises in cement. I've seen pictures of the results. The penises are extremely thin and elongated, often to well over a foot long. It appears that the penises are basically urethral tubes with skin on them. These practices have pretty much destroyed their erectile tissue. This is the guy you don't want to be behind in the line for the bathroom!

Some of these practices are depicted in the documentary "Short Cut to Nirvana". This movie shows a man wrapping his elongated penis several times around a stick and letting a kid hang on the stick. In addition to modifying their penises, sadhus do other unusual practices such as slithering on the ground instead of walking, putting hot barbecues on their heads, or taking a vow to hold one of their arms in the air for years at a time.

LET'S NOT FORGET ABOUT THE SCROTUM AND TESTES

The penis is not the only male organ subject to trauma. There are a number of mishaps that can befall the scrotum and testes. One of these is testicular torsion. In this instance, the spermatic cord, from which a testicle is suspended, twists and causes loss of blood flow to the testicle. The symptom of this is extreme pain in the testicle. This is an emergency situation. It's usually caused by a congenital malformation but can be caused by trauma. It can also occur intermittently and resolve itself.

I also heard about a case in which a man had read that before you are born, your testes are inside your body cavity. This is true. He also read that you can push your balls back in and tried to do so, with understandably painful results.

Injuries to the testicles caused by kicking are common. They usually occur while playing sports. Most of the time these injuries will heal quickly, but in some cases, gangrene can develop and result in amputation of a testicle or even death.

Another man heard that putting Ben-Gay lotion on your balls would provide unusual sensations. This is true, if "unusual" means "painful".

Another condition that can occur in the region of the testes and scrotum is a groin hernia. This occurs when the bowel exits or protrudes through the wall of its normal cavity, causing a bulge near the scrotum. The danger is that the bowel will become trapped. This is a life-threatening emergency requiring surgery. The problem is a lot of men know they have a hernia and don't do anything about it. The bulge can become so large that is can push the penis and scrotum to one side and cause erection problems.

One of my doctors once told me a case she saw when she interned in the emergency room. This very overweight man (well over six hundred pounds) walked (!) into the emergency room complaining of pain. When the medical personnel removed his clothes, they saw that his scrotum was so stretched due to a hernia that it was bouncing against his lower legs when he walked. The hernia (the weak spot or opening in the wall) was so large that his penis and one of his kidneys had fallen into it. The doctors were all scratching their heads wondering how this guy was still alive. Miraculously they were able to save his life.

SAFE SEX RULE
Don't put off that needed surgery. Do it while it's still elective.

I heard this one from Timothy Leary, of all people. (Yes, that Timothy Leary). I met him because I had a friend who was in that society where they arrange to have their bodies frozen after death (cryonics). Timothy Leary was a member and every year he gave a Christmas party for this group.

There was a guy at this party who was kind of odd—not effeminate, exactly, but there was just something weird-looking about him. I asked Tim what his story was.

Apparently, when he was about twenty, he was so disturbed

by intense sexual desire that he wanted to get rid of his male hormones. He read a medical book about how to perform castration and surgically removed his own testes.

You can imagine my reaction—"He told you this?"

"He told everybody this!"

Incidentally, Timothy Leary did not have himself frozen. He left the group, because, as he put it, "What if this actually works, and they thaw me out and all these assholes are still around?"

Instead, he opted to have part of his cremated remains shot into outer space. I have to say, even though I only knew him for about a year, Timothy Leary was one of the smartest and most interesting people I ever met. If he was still alive, I'm sure he would give this book an endorsement.

THE URETHRA

Some men get into trouble and it's their own fault. They try to insert objects into their urethra just out of curiosity or for sexual pleasure. This has a name—polyembolokoilamania. Really. It means inserting objects into your body orifices for sexual gratification. Or maybe it means "the world's longest word that has to do with something kinky". I focus more on this type of masochistic practice in a later chapter, but I include injuries to the urethra here.

In one case, a man was staying in a hotel and was curious about what it would feel like to insert a coffee stirrer into his urethra. The verdict—it did not feel good.

Men show up in the emergency room claiming to have blood in their urine and the inability to urinate. It turns out they stuck objects into their urethra. Some of the objects removed from the urethra and bladder include safety pins, needles, thread, metal hooks, razor blades, Christmas tree lights, speaker wire, tweezers, and telephone cables.

In extreme cases of objects inserted into the urethra and left there, it might be necessary to reroute the urethra so that urine comes out above the penis. This is called a suprapubic urinary diversion.

WEIRD CREEPY HISTORICAL MEDICAL FACT
In the early part of the twentieth century, one of the treatments for impotence and sexually transmitted infections was to stick a heated, irradiated or electrified rod into the man's urethra.

In one especially extreme case, a guy inserted some kind of tubing into his penis. Somehow, it became tied in a knot. While attempting to remove it, he tugged really hard, and pulled his urethra, from the base of the penis to the tip, out of the penis. The medical journal article in which I read this included photographs. Thank goodness they are not reproduced here.

My head is still reeling to the point that I can't think of a safe sex rule for this—"Never pull your urethra out of your penis?"

I see a urologist a couple of times a year, and last time I saw my doctor, I asked him if he ever had a case of someone who inserted an object into his urethra for sexual pleasure. I already had enough material to write the chapter, but I wanted it to have a bit more of a personal connection. He immediately came up with three cases, which have never been published.

UROLOGIST CASE #1
My urologist performed surgery on a man to remove fourteen paper clips from his urethra. The paper clips were not hooked together and were unfolded and inserted separately. They were the size that are about an inch and a half long. When my doctor talked to the patient after the surgery, he asked him "Why fourteen?" thinking that maybe the number fourteen

had some significance. The man said, "I ran out of paper clips." (Patients in his waiting room could have heard us both laughing at this one).

UROLOGIST CASE #2

When my doctor was a resident at a hospital back east, a man was found in his car in the parking lot with blood all over him. It turned out that while high on cocaine he became psychotic (out of touch with reality) and believed that the devil was telling him to cut off his penis. So he took the mirror he was using to snort the cocaine, broke it, and used it to cut off his penis and then drove himself to the hospital where a team of urologic surgeons and neurosurgeons were able to reattach it.

This wasn't some young drug addict. This was a forty-something-year-old businessman and the day after the surgery he was sitting up in bed reading the Wall Street Journal and acting like nothing had happened! Wow, that devil really gets around, doesn't he? You'd think he would want people to hang onto their penises so they could continue to sin with them.

UROLOGIST CASE #3

A man wanted to pee sitting down like a woman. Instead of just sitting down on the toilet and peeing, he took a large knitting needle and tied a piece of string around the non-pointed end. Then he stuck the pointed end into his urethra and hammered it in so that it came out his perineum (the area between the back of the testicles and the anus). He pulled the knitting needle through which made a passage that was held open by the string. This is called a seton—a passage in tissue kept open by a string or cord. (Class, we learned a new word!) Needless to say, he developed a massive infection.

My point here is that my urologist is only one guy. What if every urologist in the U. S. had stories like this? Or even urologists in other countries—many of the cases I researched to write this chapter appeared in European or Asian medical journals. This penis craziness may be more widespread than we suspect.

A FINAL EXAMPLE

Let's go back to the Quad S presentation. The doctor showed us a slide and asked for our opinion about what was wrong with this man. His body was a mess. It was a huge mass of scar tissue, kind of Frankenstein-looking, and his penis and scrotum were pushed all the way to one side, almost to his hip. Our guesses included car accident and shark attack. It turned out the patient had flesh-eating bacteria (necrotizing fasciitis). He had skin grafts over his whole body and the surgeons had moved his penis and scrotum over as far as they could to save them. Then the doctor showed us the after picture, in which he had moved and reconstructed the man's genitals. No wonder I think this guy is a genius.

PENIS ENVY—I DON'T THINK SO!

After doing the research and writing this chapter, there is no way I would want to have a penis. Too much trouble! Let's move on to another subject, one more near and dear to my heart—vaginas. That comment showed a serious misunderstanding of female anatomy, didn't it?

CHAPTER 4
VAGINACOLOGY 101

Are you a fan of the Wayans brothers? I am. My favorite movie of theirs is "Dance Flick" and that's where I got the title for this chapter and the next one. In one scene an African-American man is telling his white girlfriend that he just got accepted to college and wants to be a doctor. She asks him what kind of doctor and he says, "A vaginacologist. I want to study vaginas."

It has since come to my attention that there are professionals called "vaginapractors". These are people who advise women how to monitor their fertility and avoid getting pregnant while not using the pill. Apparently there is a trend toward women not wanting to use the pill.

FEMALE ANATOMY
Our discussion of women's safety and health issues begins with an anatomy lesson, and yes, there will be a test on this. The vulva is the word for the parts of female genital anatomy that can be seen from the outside. Before modern understanding

of anatomy, there was an erroneous belief that the female genitals were the same as the male genitals but turned inside out. This is not true. Male and female internal and external anatomy are different although they arise from the same embryonic structures. They are different due to the influence of chromosomes and hormones.

The vulva includes the pubic mound, the labia majora, the labia minora, the clitoris, the vaginal opening, the vestibule, and the hymen. The pubic mound is the triangular fatty pad between your legs that's covered with pubic hair if you don't shave. It cushions the pubic bone during intercourse.

The labia majora are the outer vaginal lips and the labia minora are the inner lips. Their function is to protect the vaginal opening. The outer lips on most women are larger than the inner lips, but that's not always the case. In some women, the inner lips are larger and longer and can protrude from the vaginal opening. This can be painful, as they can get chafed from clothing or tugged uncomfortably during sexual intercourse. It's possible for a woman to be born without vaginal lips. Every woman's lips look different and they are not symmetrical. Some women don't like the way their vaginal lips look because they are large or are not the same size. There is a form of cosmetic surgery in which the size of the lips is reduced.

The clitoris appears to have no function other than sexual pleasure. In the very early weeks of development in the uterus, the embryo, whether XX or XY, has a generic external genital organ called a genital tubercle. Under the influence of male hormones in a male embryo, that organ will grow and become a penis. If no male hormones are present the organ will remain small and become the clitoris. Because the penis and the clitoris come from the same embryonic structure, we call them homologous organs. They have similar structures although they are quite different in size. With the penis, you can see about ninety percent of it on the outside and there is another ten percent you can't see. With the clitoris it's the opposite—you see about ten percent of it and the remaining ninety percent is under the surface anchored to the pubic bone. Like the penis, the clitoris has a shaft, a head, and a foreskin. With the clitoris, the foreskin is called the clitoral hood or the prepuce. In contrast to the penis, the clitoris contains only two cylinders of erectile tissue—two corpora cavernosa, but no corpus spongiosum, because the urethra does not exit through the clitoris. It exits between the clitoris and the vaginal opening.

There are some medical conditions that can affect the clitoris. One is called congenital adrenal hyperplasia (CAH). In this condition a female embryo is masculinized because the mother has a tumor on her adrenal gland that produces male hormones. When this baby is born she is female but may have an enlarged clitoris and initially be misidentified as male. This is cleared up when she urinates.

What can be done in a case like this? Thirty or forty years ago when this happened, parents panicked and begged doctors to do surgery on the girl's clitoris right away to make it smaller. This is not a good idea for two reasons. One is that an infant is not capable of giving consent to what is in effect genital mutilation. Sometimes when this happened, the whole clitoris was inadvertently removed.

The second reason this is not a good idea is that you have no idea what's going to happen to the clitoris at puberty. If there are no medical problems associated with the enlarged clitoris it's best to leave it alone and let the girl make her own decision about cosmetic surgery after puberty. Some women opt for surgery and some just decide to leave it alone. An unusual finding is that women who have CAH tend on the average to be more likely to have a lesbian or bisexual orientation than women who do not have this condition. We don't know why. If CAH is recognized early enough before birth, a hormone can be delivered to prevent it, causing some gay activists to be upset.

CLITORAL CONTROVERSY

Here's a history lesson. In the 1920's a wealthy European woman named Marie Bonaparte went into psychoanalysis with Sigmund Freud because of her problem with "frigidity"—the old term for not being able to have an orgasm. Unsatisfied with her treatment, she decided to do some sex research. She believed that the reason she couldn't have an orgasm was that her clitoris was too far from her vagina. She measured the distance between the clitoris and the vagina in over two hundred women and was convinced that this variable made a difference in the ability to have an orgasm. She persuaded a doctor to operate on her to move her clitoris closer to her vagina. It didn't work, so she had the doctor do it again! She later trained as a psychoanalyst in her own right and she was instrumental in paying the bribes that allowed Sigmund Freud to get out of Austria and escape to England in 1938.

Here's another kind of weird clitoris story that I read somewhere. I tried to look this up and had no luck. Back before Masters and Johnson did their research on the sexual response cycle, people who were having sexual problems had no choice but to go to a psychoanalyst, as it was the only form of psychological treatment available. Women went to analysts complaining that they couldn't have an orgasm. The analysts told them that they either had clitoral adhesions that needed to be removed or they needed to have the hood of the clitoris removed to make the clitoris more accessible.

The hood of the clitoris has tiny glands in it that secrete a fluid. If a woman never washes her clitoral area that fluid builds up and causes the clitoral hood to stick to the clitoris. That's what a clitoral adhesion is. It's similar to what we saw in the chapter on the penis with men having to get an adult circumcision due to foreskin adhesions but on a much smaller scale.

So, anyway, all these women went to doctors and had these painful operations which probably weren't necessary, and probably didn't work. What I was surprised to find out when I researched this was that there are a lot of doctors who are still doing these surgeries.

I've never heard of a case of a woman born without a clitoris, but I suppose it could happen. I did see a picture once of a woman who was born with two. This was some kind of birth defect where the woman's pelvic bones failed to fuse and she literally had two clits about three inches apart. She did opt for cosmetic surgery.

The vaginal opening is just what it sounds like and is considered a separate structure. The vestibule is the skin area surrounding the vaginal opening. It's an appropriate name because it's like the opening to the holy city.

When young girls are born, they have a membrane across the opening of their vaginas called the hymen. It is usually attached to both sides of the vaginal walls and often has openings in it so the girl can menstruate at puberty. The hymen has a lot of mythology associated with it. If you have an intact hymen, the first time you have sexual intercourse, it will tear and may bleed. It might be so tough that it doesn't tear and might have to be removed by a doctor.

In cultures in which a bride price is paid the hymen is significant because the groom's family wants to make sure they got a good deal by getting a virgin. Wedding guests would wait outside the room where the newlyweds had sex. When they were done, they would hang the bedsheet out of the room to demonstrate that the bride's hymen bled. (Personally, I can think of a number of ways to fake that).

In modern Western societies, most girls lose their hymen before they have sexual intercourse, by doing sports such as gymnastics, cycling, or horseback riding, or by using tampons or inserting other objects into their vaginas. So just because a girl doesn't have an intact hymen, it doesn't mean she's not a virgin. In cultures where the hymen is important, some women have surgery to replace the missing hymen with another piece of tissue so they will bleed on their wedding night and be able to show they were a virgin.

In a previous chapter I talked about male circumcision and here I'll talk about female circumcision, also called female genital mutilation (FGM). Male circumcision mostly occurs in Western society and is done by medical personnel, except for Orthodox Jews who use a specially-trained rabbi called a mohel. Female circumcision usually occurs in cultural enclaves in Africa and the Middle East. It is a cultural practice, not a religious practice.

There are several types of female circumcision. They are sometimes described as Type I, II, or III, or Type 1, 2, 3, or 4. Since there is no agreement I'll just describe them without giving types.

One type is symbolic circumcision and it's done at birth. The clitoris is pricked with a needle and three drops of blood are squeezed out. This is not common. Another type of circumcision is similar to male circumcision. The clitoral hood is removed. Again, this is also not common. The type of circumcision that is most common is called Pharaonic circumcision. In this practice, the girl's clitoris and inner lips are removed. This is usually done on girls between the ages of five and twelve—before puberty. In an even more radical form of circumcision, parts of the outer lips are removed also.

Circumcision can also be accompanied by infibulation. In this practice the remaining sides of the lips are stitched or hooked together. In the most extreme cases only a very small opening is left for urination and menstruation. In another practice called introcision, part of the internal musculature of the vagina is scraped away.

It's tempting for us to look at these practices and say, "How barbaric!" But keep in mind that male circumcision is genital mutilation without consent also. In the enclaves in which female circumcision practices are well-entrenched, they have thousands of years of history behind them.

When I belonged to Quad S, one of the conferences I was to attend included a panel discussion of FGM. Everyone was very eager to attend this, as we were just becoming aware of these practices. When we all showed up and crammed into the conference room it was announced that the panel was canceled. Quad S had searched worldwide and was not able to find a professional person who was willing to defend these practices.

It would also be easy to say, "Well, that's just another example of a patriarchal society. Look how far they'll go to keep women in their place." FGM is performed on girls by women, not by men.

A weird coincidence occurred as I was writing this material. I was reading the book "The Handmaid's Tale" by Margaret Atwood. There is interest in this book published in 1985 because of the Hulu series in 2017. If you are not familiar with this book, it describes a dystopian patriarchal society in which some young women live as virtual slaves and are forced to get pregnant by powerful men. The very day I wrote the above paragraph I read the following quote from that book—"the best and most cost-effective way to control women for reproductive and other purposes was through women themselves." Makes you think.

In enclaves where FGM is practiced the rationale is that it is a rite of passage into womanhood. It is also a way to protect a woman's virginity. In these cultural enclaves, both men and women are taught that intact genitals are unclean, disease-ridden, and smell bad. They are taught that intact genitals are a sign of a woman with no family or a prostitute. Women are taught to be extremely afraid of rape. The practice is used to prevent masturbation. Men are taught to prefer childlike genitals. Girls who are about to undergo this procedure are not told what will happen to them. They are then told the clitoris will grow back and that the procedure will enhance their fertility.

The reality is quite different. Some of these procedures take place in a hospital under sterile conditions but most do not. Often the procedure is performed in a hut and the cutting instrument (a knife or even a sharpened shell or stone) is not cleaned. No anesthesia is used.

Complications include infections, scar tissue, cysts, lifelong pain, urination and menstrual problems, and childbirth complications. This is all in addition to the loss of sexual pleasure. I can't begin to see an upside here. It's also true that in the enclaves in which this practice is prevalent, young girls who have had the procedure may make fun of girls who haven't had it.

As an aside, one of the reasons sex is fun is because during intercourse, one of the things that feels good is the vagina has a muscular structure that grips the penis with each stroke. That can't happen here because in most of these cases, so much scar tissue has formed that the vagina loses its elasticity.

I didn't think that anything could be done to help women who had the clitoris removed. But as of this writing, a charitable organization called Clitoraid has funded a center in Kenya. Doctors there are treating victims of circumcision using a surgical technique to remove scar tissue and improve sexual functioning by cutting ligaments to allow the clitoris to descend so that some of it that is left is available for stimulation. Recall that a similar technique is used to lengthen penises, so this makes sense. The clitoris has suspensory ligaments the same way a penis does. I'm glad somebody finally thought of this!

Another couple of structures that are sort of on the outside but aren't really part of the vulva are the pubococcygeus (P. C.) muscle and the Bartholin's glands. The P. C. muscle surrounds the opening of the vagina and supports the pelvic floor. It has several functions. In childbirth it's the muscle group that the woman pushes with to give birth. It's the muscle group that spasms when a woman has an orgasm. It's also the muscle group that helps you maintain urinary continence. That's why it's important for all women, not just pregnant women, to exercise this muscle group on a daily basis using the Kegel exercises. These exercises have been written about extensively so I won't repeat them here.

Bartholin's glands (also called the Bartholin glands or the greater vestibular glands) secrete a small amount of clear lubrication into the opening of the vagina. Unfortunately, one of the glands' ducts can become clogged and create a huge cyst which has to be dealt with medically.

INTERNAL ANATOMY

The vagina is the tubular organ for sexual intercourse and is also the birth canal. It has three layers. The inner layer is mucous membrane and when a woman is aroused, blood flows into that area, forcing lubrication into the vaginal canal. The middle layer is muscular, and the outer layer is connective tissue that holds the vagina in place in the pelvic cavity. You can imagine what an amazing muscular structure the vagina must have to be able to stretch to the size of a baby.

There has been a lot of mythology surrounding the vagina. People can't see it, so it's mysterious and they're scared of it. The myth of vagina dentata says that the vagina contains teeth that will bite off a man's penis or castrate him if he tries to have sex with a woman. This is a folktale in many cultures and was probably used to convey the dangers of women, or to prevent rape. There is a fairly recent film called "Teeth" that illustrates this myth. It's a horror movie in case that wasn't clear.

The vagina also involves the myth of the evil eye. According to European legends, one way for a woman to curse someone is to raise her skirt and flash her vagina at the person.

The cervix is the opening to the uterus. The uterus is the organ that holds the developing embryo. In a woman who is not pregnant and not sexually aroused the uterus sits on top of the vagina about two-thirds of the way up.

The ovaries are located in the pelvic cavity on either side of the uterus. They contain a woman's eggs. Girls are born with all the eggs they'll ever have, unlike men who produce new sperm every day. At puberty the eggs start to mature and a woman eventually produces one every month at ovulation about halfway between periods. The egg migrates into one of the Fallopian tubes which are on either side of the uterus.

If you are a woman, I'm going to urge you to do a self-examination of your vagina. It's important not just for comfort with sexual activity. You need to know what your vulva and vagina look like, feel like, and smell like when they are healthy so you'll know if something is wrong.

Sometimes during your annual gynecological exam, the doctor will offer to hand you a mirror so you can take a look. Not all doctors will do this so it's best to do it yourself. The best time to do it is right after your annual exam when the doctor has told you that everything is healthy. You'll need a speculum, a mirror, and a flashlight.

First examine your vulva, without the mirror and then with it to see the lower area. This is much easier to do if you have shaved or trimmed your pubic hair. Gently spread your inner and outer lips apart and examine all the folds. Identify your clitoris and the other outer structures I've talked about. Note the skin color and texture. Note any moles, bumps, or anything else unusual. It wouldn't be a bad idea to take a picture with your phone, print it, and save it for future reference.

Now insert the speculum and open it so you can see the inside of the vagina. Here's what you will see. It's a tunnel that looks kind of like the inside of your mouth. The walls will be pink and they may be shiny due to lube. On top on either the left or right side, you'll see something that looks like one of those miniature powdered sugar donuts. That's the cervix. The vaginal walls will appear kind of striped or corrugated. That reflects the muscle structure. Those striped areas are called rugae. If you really pay attention during intercourse, you can and your partner can feel them.

When I took my first Human Sexuality class back in the 1970's one of our guest speakers was a woman from a local health center. At one point in her talk, she asked all the men to leave the room and she got up on the instructor's desk and showed us how to do a pelvic exam. I can't imagine doing that in my Human Sexuality class today. You'd think we'd have become more liberal over the years, but that's not the case.

When you look inside your vagina, here are a couple of

structures you can't see. You won't see the Grafenberg spot (G spot) because it's a little off the beaten track. The way to feel it is to remove the speculum, insert your middle finger, and curl it back so it's pointing at your pubic mound but from the inside. I tried to see mine once using a dental mirror but was not successful because it kept fogging up. When you touch the G spot it will feel like a rougher spot about the size of a nickel.

Another area you can't see is the anterior fornix, also called the A spot. You can't see it because the speculum will be in the way. The A spot is the upper wall of the vagina and is thought to be responsible for most of the lubrication that occurs when you get aroused.

A third area you won't be able to see is the end of the vagina, called the cul de sac. The vagina doesn't end at the cervix and uterus. There's another inch or so beyond the uterus. When a woman gets aroused, the uterus tenses up and the cul de sac is exposed.

Some abnormalities can occur in the development of the vagina. It's possible for a girl to be born with two vaginas. Technically it is really one vagina with a membrane down the middle. It's called septate vagina.

I asked my gynecologist (also known as "the caretaker of the Holy City") if he had ever seen a case of this and he said, "Absolutely." It's not particularly dangerous. Some women with this condition just leave it the way it is and don't have corrective cosmetic surgery. They just push the membrane out of the way and use whichever side is more comfortable for sex. He told me about a patient he saw with this when he was an intern. She was African-American and worked as a prostitute. He thought he was being a real smart ass and asked her, "So, how do you know which side to use?" And she said, "The larger one is for my customers and the smaller one is for my special friends."

A study indicated that three out of ninety thousand women had septate vagina. The division could occur all the way up to the level of the uterus.

It's also possible for a girl to be born without a vagina. The opening could be there without the canal, or the canal could be internal but have no opening. The whole thing could be missing. If that was the case, the infant girl would probably have other major deformities of the urogenital system. An opening or internal vagina can be constructed to form a vagina that can be used for sexual intercourse. I think it's also possible for a woman to receive a transplant from a donor if hers has to be removed, for example, due to vaginal cancer, which is rare. Congenital absence of the vagina is called Mayer-Rokitansky-Kuster-Hauser syndrome.

In a birth defect called sirenomelia (again rare, something like one out of one hundred thousand cases), an infant girl is born with her legs fused together all the way up to her pelvis. This condition is named after mermaids. I found very few journal accounts of successful surgery to correct this condition, which would obviously involve constructing a vagina in addition to separating the legs. This condition was featured on the Oprah Winfrey show in 2009.

How big are vaginas? This is a little hard to answer because it's not like a penis where you can see it and measure it with a ruler. The vagina is a potential space. It can really only be measured by the size of an object that will fit into it (or come out of it). Fortunately it has that muscle structure that allows it to stretch and spring back.

Vaginal size can be an issue, because there are some couples where the man's penis and the woman's vagina just don't fit, and it's not necessarily always about the man's penis being too big and/or the woman's vagina being too small. The shape of the penis and vagina can be an issue too. In my career, I've run across a couple men with whom I had pain during sexual intercourse. It was just something about the shape. It can be a challenge to find different positions, lube, and type of foreplay that will make you comfortable and that's part of keeping yourself safe. Childbirth and surgery may change the length or shape of your vagina also.

A friend of mine once brought over this movie. It was called something like "Monster Dildo Party" or "Monster Dildo Olympics", I can't remember. I guess it was supposed to be a porno but it's hard to imagine somebody getting turned on by it. It featured seven naked women surrounding another naked woman. None of these women were at all attractive, by the way. The seven women took turns inserting larger and larger dildos into the central woman. For the finale, they inserted an object that I swear was the size of a traffic cone. Oh, and in another scene, the central woman took a regular size vaginal dildo (about seven inches) and inserted it into her urethra and then peed all over the place, which was no big surprise. During this whole movie I was alternating between cringing and laughing hysterically and yet I kept watching, go figure.

The central woman in this movie was unusual, to say the least. When the camera was facing her empty vagina, it was so big you could see into it, which is not the case with most women. A friend of mine used to call having sex with a woman with a large vagina "throwing a hot dog down a hallway".

Part of sexual health is having a positive attitude about how your genitals look and feel, and being safe about any cosmetic alterations you make to them. Feeling good about how your vulva looks has been difficult for a lot of women. Attitudes are more positive than they were in previous eras, but there are still women who were taught not to look at yourself or touch yourself "down there".

Some of the things women have done to feel more positive about how their genitals look are removing pubic hair, getting genital piercings, and getting tattoos on the genitals, as well as temporary practices such as dying the pubic hair or gluing fake jewels onto the pubic mound ("vajazzling"). I've also heard of a process that involves cleaning the vagina using steam. A woman squats over a source of steam. I don't think this is necessary but it sounds like it might feel good.

Hair removal needs to be done safely. One option is shaving. This can be done with a regular razor with a blade or a beard trimmer. They make special shaving gels for the pubic area, as the skin is sensitive here and a razor rash can occur. You don't want your partner to get whisker burn when he's going down on you. You can shave the area on your pubic mound wet or dry but I find it's best to use a beard trimmer on the lips because it's tricky—it's kind of like trying to shave a piece of sushi.

Waxing is another option. Just doing the pubic mound and lips is called a bikini wax. The Brazilian also includes the area around the anus so you can wear a thong. In this practice, strips of hot wax are put on the area. The hair sticks to the wax and then the wax strips are pulled off. Very painful. I could never bring myself to get this done. Plus, for this to work, you have to let the hair grow out to at least a quarter inch for it to stick in the wax. No way! My husband and I have an ongoing discussion about how much money it would take to induce me not to remove any hair from my body for a year. We haven't reached an agreement on the amount yet, but it's approaching an amount somewhere near the national debt.

Electrolysis involves destroying individual hairs at the root using an electrical current. This is somewhat painful and may need to be repeated several times, resulting in a major time commitment and expense.

Laser hair removal is even more expensive and there are no guarantees it will be permanent. Results may vary according to hair color, hair texture, and skin tone, with best results on people who have dark hair in contrast to light skin. This involves probably about the same amount of pain as electrolysis.

There are some depilatory (hair removal) creams made specifically for the bikini area. I really don't know how well they work, but again, to use them successfully you have to let your hair grow out somewhat.

Pubic hair removal has major benefits for women. I can't believe it didn't become more popular sooner than it did. Removing pubic hair makes it so much easier to do a vaginal self-exam, and so much easier for a man to go down on you and find the most pleasurable areas. It eliminates odors in the genital area. Best of all, it makes oral sex so much more enjoyable!

Of all of the above methods, I would still stick with shaving as long as it doesn't irritate your skin. It's cheap and if you don't like the results you can always change your mind and let the hair grow back. Injuries that can result from shaving include cuts, abrasions, ingrown hairs, itching, rash, and infection.

Genital piercings are a different safety story. Some women have rings pierced into their labia. Some have a stud put into the clitoris. Reasons for piercing include appearance and the idea that sex feels different when the piercing is tugged on.

I rate genital piercing for women as a fairly dangerous process. Consequences could include infection, torn skin, scarring, and having the piercing become embedded into the skin. This could require surgery. If you are going to get a genital piercing, make sure you inquire about the professional's experience.

I'm a nudist, so I've seen a lot of pierced genitals (not on myself). I've seen women with rows of rings in both lips with a ribbon tied through them so the vagina was laced together. Nudist resorts are one of the few places people can show this off. I think that makes your vagina look like a shower curtain rod, but to each his own.

Tattooing can be done on the pubic mound and is quite popular. I saw a woman, again at a nudist resort, who had a five-by-five inch rose tattooed on her pubic mound. It's probably not any more dangerous than a tattoo on any other part of your body, as long as it's done by a trained and experienced professional. That reminds me of a joke.

Back in the 1970's, a woman went to see "The Sting". She thought that Robert Redford and Paul Newman were the best-looking guys she'd ever seen. So she went to a tattoo parlor and told the tattoo artist she wanted a picture of Robert Redford tattooed on one of her upper inner thighs and Paul Newman on the other. When the work was completed and the tattoo artist gave her a mirror to look at it, she wasn't happy. She said it didn't look like them and he disagreed. He said, "I could get anyone off the street and they could look at this and know exactly who those men are." So he went outside and grabbed a wino off the street and asked him, "Who are these men?" And the wino gazed carefully at the tattoos and said, "Well, that one on the left is a very good likeness of Robert Redford. And the one on the right is an excellent likeness of Paul Newman." And the tattoo artist said to the woman, "See?" And the wino said, "And who's that guy in the middle? Willie Nelson?"

PHYSIOLOGY

How do the female parts work? This section will deal with the female sexual response cycle, erections (yes, erections), muscle tone, hormones, lubrication, the menstrual cycle, and orgasm. This is based on the work of Masters and Johnson.

When a woman becomes sexually aroused, the vulva and vagina change in appearance somewhat. As a woman goes from desire to arousal to orgasm, the outer and inner lips engorge with blood and turn darker, to red or even purple. The area between the clitoris on the outside and the G spot on the inside swells. The vagina expands. When a woman is very aroused, the muscles that support the uterus tighten up and the cul de sac of the vagina is available for penetration. When a woman is very aroused, the middle third of her vagina gets tighter. Masters and Johnson called this the formation of the orgasmic platform. After orgasm, blood leaves the pelvic area and the genitals return to their unaroused appearance. So none of the above changes are anything to worry about.

Do women get erections? Yes, they do. When a woman gets aroused, the erectile tissue in the clitoris, the two corpora cavernosa, fill with blood and the clitoris enlarges. But that's not the whole story. When a woman gets aroused, blood flows to the whole genital region and the whole area swells up. Picture yourself cupping your vulva with your hand. The internal area of tissue that surrounds the urethra is called the vaginal sponge or the paraurethral sponge. When a woman gets aroused, this area engorges with blood and this is the female erection response.

Three are two sources of muscle tone in the vagina. The P. C. muscle at the opening of the vagina can be tightened and relaxed voluntarily. The entire length of the vagina has striated muscle in the middle layer. You can get some voluntary control of these muscles by exercising them using vaginal balls. These are small metal balls that you insert in your vagina and try to move around. Sometimes these are called Ben-Wa balls.

Exercising both the P. C. muscle and the internal vaginal muscles on a regular basis can often make your vagina somewhat tighter. Even better, developing these muscles allows more blood to flow to the genital area when you get aroused, resulting in more pleasure.

There are three sources of female lubrication. The Bartholin's glands secrete a small amount of clear fluid directly into the vagina. Most women don't notice this because it's such a small amount and is overshadowed by the lubrication in the vaginal walls.

When a woman gets aroused, blood flows to her pelvic area and causes the vaginal walls to swell, which forces lubrication into the vagina. This is called vaginal sweating. The technical term is transudation.

Women vary greatly in the amount of lubrication they produce. Some women produce very little lubrication even though they are otherwise psychologically and physically turned on. Other women produce so much lube that it's almost embarrassing. So lack of lube cannot be interpreted to mean that a woman is not turned on.

Even if you produce a lot of lubrication, you may still need to use a lubricating product, especially as you get older and the vaginal walls start to thin. It's always good to err on the side of too much lube rather than too little, because having sex when your vagina is too dry can cause abrasions and pain. You'll wake up the next morning thinking, "Really should have gone in the bathroom and taken that lube out of the drawer."

Finding the right lube for yourself is key. There are so many choices. I don't recommend or endorse particular products because I'm not getting paid to do so. Generally, you make a choice between an oil-based product or a water-based product. Every source I've read on this subject says Vaseline is not recommended. I don't know why, I've never had a problem with it. One thing to keep in mind is you might have an allergy to certain products so try them on your hand first. I prefer an oil-based product such as mineral oil (generic) or coconut oil (also generic) but that's me. Another thing to keep in mind is if you're slathering lube all over your vagina, it should be something that is not harmful if your partner goes down on you.

Sometimes women get into trouble with lube because they weren't planning to have sex and weren't prepared. Women have used skin lotion, tanning oil, vegetable oil, and other substances for lube. Any of these products could affect the chemical balance in the vagina.

A third possible source of female lubrication is the G spot. Some women report that when their G spot is stimulated either through intercourse or the use of a curved dildo, they experience intense lubrication. This can be so much fluid that it's called female ejaculation or a gusher. Not all women have experienced this.

Believe it or not, the G spot is still controversial so many years after the publication of the book by Beverly Whipple and her colleagues in 1982. It's clear that stimulation of that area can be quite pleasurable and trigger an orgasm. It's also clear that many women experience this gushing of fluid. What's controversial is that anatomical studies have shown no difference between the structure of the G spot and the vaginal tissue surrounding it. All I can say is, if you've ever experienced this phenomenon, you know that there's definitely something going on there, whatever you want to call it.

Women's hormones are quite complicated. But I'll try to keep it as simple as I can. The two main female hormones that are produced by the ovaries are estrogen and progesterone. They run on a monthly cycle. Sometimes they're both high and sometimes one is high and the other is low. Estrogen regulates ovulation, development of the endometrium (the lining of the uterus), and female secondary sex characteristics such as breast development. Progesterone regulates the release of the ovum and implantation of a fertilized egg into the uterine wall. Both of these hormones are controlled in the brain by the hypothalamus and pituitary gland. When estrogen is high, for example, right before your period, you may experience premenstrual symptoms such as nausea and swollen breasts.

The interaction of these hormones results in the menstrual cycle which regulates a woman's fertility and allows for conception and pregnancy. Unlike men, who make sperm constantly, women in theory are only fertile when an egg is released in the middle of the monthly cycle. Preventing unwanted pregnancy is a huge safe sex issue and will be dealt with in a separate future chapter. The focus here is on safety issues involved in the menstrual phase of the monthly cycle when you are actually having your period.

Having your period presents a couple of safety issues. It's safe to have sex during your period. A lot of people don't, just because it can be messy.

Throughout history, people have developed mythology about menstruating women. They were either seen as very powerful or as tainted or unclean. In some cultures, menstruating women were banished to a special hut and weren't allowed back into the tribe until they underwent a special cleansing ceremony.

Even up to the end of the twentieth century, some people believed that having your menstrual period was like an illness—you're sick and should not do normal activities like play sports. Some women do experience debilitating cramps during their period, but there is no medical reason you cannot have sex. There is some evidence that having an orgasm can help with uterine cramping. Also keep in mind that when you are actively menstruating, if you have sex with someone who has a bacterial or viral STI, you are more likely to catch a disease than you would be if you had sex at another phase of your cycle.

There was a rumor going around about camping which said that you are more likely to get attacked by a bear if you're on your period because they can smell the blood. Some researchers took this seriously enough to do a study on it. They made up bear food packets, either with dog food or used tampons from female park rangers. It turned out the bears preferred the dog food to human blood.

Some people think you're more likely to be attacked by a shark if you swim in the ocean when you have your period. This one might be true—nobody's been crazy enough to do a study on it as far as I know.

SAFE SEX RULE
You shouldn't really be hanging out any place where you even think there might be bears or sharks, whether you're on your period or not.

Having your period requires that you use protection in the form of pads, cervical cups, or tampons. Did you know that in some countries in Africa, commercial menstrual products are not available and so girls use leaves or actually squat over a hole while they flow? They often miss several days of school a month because of this.

Problems obtaining feminine hygiene products are not limited to third-world countries. There is a trend in the U. S. toward recognizing that charging tax on menstrual products and high prices for them is unfair and discriminatory toward women. Female students in the U. S. also sometimes miss school because they can't afford menstrual supplies or otherwise don't have access to them. Homeless women often have to make a choice between buying food or buying menstrual supplies.

Pads and cervical cups are safe to use. However, they're messy to remove and change. Pads, especially, can be uncomfortable.

Tampons are safe also, but as they are used internally, they can present a bit of a challenge. They must be used correctly.

Back in the early 1980's, there was a major health scare involving tampons. Some women who used the then-popular super absorbent tampons such as Rely became ill with a potentially fatal bacterial staph infection called toxic shock syndrome (TSS).

Tampons did not cause TSS. Nobody knows what caused it. If this particular staph bacteria gets into your body it produces a poison. People who didn't use tampons sometimes got TSS too. The symptoms were quick onset and included fever, muscle pain, delirium, loss of consciousness, and possible death. One of the weirder symptoms was skin peeling off the ends of your fingers.

What happened with the tampons was that because they were so super absorbent, women were leaving them in too long. Women liked the convenience of not having to change so often during a heavy flow. But that caused a large accumulation of blood in the vagina and set the stage for toxic shock.

Because of that health crisis, the government now regulates tampons. They come in standard sizes—junior, regular, super, and super-plus—based on their rate of absorption in grams. Prior to this if a box of tampons was labeled "Super" or whatever, it could mean anything. So now you know exactly what degree of absorbency you are getting if you buy a box of tampons.

Here are some other suggestions for the safe use of tampons. Insert them at the correct angle as shown on the package. Otherwise they will be uncomfortable and will not absorb well. Use the least absorbent tampon you can for the particular phase of your period. Don't leave a tampon in for more than three or four hours without changing it. Use tampons only during your period and not just to absorb vaginal discharge at other times. This is especially important. Using tampons and pulling them out when they are relatively dry can cause vaginal abrasions or even vaginal ulcers. Don't forget to remove the last tampon at the end of your period. Most gynecologists have had experiences where a woman came in with a horrible vaginal odor and it turned out the woman had inadvertently left a tampon in for several days and forgot about it.

A few years ago there was a concern that some brands of tampons might contain toxic substances such as dioxin or asbestos. This is not true.

I also looked into whether it is dangerous to go in a hot tub during your period. What I found is that it is apparently no more dangerous than when you are not on your period.

The next chapter is about medical conditions and injuries that can affect the female reproductive organs.

CHAPTER 3
ADVANCED VAGINACOLOGY

The previous chapter dealt with normal female anatomy and physiology. This chapter deals with some of the things that can go wrong.

SEXUAL PAIN

Pain in the vaginal and vulval areas is not normal. It indicates something is wrong. The pain could occur only during intercourse or be there all the time. Genital pain that causes personal distress and impairs functioning can become so severe it is considered a mental disorder.

Let me explain a little bit about how mental problems are diagnosed. There is a book called the Diagnostic and Statistical Manual of Mental Disorders (DSM) that is used by most mental health professionals. Its most recent edition was published in 2013. In the most recent version of the manual sexual pain in women is called genito-pelvic pain/penetration disorder.

Here are the criteria for its diagnosis—difficulty with penetration, vulvovaginal or pelvic pain during intercourse attempts, fear or anxiety about pain during sex, and tightening of the P. C. muscle that prevents penetration. This is very confusing, because the definition seems to be mostly about penetration and not so much about the pain. The DSM contains a strong heterosexist bias when it comes to diagnosing sexual dysfunctions. The authors make it sound like vaginal pain is not a problem unless you're trying to have intercourse, and this is not true, as we'll see.

A little history lesson. In the previous DSM-IV-TR, female genital pain during sexual activity was divided into two categories—vaginismus and dyspareunia. Vaginismus is a psychological anxiety-based condition in which a woman is afraid to have penetration and the P. C. muscle that surrounds the opening of the vagina tightens up and causes pain if penetration is attempted. Some women with vaginismus tighten up only at the prospect of intercourse. Others have such severe cases of vaginismus that they can't even use a tampon and have to be sedated to have a pelvic exam. Again, this is a psychological condition due to anxiety. This is often caused by sexual trauma, or lack of knowledge and/or sex education.

Dyspareunia is pain during intercourse. In previous diagnostic schemas, it could occur in women or men. It usually meant psychologically-based pain during intercourse. That meant for a diagnosis you had to rule out a huge number of medical conditions and when you ruled out every medical possibility you were left with dyspareunia and it was treated psychologically.

Pain, whether during intercourse or not, is much too common, especially in young women and post-menopausal women. I'm going to go into every condition I know about that could cause pain in the female pelvic region. You have no idea how many things can go wrong with your vagina and how many things you have to watch out for. First, I'm going to tell you what it feels like to have a vagina, for those of you who don't have one. I don't know what it feels like to have a penis, because I don't have one. But I imagine it feels kind of like having a fish in your pants. Sometimes (rarely) the fish is asleep, but most of the time it's flopping around down there and you're aware of it.

This is not true of a vagina. It's more like a nose. Most of the time you're not aware of it. You're only aware of it if it's swollen because you're aroused, or it's inflamed or has something in it.

Here are some issues to consider. The nature of pain is subjective and so it's difficult to describe it to a doctor. If you are experiencing pain in the genital/pelvic region your doctor will ask you to rate the intensity, probably on a 1 to 10 scale. The doctor will ask the location of the pain. Does it appear to be coming from the vulva area or deeper within the vagina or pelvis? Is it on only one side or both? Describe the nature of the pain. Is it searing, burning, aching, throbbing, shooting, acute, or dull? How long have you had the pain? Does it come and go or is it ongoing? These are all important for the doctor to know in order to diagnose your problems and treat them.

At the most basic level, vulvovaginal pain can be caused by lack of lube and/or rough sex. Keep yourself safe and pain-free by using lots of lube, not having dry sex, and taking a day or two off to let your vagina heal up. I know it's tempting sometimes to have rough sex, because when you're really aroused you don't feel pain the same way you normally would.

I get it. That's why it's so important to use lube even if you think you don't need it.

Another possible source of vaginal pain is STI's and vaginal infections. These are dealt with in detail in a later chapter, but I'll mention them a little here. Gonorrhea and chlamydia can cause burning pain on urination. Often they don't have symptoms and can travel into your Fallopian tubes and cause an infection called pelvic inflammatory disease (PID). Symptoms of PID are major abdominal pain and high fever.

A yeast infection can cause pain due to cracking of the skin of the vulva. This can be diagnosed by looking at it. So can herpes, which can cause major pain. It can be diagnosed by looking at the blisters.

Uterine fibroids are benign tumors in the middle layer of the uterus. If they become too large they can press on other organs and cause pain in the abdomen. Treatments include hormones, embolization (cutting off blood supply to the fibroid), or surgery.

Cysts are sacs of fluid and they can occur on the ovaries. There are many different kinds of ovarian cysts. The most common kind flare up when you ovulate and cause severe pain on one side of the pelvis during intercourse. Treatment can consist of birth control pills.

I suffered from ovarian cysts in the 1970's when I was a mail carrier. They were quite painful. In addition to causing pain during intercourse, they also caused back and shoulder pain, which affected my job. One time I came back to the office from doing my route and my supervisor said, "I saw you out on the street and you weren't carrying your bag." (We were supposed to carry our mailbag even if we had a light load and didn't need it). I said, "My doctor told me not to carry it because I have cysts on my ovary". Of course he replied, "Where are you trying to carry it?" Everybody's a comedian, hunh?

Endometriosis is a condition in which the endometrium (the inner lining of the uterus) grows outside the uterus into other areas of the pelvic cavity. This can be quite painful during the menstrual phase of the cycle because the tissue swells, bleeds, and scars. Treatment is surgery.

There are several kinds of cancer that can affect the female pelvic area. Cervical cancer is usually not painful in the early stages. It is diagnosed with a Pap smear and by looking at it. The main symptom is bleeding after intercourse and the major risk factor is unprotected sex with multiple partners. Uterine cancer is usually not painful in the early stages. The main symptom is irregular bleeding or bleeding from the uterus after menopause. It is diagnosed during a manual pelvic exam or by a scan. The main symptom of ovarian cancer is abdominal discomfort or bloating. It is also diagnosed by a manual pelvic exam or by a scan. Family history is important to monitor here. Treatment can be a combination of surgery, chemotherapy, and radiation.

This is why it's important to have a Pap smear and internal exam regularly. It's confusing at this point in time because the rule of thumb used to be easy. It was, "Have a Pap smear every year starting when you turn eighteen or when you start having intercourse, whichever comes first." Now, because of changes in healthcare funding and the way insurance companies evaluate risk, they're saying that women can probably safely go two or three years between exams. In other words, the insurance companies will only pay for an exam every two to three years instead of once a year. In my opinion, if you are having unprotected sex with more than one person, you should get an exam every year, even if you have to pay for it. Insurance companies have determined that it saves money to wait until a person gets cancer and pay for the treatment, rather than pay for millions of Pap smears a year. Sad but true. Don't get me started.

THE "DYNIAS"

There is another type of vulvovaginal pain that is kind of mysterious. It's called vulvodynia. It was brought to public awareness when one of the characters on "Sex and the City" was diagnosed with it. The symptoms are searing burning pain all the time, even when you're not trying to have intercourse. I say trying, because it's not going to happen, this can be so painful. Sometimes this is called burning vagina syndrome. Another form of this is vestibulodynia, also called vulvar vestibulitis, in which the pain is confined to the vestibule, the skin around the opening of the vagina. Clitorodynia is pain in the clitoris. This could be caused by clitoral adhesions.

I call these conditions mysterious because nobody knows what causes them. Everybody has their guess. Is it excitation or inflammation of a nerve? Is it chronic tension in the P.C. muscle? Is it an autoimmune reaction in which a woman develops an allergy to the skin of her vulva? Is it psychological? It's mysterious because the woman is complaining of this searing burning excruciating pain, and yet when the doctor looks at her vulva, it appears normal. There is no sign of injury or disease.

Because we don't know what causes it, we don't know how to treat it. The most basic instruction to a woman with this complaint is to keep all chemicals away from the vulva—I mean all. This is in case the condition is an allergic reaction. Don't wash your underwear in products that contain chemicals. Don't use soap on your vulva. Don't use toilet paper that contains chemicals. And on and on. Sometimes this relieves the symptoms, if an allergy was involved. Estrogen cream or cortisone cream may be prescribed.

The next step is psychological treatment including relaxation, meditation, biofeedback, or antidepressant drugs, in particular the tricyclic antidepressants. These methods could work if there is a psychological component to the condition.

Painkillers will no doubt be prescribed. If a nerve condition is suspected, an anti-convulsant or anti-epilepsy drug could be used. Sometimes spinal misalignment due to an accident might cause nerve pain. If an autoimmune condition is suspected, interferon could be prescribed. The last resort is surgery, which is called vestibulectomy. This is the surgical removal of all the skin of the vestibule. It only works about half the time.

For some women, the search for relief for this condition has been a years-long struggle, taking an immense toll on the woman's mental health and intimate relationships. Weirdly, sometimes the condition goes away by itself.

Another source of pain is pelvic trauma. The trauma could be injuries due to an accident. Some women have chronic genital or pelvic pain due to injuries suffered during childbirth, surgery, or a brutal rape.

Hysterectomy—removal of the uterus—is a commonly-performed surgery due to cancer or benign conditions such as fibroids. I know women who had hysterectomies and suffered chronic pelvic pain for years, and doctors were unable to help them. Surgery to remove cancerous tumors could also cause chronic pain especially when accompanied by chemotherapy or radiation. Radiation in the pelvic area can thin or shrink the vagina and make intercourse very painful.

In addition to pain, other causes for concern are bumps, discoloration, redness, rashes, odors, growths, and itching. Odors usually signify an STI. A growth in the vulval area could be benign or something worrisome. If there is a change in the skin of your vulva that concerns you, definitely get it checked by a doctor. Vulval cancer is rare but it can occur. A melanoma tumor could arise in an existing dark mole. It's best to have moles removed before they can turn cancerous.

There are a number of skin conditions that can affect the vulva. Some of these are really nasty. Dermatitis or eczema can occur on the skin of the vulva. Symptoms are redness, cracking, and itching. Treatment is cortisone cream.

Lichen sclerosus is a condition in which scaly white patches grow on the vulva. It's called that because it looks like lichen growing on a rock. I know you're thinking, "Oh great. I haven't used it in so long it's growing moss down there." Nobody knows what causes it, although it does appear to run in families. It's diagnosed by biopsy. Treatment is potent steroids. Women with this condition are also advised to avoid tight clothing and to quickly change out of wet bathing suits and exercise clothing. If you are diagnosed with this, you really need to get a referral to a gynecologist who specializes in the vulva, because most gynecologists don't—most of them specialize in pregnancy.

Lichen planus is a skin disease that can occur in many body areas besides the vulva. The cause is unknown although it may be autoimmune and the use of some medications may make it worse. The main symptoms are itching and the erosion of the skin surface. The inflammation associated with this can cause scarring so bad that it can change the structure of the labia and clitoris. It can become so severe it can actually cause the vagina to close up. It's chronic and treated with painkillers and cortisone.

Wow! Kind of scary, hunh? I'm going to stop here with the diseases. For more information, you absolutely need to read "The V Book" by Elizabeth Stewart, M. D. This is the best book about the vulva and vagina that I've ever read. It's kind of technical but well worth it. On that happy note, let's get away from diseases and get into some tips for keeping your vulva and vagina healthy.

Hopefully you will never have any of the medical conditions I've described earlier. You still have to take care of your vulva and vagina. The pH balance of the vagina is very delicate and using certain products or inserting objects can upset it. Here are some of the things doctors recommend.

Don't douche unless it's recommended by a doctor. Sometimes douching with Betadine is prescribed for the itching that's involved in bacterial vaginitis. Other than that douching is not recommended. I know when you douche you feel cleaner, but research shows it's associated with increased risk of vaginal infections as well as cervical cancer. The vagina is self-cleaning. Let it do its job. After intercourse, shower and remove semen with your fingers.

The use of feminine hygiene products is also not recommended. Women use them because they perceive a negative odor and want to cover it up. A bad odor could signify an infection and using a vaginal deodorant is only going to prolong the problem.

The source of vaginal odor is a combination of normal vaginal secretions and perspiration which gets trapped in the pubic hair. Solution—remove the pubic hair. No more odor.

Normal vaginal discharge contains a number of substances including sweat and dead skin cells. It may be white or yellowish. The thing you have to be aware of is that normal vaginal secretions do not burn, irritate, or itch. Burning, irritation, and itching are signs that something is wrong.

Using products containing any talcum powder in the vaginal area is another huge no-no. Believe it or not, the extended use of talcum powder products in a woman's vaginal area is highly associated with ovarian cancer! In fact, in 2017 as I was writing this book, the first lawsuit came to court involving talcum powder and ovarian cancer. One of the allegations is that Johnson & Johnson, the largest manufacturer of baby powder, should have to put a warning label on it.

The other night I was watching the movie "Blazing Saddles" for the millionth time. There was a scene in which Lili von Schtupp, played by Madeline Kahn, is sitting in her dressing room and putting talcum powder all over her upper thighs. Didn't she die of ovarian cancer?

Some women are allergic to bath soap or laundry soap, or to the chemicals that are found in some scented toilet paper. Even the underwear you wear can be a problem. Most underwear now has a cotton crotch because it's safer in terms of preventing infections. Wearing thong underwear can cause fissures in the perineum or anal area. Save the thongs for a special occasion.

You should never insert food into your vagina. I know, maybe you think it sounds sexy to have your partner eat whipped cream or some other food off your vulva. Bad idea. Foods can seriously affect the pH of the vaginal area. I also read a case of a woman who inserted a carrot into her vagina for masturbation and got an embolism and died.

SAFE SEX RULE
Dildos are made for vaginal penetration. Cucumbers are not.

There is a sign in the classrooms in which I teach, which students never pay attention to. It says, "No food or drink allowed in this area." This should be your motto when it comes to your vagina.

The penis is made to go inside the vagina. Dildos are phallic-shaped objects used for sexual stimulation. The idea of using a dildo for sexual pleasure is thousands of years old.

Archaeological digs have uncovered dildos made of stone and marble. Today's models are mostly made of rubber or plastic. It's safe to insert dildos into the vagina as long as they are cleaned with water after each use.

Vibrators are usually used on the clitoris. Some women insert vibrators that are shaped like penises into their vaginas. This is probably okay as long as you use the slow speeds and don't thrust too hard. The problem is that a vibrator especially on high speed can leave your vagina kind of numb and you might not notice that you are thrusting too hard and possibly damaging your vaginal walls or cervix. Here are some weird vagina stories.

Back in the early 1990's a friend of mine wanted to pay me to model for a statue. The sculptor was a guy who worked in La Presa outside of Tijuana, Mexico. His usual specialty was replicas (i. e. ripoffs) of Frederick Remington Western statues but he did original artwork as well. The process consisted of me lying on a table and having plaster poured on various parts of my body and waiting for it to harden and be removed.

Where does a vagina come in here? While I was lying on his table, I had a view of one wall of his studio and there were all these weird-looking sculptures hanging there. They were all sort of similar shapes, but glazed in different colors. Suddenly I realized what they were—they were plaster casts of women's vulvas. We started talking about them and he asked me if I wanted to contribute mine to the wall and I agreed. Looking back, I'm thinking, "Wait, what? I agreed to let someone pour plaster on my pubic area?" What if it didn't come off? Seriously, that can't happen. They put Vaseline on the area to make the plaster easy to remove.

The thing about plaster, if you ever had a cast made of your hand in kindergarten, is that when it sets, it gets warm. Hot actually. A few moments of discomfort there, but in a good way. So a sculpture of my vagina is hanging in an art studio on the outskirts of TJ. I don't know if I would recognize mine out of the many that were hanging there as I didn't see the finished product so I don't know what color he glazed it. The colors were not meant to be realistic—some of them were green, blue, purple, black, or whatever he felt like.

Here's a funny vagina story. Back when I was in my twenties, I had a friend I worked with. Like most of us back then (then?) she was horny and liked to drink. We all went out drinking one night after work and she went home to find that her boyfriend was out for the night with his friends. This is before cell phones so she couldn't call him. So…she drank some more and called a couple other men she knew but nobody was available so she got her vibrator out and started working on herself. She was so drunk she passed out with the vibrator inside her. She had forgotten that she had told her landlord it was okay to come over to look at the refrigerator which had something wrong with it. The landlord knocked on the door, didn't get an answer and entered the apartment to find her passed out in bed naked with the vibrator hanging out of her, still buzzing away. For the safe sex rule here I'm going to invoke one from a previous chapter—never operate heavy equipment while under the influence of alcohol.

In a case I read about online, a woman and her boyfriend were having sex and the woman claimed she wasn't getting enough stimulation. So her boyfriend took a rubber dildo and went into the garage and put the dildo on the end of a saber saw. He stuck the dildo into the woman's vagina and turned on the saw, which of course shredded the dildo and started cutting up her vagina. Through some miracle this woman didn't die and recovered following surgery. The vaginal tissue appears to be amazingly resilient. I guess it would have to be to survive childbirth when you think about it. Still, that's no reason to go at it with a sharp appliance.

SAFE SEX RULE
Break loose with the money already and buy a vibrator with varying speeds.

A sex therapist I worked with told me this one. A female client came to him because she and her husband were not getting along sexually. She started seeing another man who was a dentist. She met him after hours in his dental office and they were doing all sorts of foreplay and he started going at her with the drill apparatus, sticking it in her vagina and turning it on (without a needle in it, thank goodness). After some major reconstructive surgery she was ready to go back to her husband and get their sex life together, but first she had to work through some major emotional issues she was having (ya think?)

FAMOUS VAGINAL INJURIES
When Frida Kahlo, the Mexican artist, was a teenager, she was riding on public transportation that collided with a trolley. A handrail pierced her back and came out her vagina. She survived her injuries and went on to have sex with a number of people, both men and women. She also had lifelong health problems from polio she had suffered as a child.

In 1997 Eve Babitz, the California writer, was smoking a cigar while driving. The cigar fell into her lap and her entire skirt caught fire. The lower half of her body sustained third-degree burns, including her vagina. She barely survived her injuries and some of her former lovers such as Harrison Ford and Steve Martin raised money to pay for her medical bills. Three of her best-known books have recently been re-released.

Some women stick unusual objects in their vaginas themselves for sexual purposes. I think it's equally or more likely that women are assaulted by men who stick dangerous objects into the vagina without the woman's knowledge or prior consent.

Some women stick objects in their vagina or perform tricks with it for entertainment purposes. People I know claim to have seen women open beer bottles with their vaginas, shoot ping pong balls out of them, or smoke cigarettes with them. Personally, I always thought those stories were made up but they could be true.

Women have also stuck objects into their urethras for sexual pleasure. There are a number of problems with this. The urethral opening is very delicate and the urethra is highly subject to infection. Objects can injure the area or become lodged in the urethra or the bladder, causing pain, bleeding, and inability to urinate.

I have a girlfriend who is a nurse and when she was training in the ER a woman came in with a mascara brush lodged in the opening to her bladder. The doctor asked her how the mascara brush got in there and she said, "My husband and I are British and we like to experiment."

SAFE SEX RULE (NATIONALITY ASIDE)
Do not insert foreign objects into your urethra and/or bladder.

Well, this has certainly been a lot to take in, hasn't it? I'll tell you, these two chapters were the most challenging to write in the whole book, which shows that having a vagina can be really challenging. I think the lesson here is to be as kind as you can to your lady parts—no foreign objects, no sharp objects, no chemicals. Also, the vagina is subject to injury in an accident the same as any body part would be.

In the next chapter I examine various ways people can get themselves into trouble with their sexual behavior.

CHAPTER 5
WHO, HOW, WHAT, WHERE?

This chapter is about sexual behavior—which behaviors are safe and which are less so. Relative safety depends on who you have sex with, how you do it, what you do, and where you do it. Sexual behaviors include fantasizing and masturbation, which are usually considered solitary sexual behaviors. Behaviors that are usually done with a partner include forms of foreplay such as kissing, fondling, and oral sex, as well as sexual intercourse done in a number of positions. I'll cover anal sex in a later chapter.

FANTASY

A sexual fantasy is a private mental experience that includes thoughts and images that are sexually arousing to an individual. While men's and women's fantasies often contain common themes, people have personal turn-ons that they use as fantasy material. Fantasizing is one of the safest sexual behaviors that you can do. However, it's possible to run into trouble in a couple of ways. If fantasizing is the only way you can get turned on enough to have sex with a partner, that could cause relationship problems. If you fantasize about one person while you're having sex with another person, that could be problematic especially if you yell out the wrong person's name when you get excited! You'll definitely have some 'splainin' to do.

Some people worry that their fantasy content is abnormal. They worry about whether they will eventually have no choice but to act out what they consider an abnormal fantasy, for example having sex with an animal or a child. There are two schools of thought on this. The first says that fantasy is a harmless catharsis that allows you to explore the range of forbidden sexual behaviors without putting yourself in physical danger. The second school of thought is more Freudian. It says that fantasies (and dreams) are always wish fulfillment and no matter how hard you try to stop yourself, you will be compelled to act out your fantasy.

I think school of thought number one is true of the majority of people. Most of us can pretty much fantasize about any sicko thing we want and be relatively sure we won't need to act it out and put ourselves at risk. However, there's a small subgroup of the population, sexually sadistic serial psychopaths, for whom the relationship between fantasy and behavior is disordered. These people feel compelled to repeatedly act out destructive harmful fantasy scenarios. The rest of us are okay. It's not 1984 and we don't have the thought police looking into our brains, so go ahead and fantasize about whatever gets you going.

Should you share your sexual fantasies with your partner? A lot of sex experts say yes, that this can increase intimacy for a couple. I tend to say no. Your fantasies are private and their content may offend your partner. Do you think that sharing with your partner the idea that you've always wanted to pork her sister will bring the two of you closer together? It probably won't.

Seriously, there are some couples who do not have any sexual jealousy. You know who you are. You're the type of people who feel comfortable telling each other that you fantasized about banging your grandfather or the Green Bay Packers. But most people aren't like that. Only you and your partner know whether you will be comfortable listening to each others' fantasies. Don't forget—once you've told it, you can't take it back. "Oh no, really. I was just kidding!"

MASTURBATION

Masturbation is self-touch of the genitals for sexual pleasure. Most people masturbate by themselves but mutual masturbation is common and is considered a form of safe sex because body fluids are not exchanged. Masturbation is extremely safe, as long as you're not into some of the extreme masochistic practices described in a later chapter on the paraphilias.

Masturbation and fantasy often go along together. Given that masturbation is safe, fun, and doesn't cost any money, how did it get such a bad reputation? It started with the Old Testament of the Judeo-Christian Bible. In the times of the ancient Hebrews it was a common practice that if a man was killed in warfare and he had a brother, it was the brother's duty to marry the widow. A man named Onan had a brother who was killed and Onan was expected to marry his brother's widow. He refused to marry her and masturbated instead. The exact quote is, "And Onan spilled his seed on the ground, and that was displeasing to God." I think that's from the King James version of the Bible. I know the quote because one of my students made a computer banner out of it and gave it to me. Masturbation is sometimes called onanism or the sin of Onan.

But it was all a misunderstanding. People interpreted this to mean that God didn't like masturbation. Let's face it, I'm no Biblical scholar. But I'm interpreting that quote to mean that Onan was disrespectful and disobedient and that was the problem, not the masturbation itself. It's like he was saying, "Marry her? Are you kidding? I wouldn't fuck her with somebody else's dick!"

So masturbation was considered a sin for thousands of years. Then starting in the 1700's with the rise of science, doctors started believing that it was bad for you and caused all kinds of physical problems. This kind of thinking peaked in the late Victorian Era. Mothers were exhorted to make sure their kids didn't touch their own genitals. Devices were sold that parents could put on their kids' genitals before they went to bed to keep them from touching themselves or to keep boys from having erections. Parents were also told not to feed their kids spicy foods because that would make them horny. Instead they were told to feed their kids bland foods to prevent masturbation. Kellogg's Corn Flakes and Graham Crackers are two of these foods.

Masturbation was thought to cause impotence, insanity, sexual inversion (homosexuality), blindness, fatigue, hair loss, tuberculosis, epilepsy, sterility, acne, memory loss, hairy palms, genital cancer, and a small penis. It causes none of these things.

In fact, in most cases, masturbation is actually good for you. It helps you learn about what turns you on, which is especially good for women before they start having sex with a partner. It raises your sexual self-esteem. It's used in various forms to treat sexual problems such as desire, arousal, orgasm, and anxiety disorders. Masturbation in most cases is so safe that former Surgeon General Joycelyn Elders suggested that it would be a good practice for adolescents to do instead of having sex with each other. Most people were not ready to hear that message and soon she was out of a job.

There is a situation in which masturbation can become a problem. That's if it becomes compulsive. If you masturbate so much that it causes you personal distress and impairs your functioning in other areas of life, this is considered problematic.

Most people are geared toward wanting to have sex with another person at some point in their life. Other people have more of an autoerotic focus—they only want to have sex with themselves even when there are other sexual outlets (Kinsey's term) available. And that's okay. As Woody Allen said, "It's having sex with someone I really like."

The way some men masturbate may create problems when they try to have sex with a woman. Men who always masturbate very quickly may develop premature ejaculation when they have partner sex. Men who masturbate frequently, do it for a long time, do it with an extremely firm stroke, and clench and unclench their PC muscle while doing it often build in a tendency toward delayed ejaculation when they are with a partner. None of these practices are unsafe but they may cause frustration for both partners.

I don't know whether to call the following practice masturbation or not. There is a company near San Diego that sells very realistic sex dolls. They are very expensive and made to order with custom sizes, hair color, and skin color. I guess this is really the epitome of safe sex.

The reasons most people masturbate are to reduce sexual tension, to relax, to help them sleep, or to relieve boredom. Others masturbate because they don't have a current partner or they are afraid to catch an STI.

People still have the urge to masturbate even when they are

in a committed relationship. This can create conflict between members of a couple. Some men get jealous if their partner wants to use a vibrator. It's no reflection on you, really. She just needs a different kind of stimulation once in a while.

Women sometimes get upset if they catch their partner masturbating. I've heard women say, "I don't know why he needs to masturbate when he has me." That's actually kind of humiliating when you think about it. Are you just a sperm receptacle? Would you really want to have sex with your partner when you know all he wants to do is just get off? Wouldn't you rather wait until you could have a nice intimate experience in which you both get satisfied?

He just needs something different once in a while. It doesn't mean you're not having enough sex. In fact it's just the opposite. People who are having a lot of partner sex tend to develop a higher sex drive over time and may feel the need to masturbate more often. People in the Victorian Era believed that men only had a certain number of ejaculations in their lifetime and they didn't want to waste them. This is not true. Men manufacture sperm constantly and in many cases are capable of multiple ejaculations in relatively short time frames.

Most men masturbate by gripping their penis and moving their hand up and down. This tends to mimic the stimulation you get during sexual intercourse. Some men touch their balls or anus. Inserting objects into your urethra is dangerous as described in an earlier chapter and the same goes for inserting objects into your anus as described in a later chapter. The future chapter on the paraphilias describes dangerous autoerotic practices such as cutting off your air supply when you have an orgasm

Some men masturbate by rubbing their penis on the bed or a rug. This is not dangerous but I've noticed a trend—men who tend to masturbate in this way often have issues with delayed ejaculation.

Most women masturbate by rubbing their clitoris. Other women like to insert an object to simulate the sensations of sexual intercourse. Just don't insert sharp objects or food items as described in a previous chapter. Clean any sex toys after you use them. Don't insert an object so large that it causes pain.

A vibrator on the clitoris feels great to a lot of women. There are so many different kinds of vibrators available now, and they are sold online and in nicer shops where you don't feel sleazy. It's difficult to know which type of vibrator is best for you until you've tried a lot of different kinds. Don't just go into your kitchen cabinets and say, "I wonder if this might feel good if I stick it in my vagina."

HISTORY LESSON

Much of what we know about female masturbation comes from the research of Masters and Johnson. Maybe you've seen their research dramatized on television in the series Masters of Sex. The researchers had single people and couples come into their laboratory and they hooked them up to devices that measured their heart rate, blood pressure, respiration, and other vital signs. They wanted to find out the physiological changes that men and women go through as they go from stimulation to arousal to orgasm.

For women who were being measured individually, the researchers inserted a device into their vaginas called a vaginal photoplethysmograph. It's about the size of a tampon and measures heat and moisture in the vagina. Then the researchers told the women to masturbate, preferably to orgasm if they could. From this research, Masters and Johnson concluded that the source of all female orgasms was the clitoris, which we now know is not true. I think you can see the problem here.

When they told the women to masturbate, they all reached

for their clitoris, because their vaginas were already occupied! I think all of us would do the same in this position. The clitoris may not be the ground zero for female orgasm, but it's definitely "Old Faithful" for most women.

KISSING

Kissing is considered very romantic by many people in our culture, but that's not the case worldwide. In some cultures, it's considered neutral or even disgusting. It's usually safe unless one person has a herpes sore or a cut in their mouth. In theory, HIV could be transmitted through mouth kissing, but I don't know that there's ever been a proven case. Transmission would probably require blood-to-blood contact. Kissing is not considered safe sex due to the exchange of body fluids.

Of course we have all heard of people who sustained injuries to their mouth due to kissing. Enthusiastic kissers have gotten chipped teeth or sore lips because of a kiss being too vigorous. A partner's lips could get caught on orthodontic braces or a tongue piercing. I've heard it's also possible to get a blood clot from a hickey if your partner sucks on your skin too hard.

FOREPLAY

Rather than jump right into sexual intercourse, most people prefer to do a little foreplay if they have time. It serves a purpose, especially for women. Caressing the arms, legs, and breasts causes blood to flow toward the center of the body and into the genitals.

One common form of foreplay is finger fucking in which a man inserts his finger into a woman's vagina and moves it in and out. Guys, beware of this one—a lot of women don't really like this. It's one thing to gently caress a woman's fully lubed genitals. It's a whole other thing to jam your stiff finger in and out. A stiff finger doesn't have the give a penis does, so be sure and check with your partner as to how much pressure she prefers.

ORAL SEX

Oral sex is extremely common in our culture, much more so than it used to be. There are a number of reasons why oral sex is so much more popular now than it was, say, in Kinsey's day in the 1940's and 1950's. One reason is better hygiene. In Kinsey's day, many people still didn't have indoor plumbing or the means to take a bath on a daily basis. Shaving of the pubic hair was not popular.

Another reason is that a couple of generations ago, society was not as affluent in general as it is today. Many couples could not afford a place to have sex in private or had to borrow a car. When you're having sex in a car in a semi-public place, you don't have time for oral sex—you go right for the main event. It's especially difficult to perform oral sex on a woman in a car.

One thing that many of us today overlook is that before the Sexual Revolution of the 1960's and 1970's, oral sex, even between a man and a women, was against the law in many venues. It was covered under the sodomy laws in some states. Sodomy usually means anal intercourse between two men, but some of those laws forbade any sexual behavior that wasn't male-female intercourse.

During the Sexual Revolution, most sexual behaviors became more popular and frequent including oral sex. But the main reason oral sex is so much more popular now than it was seventy years ago is that the population in general is a lot more educated. This doesn't mean that they teach you to have oral sex in college, although oral sex is the subject of one of my Human Sexuality lectures. It means that a college education is a liberalizing experience for most people. People often start college with traditional values but are then exposed to people with much more liberal attitudes and more experience, and the flow of influence usually goes in the direction of the more traditional students being influenced by the more liberal students and professors. Nobody comes out of college with less sexual experience than they went in with.

Is oral sex safe? It can be depending on a number of factors. It's not considered a safe sex practice despite what a lot of teenagers think. It does involve the possible exchange of body fluids including vaginal discharge, semen, and blood.

The most important factor to keep in mind about making oral sex as safe as possible is to know your partner and be sure your partner does not have an STI, because many STI's can be transmitted through oral sex.

Beyond that, injuries have occurred during oral sex, due to the use of the teeth. This is usually a problem with somebody who doesn't have a lot of experience. Pubic hairs can get caught in teeth. Earrings can get caught in the skin of the scrotum.

If there is a bizarre oral sex-related injury you can think of, it's probably happened to somebody. In one case a man ate watermelon and went down on a woman. She was allergic to watermelon and she went into anaphylactic shock and almost died. In another case, a man was going down on a woman so hard and with his neck so stiff he actually tore his cerebellum. (This is a structure on the back of your brain that controls voluntary movement). He was taken to the hospital unable to stand upright without dizziness. Of course hospital personnel initially mistook his condition for drug intoxication.

A case was reported on the Internet in which a woman choked to death on her partner's penis, which apparently was large. There was a trial involved and the man in question actually seemed proud of this.

Suggestions for making oral sex better (and safer) include washing and shaving. It's safe to eat food off a penis but not a vagina. Never use alcohol products on the genitals. It might sound romantic to take a sip of champagne in your mouth and go down on your partner, but there will be nothing romantic about their screams. Mouthwash has alcohol in it. Don't go down on your partner after eating chili peppers.

To prevent injuries during oral sex, keep it relaxed. Keep your lips, tongue, chin, and neck relaxed. Keep it sensual. Every once in a while, focus and slow down.

SEXUAL INTERCOURSE

Intercourse is any activity in which the man inserts his penis into a woman's vagina. It can be performed in any number of positions but the positions are divided into four basic types.

In a male superior position, the man is physically on top. In a female superior position, the woman is physically on top. In a side-to-side position, the man and the woman lie on their sides so nobody is on top. In a rear entry position, the man puts his penis into the woman's vagina from behind.

No sexual position is inherently less safe than any of the others. However, the positions differ in the amount of physical and emotional stimulation obtained from each. I'll give you a quick rundown of the advantages and disadvantages.

The male superior position (also called the missionary position), is still the most commonly used position in Western culture. It tends to be less stimulating for the woman as the penis does not go into the vagina very deep and there is no contact with the clitoris. It tends to be most stimulating for the man and not necessarily in a good way. Some men get aroused too quickly in this position because they have to support their weight with their upper body and so can't pay as much attention to their genitals.

From a psychological standpoint, this position can be arousing to both partners because it allows eye contact and touching of other parts of the body besides the genitals. It also conforms to many peoples' idea about appropriate gender roles—that the man should be the initiator of sex and that he should be on top.

There is a version of the male superior position that is much more stimulating for women. Instead of lying on top of the woman the man kneels in front of her. The woman tilts her pelvis back and puts her legs as far back as is comfortable. This allows deeper stimulation of the vagina. In this position the man does not have to support his weight with his upper body and so can last longer.

Sex therapists agree that of all the intercourse positions, the female superior position provides the best chance for female arousal and orgasm. In this position the woman is in charge of the angle, depth, and speed of penetration and she can stimulate her clitoris with her hand or a vibrator. Some men get very physically stimulated in this position because they can see a woman's breasts. On the other hand, some men have difficulty getting physically stimulated in this position because it may be difficult to move enough to match a woman's thrusts.

Psychologically, the female superior position is intimate because it allows eye contact and touching of the body parts besides the genitals. However, some people are uncomfortable with this position because it goes against what we consider traditional gender roles in sexual behavior. The woman on top position is often considered the "bad girl" position.

In the most common version of the side-to-side position the man lies on his side and the woman lies on her back perpendicular to him. He inserts his penis and they wrap their legs around each other. This position is usually the least physically stimulating for both partners. So why use it? Neither partner has to support their own weight so it's a comfortable position. It's often used in sex therapy to treat premature ejaculation because it is less arousing than the other positions. It's also intimate and allows eye gaze and body touching. It is a very egalitarian position because nobody's on top.

I use this position a lot because being post-menopausal, I tend to take a long time to lube up for intercourse. This position allows me to take my time getting wet before the main event. In my household we refer to this position as the "pre-game skate" in which hockey players warm up on the ice before the actual game.

In the most common version of the rear entry position, the woman kneels on all fours and the man kneels behind her. From a physical standpoint this position allows depth and speed of thrusting. It can stimulate the G spot and cervix area. You can really get some good pounding in this position if that's your thing. The man or woman can stimulate the clitoris by hand.

Some people don't like this position because they think it's primitive, animalistic, and not intimate. Other people really like this position because it's (you guessed it) primitive, animalistic, and not intimate.

No sexual positions are inherently right or wrong or good or bad. They are only more or less stimulating or more or less safe. The reason the missionary position got its name is when the Christian missionaries came to the Pacific islands in the early 1800's, they found the natives having sex in the rear entry position. They believed this was sinful and tried to teach the natives that the only okay way to have sex was at night in the dark with both partners fully clothed, under a blanket. I repeat, no intercourse positions are bad, wrong, or immoral.

When you are deciding what positions to use for intercourse, you're making a decision between boredom and burnout. If you use the same position all the time, you will get bored. If you try to use every position you know in every sexual session, you'll get burned out.

People are curious and want to have sex in novel settings. Let's go through some of those and look at the possible safety aspects.

It's much safer to have sex in daylight or with the lights on than in the dark, because you need to inspect your partner's genitals to make sure there are no STI symptoms present. This will be the focus of a future chapter.

Every year a number of people are injured severely enough by their bed or bedding to require medical care. This is without even adding sex into the mix. Think about banging your head into a headboard hard enough to get a concussion or lose consciousness. It's happened. Falling out of bed, elbowing a partner in the face, rolling over onto a penis—they've all happened as well as any other mishaps you can think of. In one episode of Sex Sent Me To the E R I watched a woman's head get caught between the bars of the headboard of a brass bed and the fire department had to be called. I know these are reenactments but they're based on true stories.

Another source of injuries is allowing animals to sleep in your bed. Not only is this dangerous, it's also a recognized source of sexual dysfunctions such as low desire.

You know what I think would be a cool T.V. show? A combination of America's Funniest Videos and Sex Sent Me to the ER. Plenty of people like to record themselves having sex and I'm sure there have been some mishaps that AFV won't show. Heck, there probably already is a show like this and I'm just too out of it to know.

The shower is a popular place for sexual encounters. Bad idea, as far as I'm concerned. Combine a slippery floor and a breakable glass door and I'm sure you get the idea.

Some places sound really romantic for having sex. Who hasn't fantasized about sex on a deserted moonlit beach? But who has actually done it, with a two hundred pound man on top of her pounding her lower back into the hard-packed sand, with sand going up every orifice?

Hey, I'm not trying to ruin your good time. As I said in the Introduction, I've done most of this stuff, and lived to tell about it. I once had sex in a cow pasture (with a person). I had sex on the side of a volcano.

Sex in a pool or hot tub sounds great too. But chlorine dries out your vagina, the hard rims can pound into your back, and there's the danger of drowning. In general, I stay away from sex on hard surfaces, and I include carpet in that. Rug burns can take forever to heal. And they can leave scars.

The Great Outdoors is another popular place for sexual activity. I admit, it feels great to have sex outside in good weather. There's something really sensuous about feeling the air on your body. The possibilities of injury are unbelievable. Poison ivy. You could be attacked by insects, snakes, or other animals, including bears. In one case in Zimbabwe, a couple were having sex in some bushes and a lion ate the woman. The man managed to escape.

SAFE SEX RULE

It's a jungle out there. Or in this case, it was probably a savannah.

In another case in Los Angeles, a man and woman were having sex on a hotel balcony. He had her balanced on the balcony and he was standing up and screwing her, and she fell off the balcony. That one was ruled a homicide.

From an evolutionary standpoint, one of the reasons humans started to have sex face to face versus in the rear entry position is that mammals are extremely vulnerable to predators when they are having sex and both of them are facing the same way.

A number of famous people have died during sexual intercourse. Among them are a former French president, Nelson Rockefeller, the former vice-president of the United States, John Garfield, the actor, and Attila the Hun (although I'm wondering how anyone could know that). Add to that the father of actor Matthew McConaughey. True—his mother even wrote an article about it, almost as if she was proud of this. These people died while having regular heterosexual intercourse, not in conjunction with sado-masochistic sexual practices.

How could you avoid having this happen to you? Most people who die during sex die of undiagnosed heart problems or cerebral aneurysms. I think we all know the guidelines for preventing heart attacks in general—try to stay at a healthy weight, don't smoke, get plenty of exercise, eat a good diet, etc. That's all great advice, but there are a few other suggestions too. If you've had a previous heart attack and/or surgery, get your doctor's okay before starting to have sex again. Don't have sex right after you've eaten a heavy meal. Don't have sex if you have chest pain.

To summarize, people get turned on by novelty. If that wasn't true, everybody in the world would have sex in the same position the same way all the time. People get turned on by having sex in unusual settings. Popular settings for sex are the workplace, restaurants, different rooms of the house besides the bedroom, and cars, elevators, boats, and airplanes. Part of the excitement here is that you might get caught. Literature is full of stories about people getting caught having sex by parents or roommates. When people tell you they'll be gone for a certain amount of time, don't trust this. Anything can happen.

I have a few general rules for staying safe in these locations. Avoid hard surfaces, especially ones in which you might hit your head. Avoid confined spaces. If a part of your body stays in one position for too long, you risk loss of blood flow and possible permanent injury.

Do not have any form of sex in a moving car, especially oral sex. You may be a confident driver but you have no idea what other drivers are going to do. Remember the scene in "The World According to Garp" in which Garp's wife was going down on her lover in a car parked at the bottom of their driveway? Garp and the kids came home, coasted down the driveway, and hit the other car, causing Garp's wife to bite her lover's penis off.

Even sex in a parked car can be dangerous depending on where you are parked. You want to be in a secluded area, but this leaves you vulnerable to possible police harassment or robbery. People have died because they had sex in a parked car with the engine running on a cold night. They died of carbon monoxide poisoning.

ALCOHOL AND DRUGS

One huge factor in whether your sexual activity is going to be safe or less so is the use of alcohol and other drugs. Drugs can impair your functioning in many areas, not just sex.

We usually divide drugs into four main categories—depressants, stimulants, opiates, and hallucinogens. Some drugs fit nicely into the categories due to their primary mechanism of action but some don't. I'll discuss the different types of drugs and the possible effects on your sex life.

Most of the drugs I'll talk about are considered psychoactive.

That means a couple of things. It means they change your psychological state and they usually provide a sense of intoxication—a sense of being high in some way. Many of these drugs have addictive properties. One addictive property is called tolerance. This means you must keep taking more and more of the drug to achieve the same level of feeling high. Another addictive property is withdrawal. This means that if you are a chronic heavy user of a drug, when you try to quit using the drug, you will experience unpleasant symptoms. The rule of thumb is that the withdrawal symptoms for a drug are the opposite physiological symptoms you would get from the drug intoxication state.

Besides the mechanism of action, another drug-related factor that will affect your sex life is your pattern of use. Do you use a small dose of a drug to make sex feel better, or are you a chronic heavy user? Many drugs enhance sex in the short term, but I know of no drugs that enhance your sex life if you use them heavily and chronically. Chronic heavy drug use is not only detrimental to your sex life, but can cause specific illnesses and degrade your physical and mental health in general.

DEPRESSANTS

Depressants slow down your central nervous system. Depressants include alcohol, barbiturates, and prescription tranquilizers such as Valium, Xanax, and Ativan.

For a lot of people, alcohol and sex go together. Who doesn't like a couple of drinks before sex to help you relax? In fact, I can't recall the last time I had sex completely sober.

A couple of drinks can enhance sex for women, because a couple of drinks can potentiate testosterone, possibly causing a woman to feel more horny. Alcohol also disinhibits people and relaxes them, often allowing for a better sexual experience.

Long term heavy use of alcohol can often cause erection problems in men. (I saw that a lot when I worked as a surrogate partner). Too much alcohol at any given time will impair reasoning and reaction time. Very heavy use can lead to blackouts, stupor, or coma, or even alcohol poisoning and death. Long term heavy use is associated with heart problems, liver damage, and many forms of cancer, not to mention mental health issues and relationship problems.

Use of alcohol is associated with a number of adverse sexual outcomes. Use of alcohol by the perpetrator and/or victim is a major factor in sexual assaults. I want to make it very clear what I am saying here—alcohol does not cause rape, sexual assault, STI's, or unwanted pregnancy. However, its use is associated with all of the above. It's a relationship; there's just no proof that it's a causal relationship. Alcohol will disinhibit you and impair your judgment and that's what the relationship is. Alcohol-impaired judgment may lead you to have sex with the wrong person or make other poor sexual decisions.

Long term heavy drinkers usually lose interest in sex, not just because long term heavy use decreases your sex drive, but because people who are huge alcoholics prefer drinking to having sex.

Another type of depressant is barbiturates. These were more popular in the 1960's and 1970's than they are now. We used to know them as "reds" or "downers". Their effect on sex is very similar to the effect of alcohol. A little bit to help you relax may be okay, but long term heavy chronic use will become a problem.

Some people rely on prescription drugs such as Valium, Xanax, or Ativan. These drugs are prescribed for people who have clinical levels of anxiety. Types of anxiety disorders include panic attacks, phobias, and generalized anxiety disorder in which you worry about pretty much everything. Believe me, if you have ever suffered from chronic anxiety, you are glad these drugs exist. They are not usually used for enhancing a sexual experience as far as I know. They can be prescribed for people who have clinical levels of a phobia about sex.

Prozac and other similar drugs (called SSRI's or SNRI's) are also prescribed for both anxiety and depression. They are not considered drugs of abuse. They don't get you high. They do have serious sexual side effects. They impair desire, arousal, and especially orgasm. For this reason they are sometimes prescribed for men with premature ejaculation to take as needed. I had a client describe the sexual effects of Prozac to me. "It's like you don't want to have sex, but you don't care."

STIMULANTS

Stimulants include mild legal drugs such as nicotine and caffeine as well as much stronger ones such as cocaine, amphetamine, and methamphetamine. Nicotine is found in tobacco products and is bad news for your sex life. It causes a mild high including rapid heart rate, but its main action that impairs your sexual functioning is it constricts the small blood vessels in your body primarily in the face, fingers, and genitals, all of which you are going to need for your sex life! So, if you value your sex life, you definitely want to quit smoking.

Caffeine is similar. It's usually ingested in liquid form in coffee or soft drinks. It doesn't seem to have as strong of an effect on your sex life as nicotine does.

The above two mild stimulants are not going to get you impaired enough to make bad sexual decisions. They may impair blood flow to your genitals.

That's not the case for serious stimulants such as cocaine and amphetamine. These stimulants cause rapid heart rate, sympathetic nervous system arousal, and changes in thinking. Some people, especially men, take these because they may cause a mild form of priapism—a long-lasting erection that won't go down. They are used heavily in the porn industry.

Long-term heavy use of cocaine and amphetamine can definitely impair your sex life as well as cause medical issues such as heart irregularities. I had a good friend who was a heavy meth addict for about five years. He liked it because it allowed him to stay awake for days at a time and get a lot of work done. He developed such high blood pressure due to the meth that he almost had a ruptured aneurysm in his brain. He temporarily lost his sight, had to have surgery, and a botched eye surgery led to his eventual death. He was only forty-seven years old. How sad. I attribute his death to his meth use. At first when he started using it, he claimed it gave him great erections. A couple of years into it, he didn't even care about sex any more. All he wanted to do was use meth.

Use of stimulants can cause very poor judgment. You could develop abrasions on your penis or vagina from having sex too hard for too long. When you take stimulants you think you're invincible. Not every person has a sexual reaction to stimulants. When I used stimulants, I just wanted to talk because I thought I was brilliant. No one else thought that.

An overdose of a serious stimulant could cause you to have a psychotic episode. In more than one case, a man has cut off his penis due to stimulant intoxication. Another man injected cocaine directly into his penis. He developed an infection and had to have pretty much the whole lower part of his body removed.

OPIATES

Opiates are painkillers. They also make you sleepy. Examples are heroin and morphine, as well as Demerol, Darvon, Percodan, Oxycodone, and Hydrocodone (Vicodin and Norco). Medical use of opiates is for pain, either post-surgical pain or chronic pain such as back pain. When used post-surgically, opiates most often don't become addictive. You don't get high from them in this situation. Instead, you get rid of the pain. Opiates don't enhance sex, but they allow people with chronic incurable pain to have sex, so that's a good thing.

When you take opiates recreationally when you are not in pain, you feel good. They fill in receptor sites in your brain that normally respond to endorphins, endogenous brain chemicals that are released during intense physical activity (for example, sex).

People who are chronic opiate users often lose interest in sex. Getting stoned on heroin feels better to them than sex does. Withdrawal from opiates can be hell on your sex life. Among other painful conditions, opiate withdrawal can cause premature ejaculation, in this case flaccid ejaculation with no erection.

HALLUCINOGENS

Hallucinogens are drugs that cause unusual perceptual experiences (usually visual). Hallucinogens include LSD, mescaline, peyote, and psilocybin mushrooms. I have never talked to anybody who said they enjoyed doing hallucinogens before having sex. More than likely, if you're doing hallucinogens, you'll be so out of it you won't know if you're having sex or not. Hallucinogens often are not considered drugs of abuse because people who use them generally don't use them every day or develop tolerance. Where you could get into trouble would be getting a bad batch of LSD and getting brain damage.

Some drugs don't fit neatly into the categories. The best example is marijuana. Depending on the strain, marijuana can act as a stimulant, a depressant, a hallucinogen, or a painkiller. A lot of people use marijuana, especially now that it has become legal in many venues. A lot of people use it to enhance sex for two reasons. It can have a tranquilizing anti-anxiety action. Also, the particular kind of hallucinations it produces are conducive to good sex. Marijuana causes space and time distortions. So you could be having sex for two minutes but focusing on it so intently that it feels like a much longer time.

Unfortunately, chronic heavy marijuana use can have a negative impact on your sex life, especially for men. It can cause low sexual desire, the growth of fatty breast tissue (gynecomastia, also known as "man-boobs"), low sperm count, erection problems, and the amotivational syndrome. It also causes dry membranes, which can be a problem for women.

Ecstasy (MDMA) has a reputation for enhancing sex. It's actually a stimulant—the "A" in its chemical formula stands for amphetamine. It has hallucinogenic properties. It supposedly helps you get in touch with your true feelings and makes you feel love towards everyone. I've had friends try to convince me to do it based on the above, but I always declined. I was afraid my true feelings might be homicidal rage rather than love. Most people who use Ecstasy use it as a party drug, not necessarily for sex. The danger of overdose is significant. Most people use Ecstasy for special occasions and don't become addicted to it.

Inhalants include anything you "huff"—spray into and breathe out of a plastic bag. Substances include hair spray, spray paint, or glue. These are depressants that are usually used in common with criminal activity in teenagers, not for sex.

Another type of inhalant is amyl nitrite or butyl nitrite. They are usually used specifically for sex. They are inhaled in the form of capsules (poppers) at the moment of orgasm. They are said to enhance orgasm. They can be dangerous if you have a heart condition, have high blood pressure, or take Viagra. Again, their pattern of use does not usually lead to addiction.

Phencyclidine (PCP) is a really strange drug. It's actually an animal tranquilizer, but some people use it recreationally. It's not usually used to enhance sex. It causes disinhibition similar to alcohol use, but can also trigger high levels of physical activity that turn out to be dangerous.

To summarize, there are some drugs—alcohol, marijuana, and serious stimulants—that can enhance a sexual experience in the short term. However, for all drugs I'm aware of, long term use will have a very detrimental effect on your sex life.

ALTERNATIVE LIFESTYLES

Most people have sex with one partner at a time. Any other lifestyle involving multiple partners may cause safety risks. Here's a cross-cultural comparison.

Worldwide, the most common relationship status is heterosexual monogamous marriage. That doesn't mean that most people in the world are married at any given time. It means that most people in the world have been in a heterosexual monogamous marriage at some point in their lives. So when we talk about alternative relationships, we are talking about any relationship that is not monogamous marriage. Currently in the United States, the most common household status is a single-parent household.

No matter whether you are a fan of heterosexual monogamous marriage or not, research has shown that it provides many benefits. Married people tend to be physically and mentally healthier than their single counterparts, and they tend to report more sexual satisfaction than their single counterparts. It goes without saying that people in monogamous marriages tend to have safer sex on the average.

In today's society, with the extended lifespans that most of us can expect, it's probably unrealistic to think that most of us will stay with one partner for a lifetime. A very common alternative is serial monogamy in which you move from one fairly long monogamous relationship to another and another.

Another alternative lifestyle is extramarital sex. We don't have any accurate data about how many people screw around when they are married. This is the sexual survey question that people are most likely to lie about. Although we don't have any good information about this I feel confident saying a couple of things about it—it's probably more common than you think, and more men than women screw around.

The most common kind of extramarital sex is conventional, also called clandestine. This is where people sneak around to have sex and their spouse doesn't know about it. In addition to risking STI's or unwanted pregnancy, there's also the risk that you will be caught lying by your spouse, which may result in physical violence, relationship problems, and economic disaster. Clandestine extramarital sex, if discovered, can really take a toll.

The other form of extramarital sex is consensual, in which one or both partners has sexual contact with people outside the marriage and the spouse knows about it and is okay with it. This approach became popular in the 1970's with the publication of the book "Open Marriage" by George and Nena O'Neill. This was a how-to book that showed couples what to do to open their marriage up to the possibilities of having sex with other people while staying in the primary relationship. This book was kind of interesting because it described many different patterns of open marriage and advocated couples deciding which if any of these strategies was right for them.

Some couples are okay with opening the marriage to include a third person as long as the partner never meets the third person or as long as all encounters take place out of town. Other couples have developed an open marriage philosophy in which all encounters take place with all three people. There are other strategies in between. Some partners insist on vetting anybody their spouse wants to have sex with.

Open marriage or an open relationship can take the form of "swinging" or "the lifestyle". This used to be called mate-swapping or wife-swapping. There are a couple of ways to do this. Some couples get together regularly on an informal basis and have sex with each others' spouses or have group sex in the context of a party atmosphere.

Other couples join more formal swinging organizations or clubs. These clubs charge a yearly fee as well as entry fees for private parties. Some of these clubs sponsor larger hotel-based parties, trips, or cruises.

I want to distinguish swinging organizations from nudists or naturists. There are camps and hotels where people can enjoy an outdoor nudist environment that are not necessarily sex places. Some of them cater to families. For swing clubs the goal is not just to get naked but rather to have sex with people you don't know.

Swing clubs vary greatly in their safety consciousness. If you are thinking of joining one, you should investigate it thoroughly. Some of them are really sleazy. The more legitimate ones have security personnel, require a biological balance (an equal number of men and women), require the use of condoms for penetration, and do not tolerate any sort of sexual coercion.

I've had experience with all levels of open marriage and

swinging. Not all of the experiences have been good. Here's one thing that usually presents a red flag for me.

Someone I've been having a regular sexual relationship with tells me, "I know this woman, she's a friend of mine, she wants to get into swinging, she wants to have a three-way with us, she's never done this before." How many times did I fall for this? This is not going to work. It's a formula for disaster. The other woman is going to freak out and cause a huge scene. I've seen it happen. I would stay away from this sort of scenario. You don't want people working out their weird insecurities on you.

Couples I know who want to have a third person in their activities usually see one person they know they can trust. A good swing partner is somebody who is experienced, enthusiastic, and dependable. Sometimes that person isn't the best looking person you know.

Sometimes couples who are swingers try to initiate other couples into activity. I have a funny story about this. In the early 1980's I was dating a guy who was friends with a former boss and his wife. This ex-boyfriend of mine had this delusion that all kinds of women wanted to have sex with him. This other couple lived up in Palo Alto and we drove up to visit them. The whole way up in the car I had to listen to my ex-boyfriend telling me how much this woman wanted to have sex with him. So after dinner we were all sitting in their hot tub drinking wine and enjoying the gorgeous mountain views from their multimillion dollar hillside home. Not bad, hunh? So what happened? You guessed it—she made a move on me. We did end up swapping, and yeah, it got weird.

SAFE SEX RULE
No matter how well you think you know people, it could still get weird.

Some people can handle the weirdness and some can't, and there's no way to know that until you actually get into the situation. Even couples who actually advertise for swing partners are sometimes in it not just to have sex but to create some kind of weird jealousy or drama in their relationship. That's their own thing, and again, you don't realize it until you get caught up in it.

When I was in my twenties before I worked as a sexual surrogate partner, I had a weird experience of that type. I was taking college classes at night and this one older guy I worked with lived near the college. I knew him and his wife from work parties. He invited me over for a drink after class and when I showed up his wife wasn't there. He claimed that it was her idea for him to seduce me and that she would be along later to join us. It takes a lot to shock me, but I have to tell you, I was totally shocked. This is the last couple I would have ever thought were swingers. You just never know who might be into this swapping lifestyle.

Polyamory is a lifestyle that admittedly I know very little about. Some people define polyamory in a philosophical sense--everybody supposedly loves everybody. Polyamorists believe they are capable of having intimate loving relationships with more than one person.

Others define polyamory in terms of the logistics. This could consist of a household in which couples and threesomes frequently change relationships.

To me, being in a two-person marriage is difficult enough, without adding third parties into it. Whenever you've got three people in a relationship, you've got a situation with the potential for one of the three to feel left out and jealous. The jealous person is usually the second woman who feels second-rate because of the existing couple's "primary privilege" (a real term).

Some people evolve a relationship style that's called concurrency. In this relationship style a man or woman has sex with multiple partners although not at the same time. As an example, a woman could have sex with a different man every day of the week. This may seem good for her because maybe some of her partners are married or unavailable full time, or she has one man who's wealthy, another who's really great in bed, etc. The problem with this lifestyle is all of her partners could also be having sex with a number of other partners. The partner count here can go up very quickly. This pattern has been associated with the spread of HIV in Africa as well as the spread of other STI's.

So what is our conclusion here? Monogamy is the safest lifestyle, but if you need variety you need to become very familiar with any potential partners before you have sex with them.

CHAPTER 6
CONTRACEPTION

Knowledge about preventing pregnancy is essential for every sexually active person. I have to get political here. In the current unpredictable era, with the future of healthcare up in the air, it is becoming more, rather than less, difficult for women to obtain contraception and abortions. Women in rural areas especially may have to travel a hundred miles or more to obtain contraceptive pills. Who could have foreseen this back in the 1970's? This lack of availability results in people using contraceptive methods incorrectly. When abortion and birth control methods are not available, women end up taking very dangerous chances with their health.

Something like half the pregnancies in the United States are unwanted and unplanned. I took an anonymous survey in my class and twenty percent of women reported that they had become pregnant when they did not intend to, and one-sixth of male students reported that they had gotten a woman pregnant when they didn't intend to. Even college-educated people believe myths about contraception such as, "You can't get pregnant the first time you have sex".

Given that contraception is one of the cornerstones of safe sex, this whole chapter is pretty much one giant safe sex rule. I'll cover the major forms of contraception one by one, but first I want to say some things about contraceptive use in general.

When we are looking at the different forms of contraception, the main thing we want to know is how the method works. Is the method a barrier method that actually puts a physical barrier between the sperm and the egg? Is the method the use of a chemical that kills sperm? Or is the method hormonal, which changes a woman's natural balance of hormones to prevent conception?

Another thing we need to know before choosing a contraceptive method is the effectiveness rate. This is stated as a percentage. For example, if the effectiveness rate is ninety-nine percent, then the failure rate is one percent, meaning if a hundred women use this method correctly over a year's time, one of them will get pregnant. The contraceptive methods with the highest effectiveness rates are the hormonal methods and the intrauterine device (IUD). The failure rates for these methods are under one percent if used correctly.

The effectiveness rates listed on packaging only apply if the method is used correctly. Most people do not use their methods correctly all of the time. Hence, there are two types of effectiveness rates—the laboratory use rate and the typical use rate. The laboratory use effectiveness rate is always higher than the typical use rate and only applies if the user does everything exactly according to the instructions on the product's packaging.

Some people don't pay any attention to the instructions at all. For example, some people (mostly young teenagers) purchase spermicide (sperm-killing chemicals) in jelly form and eat it on toast instead of inserting it into the vagina. Another example of product use error occurred when the birth control pill was first introduced into India. Apparently the pills were passed out without packaging and it wasn't clear that women were supposed to take them. When there was no decrease in the pregnancy rate, an investigation was launched, and it turned out that men were taking the pills.

When deciding on a contraceptive method, another factor you want to take into account is disadvantages. Disadvantages are factors such as financial cost and difficulty obtaining the product. Contraceptives do not have advantages except that they prevent pregnancy to varying degrees. None of the methods are fun to use. One type of disadvantage is possible medical side effects.

Another factor you would use in choosing a contraceptive is reversibility. If a product is one hundred percent reversible, then the next time you have sex without using the product, you should return to a normal chance of getting pregnant.

There is no perfect contraceptive. They all have their good and bad points. For a product to be perfect it would have to be one hundred percent effective at preventing pregnancy, and no method is, not even sterilization, which has a tiny but real failure rate. It would have to be one hundred percent reversible, cause no medical side effects, be easily obtainable, and free. Clearly, we're not there yet. Before I get into the methods that are somewhat effective, here are some methods that don't work.

I consider abstinence (not having intercourse) a method that doesn't work and here's why. When people, especially teenagers, promise not to have intercourse because of pregnancy fears, they often do everything else but. If the boy ejaculates near the girl's vagina, sperm may be transferred to the vagina. There have been cases in which a girl got pregnant and was still technically a virgin. Yes, you read that right. I know people this happened to in high school.

Another reason abstinence doesn't work is that if you promise not to have intercourse you are in denial that it could happen, so you don't have contraceptives handy in case you change your mind at the spur of the moment. A couple may be having oral sex and engaging in other highly arousing practices and they just decide to go for it. They are now relying on chance, which has an eighty-five percent failure rate! The only thing you can do if this happens is immediately buy some spermicide and insert it and go to the drugstore and get Plan B, the emergency contraceptive pills that may be effective up to ninety-six hours after unprotected intercourse.

Withdrawal is another method that doesn't work. Even if a man pulls out and ejaculates outside the vagina, some live sperm may have been released. Remember Chapter One on the penis and male reproductive functions? Recall that fluid from the Cowper's glands which is secreted as a man starts to get turned on may contain live sperm.

Leaving it to chance as stated previously has an eighty-five percent failure rate over a year's time. Young teenage girls (age thirteen to fifteen) are especially likely to be in denial that they are having intercourse. If they used condoms or other forms of contraception, they would have to admit that they are actually having sex.

Some women try to prevent pregnancy by charting their menstrual cycle and only having sex during their "safe" days—days when they are unlikely to be ovulating. This does not work. Old-school Catholics call this the rhythm method. It doesn't work because every woman's cycle is different and can vary from month to month. Women use other cycle-charting methods such as taking your temperature or checking your cervical mucous in order to get pregnant, not to avoid pregnancy. Repeat after me—There is no such thing as a safe day. If you don't want to get pregnant, don't ever have unprotected intercourse. There have been documented cases in which women became pregnant while actively menstruating and continued to menstruate for several months into the pregnancy.

SAFE SEX RULE
If you don't want to get pregnant, don't even be in the same room with a penis.

Now for the methods that stand a chance of working. Spermicides are chemicals that kill sperm. Used by themselves they have about a twenty-eight percent failure rate. However, you're not supposed to use them by themselves. They are meant to be used in conjunction with a barrier method such as a condom, diaphragm, or cervical cap. Spermicides come in the forms of gels, creams, or foam and are inserted into the vagina with an applicator that comes with them. To use a spermicide correctly, you insert it into the vagina between a half hour and an hour before intercourse. Also, and this is very important, after the man ejaculates, you insert another dose and leave it in for six to eight hours. Most people can't accomplish this and that's why spermicides don't work very well. They are not harmful (except to sperm) although some people are allergic to them, plus you can't have oral sex with spermicide in the vagina, as it's not safe to take it by mouth. Spermicides should have one hundred percent reversibility once they are washed out of the vagina.

Diaphragms and cervical caps are barrier methods that are placed over the cervix. Diaphragms are round and made of rubber and come in sizes from 5 cm to 9 cm. They are placed in the vagina between the pubic bone in front and the back of the cervix.

Cervical caps are smaller and made of plastic. They fit right over the cervix. Both devices must be fitted by medical personnel. They must be used with spermicide. Failure rates are high—between six and thirty-two percent, depending on whether a woman has already given birth or not. They are difficult to insert and easily dislodged during sexual intercourse. The size you need can change depending on your weight. They are one hundred percent reversible.

Given that they are not very effective, why are diaphragms and cervical caps as popular as they are? They were one of the earliest forms of modern contraception. Early in the twentieth century a diaphragm was called a pessary and was only available to married women. Women would buy a fake wedding ring and go to a doctor. Given the poor success rate and other problems, I would only recommend a diaphragm or cervical cap for a woman who is near menopause, only has sex once a year, lies on her back, and doesn't move during sex. That doesn't sound like very much fun, does it?

Male condoms are latex sheaths that are placed over the penis. They are quite popular because in addition to putting a barrier between the sperm and the egg they may prevent transmission of some (but not all) STI's. (See the following chapter on STI's). They are also popular because they are easily obtainable and sometimes free at public health clinics.

Condoms have a number of problems, mainly related to misuse. To achieve their full laboratory rate effectiveness, condoms must be used with spermicides. They must be put on the penis before any fluid, including pre-seminal fluid, has left the penis. They must be the correct size, and the sizes are not standardized. They must be used before their expiration date. They must be used with water-based lubricant, never with oil-based lubricant that can literally make the condom fall apart. Wow, that's a whole paragraph of safe sex rules in a row. Let's look at some typical condom mishaps.

Here's the scenario. You're a guy, you're really horny, you haven't seen your girlfriend in a while, and tonight's the night. As the evening progresses to a sexual situation, you put on a condom, insert your penis, and it's feeling really good! You ejaculate, and it's such a relief. You withdraw your penis—and the condom isn't there! Oh no, where is it?

It's inside your girlfriend's vagina, of course. But this is emergency time. Because the condom fell off, you have now just had unprotected sex. You better hope your girlfriend has a package of Plan B, the emergency contraceptive, or you better obtain it as quickly as you can.

What happened here? The culprit was probably the wrong size condom. If a condom is too small and doesn't go all the way to the base of the penis, it may roll off during intercourse. On the other hand, if it's too big, it may fall off during intercourse.

Let's revisit the previous scenario and get all the way up to the point after you have ejaculated and you withdraw your penis. This time, there's only half a condom on your penis—the lower half, obviously. What happened here?

There are a number of possible culprits. Maybe you used an oil-based lubricant that caused the condom to break. Or, maybe, you forgot to leave a reservoir at the tip to collect the semen and your ejaculation blew right through the end of the condom. In a young man, semen can leave the penis at up to twenty-seven miles an hour. I don't know where I read that fact, probably a respectable sexual journal like Cosmopolitan magazine. Or, you were using a condom that was too old and it just fell apart. Condoms can fall apart if they have been stored in a warm area, like your car, for too long. Go right to Plan B after retrieving the missing condom section.

Here's one of my favorite condom mishaps. You have correctly put the condom on and are using the right size. Let's say you are having intercourse with your girlfriend on top. You both have an orgasm. In order to use a condom correctly, especially in the female superior position, one of you has to grab the base of the penis with the condom on it immediately after ejaculation to make sure none of the semen leaks out of the condom. Remember from the chapter on female sexual anatomy and physiology that when a woman gets aroused during intercourse, the inner third of her vagina tightens up? Let's says that the woman in this case climbs off and holds the base of the penis at the same time so no semen leaks out. She doesn't notice, but as she is standing up, the tip of the condom is stuck in her vagina and the condom stretches until it breaks, spraying semen all over the place. Plan B, again.

Condoms can fall off during intense sexual activity even if you did everything right. That's why they work better in the male superior position. A lot of men don't like to use condoms because they decrease penile sensations. Some women are allergic either to latex or to any spermicide that might be included on the condom. Some men have problems using condoms because they have issues with erections. This is especially likely to be a problem with older men. It's much easier to use a condom with a fully erect penis.

There is a disturbing new trend in sexuality that I read about recently. It's called "stealthing". This is a case in which a man starts intercourse with a condom on, and then takes it off during intercourse without his female partner knowing what he's doing. She thinks she was protected but she wasn't. She got excited and couldn't tell the difference between intercourse with a condom and without one. That's one of the reasons to have intercourse with the lights on and literally watch what you are doing.

The failure rates for male condoms are between two and eighteen percent. They are one hundred percent reversible.

There is also a female condom sold under the name Reality. It consists of two flexible rings with a polyurethane sheath in between. The inner ring fits between the pubic bone and the cervix like a diaphragm. The sheath hangs out of the vagina and the man thrusts into it. It's basically like having sex with a sandwich bag and the failure rate is nothing to brag about—five to twenty-one percent.

A contraceptive method that combines chemical and barrier methods is the contraceptive sponge. (I'm not even sure if this method is still available). This is a small round sponge that is infused with spermicide. You place it up against your cervix and it lasts for twenty-four hours. Failure rates are somewhat high, about the same as a diaphragm or cervical cap. You could boost the effectiveness of the sponge by combining it with the male condom. Packages of sponges are sold over the counter.

Intrauterine devices (IUD's) are based on a very old contraceptive idea that began with use in animal husbandry. If you insert a foreign object into the uterus and leave it there, it prevents a fertilized egg from implanting into the lining of the uterus because it creates a state of low-grade infection and sloughs the uterine lining off continually, not just during your period.

IUD's became popular in the 1970's as an alternative to birth control pills. A lot of women either didn't want to take birth control pills because they smoked cigarettes, or they just didn't want the hassle of having to remember to take a pill every day.

The older IUD's that were used back in the 1970's had massive unpleasant side effects, such as extremely heavy periods and debilitating cramping. Believe me, I know. I had one of them for four years and that finally convinced me to get my tubes tied when I was twenty-two. I remember working at the post office and trying to deliver mail. I was having such bad cramps I would have to sit on somebody's front porch clutching my abdomen and grimacing in pain.

In the late 1970's, IUD's suddenly plummeted in popularity. What happened? A new kind of IUD called the Dalkon shield was introduced. Instead of being a 7- or t-shaped piece of plastic with some copper wire on it, the Dalkon shield was a plastic device with sharp edges that kind of looked like a little Pac-Man, if you remember that from the 1970's. The Dalkon shield perforated the uterus of some women and led to death in some cases. The main problem with the Dalkon shield was it used a braided string instead of a copper wire that hung out of the cervix. The braided string wicked bacteria into the vagina and also caused the death of several women. I believe some of the lawsuits involving the Dalkon shield have still not been settled as of this writing.

In the 2000's, IUD's became popular again. Many of them release hormones to avoid the previously mentioned side effects. IUD's have to be inserted by medical personnel but they can last up to ten years with a failure rate under one percent and one hundred percent reversibility.

Have you ever heard of the myth of penis captivus—the idea that a man's penis could get stuck in a woman's vagina after intercourse and he wouldn't be able to get it out? There was a case in which a man couldn't pull his penis out of his girlfriend's vagina. It turned out his foreskin was caught on the copper wire from her IUD.

The most basic kind of hormonal contraceptive is the birth control pill. There are many different pill prescriptions available. Some pills are all estrogen and some pills contain both estrogen and progesterone. Common estrogen side effects include indigestion, nausea, weight gain, bloating, vomiting, headache, vaginal discharge, tender breasts, yeast infections, mood swings, depression, and low sexual desire.

Common progesterone side effects include an increase in male secondary sex characteristics such as facial hair growth, thinning scalp hair, acne, and decreased breast size. Progesterone can also cause vaginal dryness and irregular bleeding.

Birth control pills contain synthetic female hormones that stop ovulation. The simplest way to use birth control pills is to get them in packages of twenty-eight pills. You take three weeks' worth of active pills and one week of placebos. During the placebo week you will probably have a very light "fake" period.

With all of the different types of pills that are available, how do you decide which one is for you? Unfortunately, many prescribers don't look at a woman's individual needs. Instead they prescribe based on how persuasive their pharmaceutical sales rep is. In other cases, women can only get the type of pills covered by their insurance. In general, women who have gone through puberty can usually handle a stronger estrogen-based pill. Teenaged girls may need to use a milder prescription. If you are having side effects such as nausea and vomiting, you may need a weaker prescription.

Another thing a lot of people don't understand about oral contraceptives is that they may take a few months to achieve full strength. You are not automatically protected the minute you take that first pill. If you are having breakthrough bleeding, your pill is not at its full effectiveness rate. The way you know your pill is at full effectiveness is when you have a slight period that starts at exactly the same time of day every four weeks.

The most common reason birth control pills fail is that the woman forgets a pill or takes them at different times of the day. Birth control pills may not be a good idea for women who are forgetful or don't know where they will be sleeping any given night. But that doesn't mean that hormonal contraceptives are out of the picture for you, because there are other types besides the pill.

The twenty-eight-day pill prescription is not the only type. There are some brands that provide active pills for three, four, or even twelve months at a time. The thinking is that women do not need to have a period every month. In fact, many researchers believe that it's not good for women to have that many periods over a lifetime.

You could use depo-provera, which is a synthetic progesterone taken as an injection every three months, which requires some planning. Contraceptive implants, which are surgically placed under the skin of the upper arm, can last as long as three years.

Hormonal contraceptives also come in the form of a skin patch that lasts a week and a vaginal ring that lasts three weeks. The benefit is they don't have the digestive side effects of pills. I don't trust these last two. I mean, I know the FDA has approved them so they have to be at least as effective as pills. But I've heard of cases of a patch falling off in a hot tub or while a woman was exercising.

The problem is that women have different metabolisms and with the patch and the ring you're getting unpredictable surges of hormones, unlike the pill which provides a steady rate if you take it at the same time every day. I've also heard of cases in which a blood clot was blamed on the use of the ring, although this couldn't be proven.

As mentioned before, emergency contraceptive is sold under the name Plan B. It is a massive dose of hormones used after an unintended instance of unprotected sex. It can work up to ninety-six hours after the incident. It basically resets your cycle. I read that Plan B as well as other contraceptives such as condoms are now being sold in vending machines on some college campuses.

There are two other issues with hormonal contraceptives. They can be responsible for a serious loss of sex drive. This claim is not based on anecdotal evidence. There are dozens of well-controlled studies that show this.

Another issue is reversibility. In theory the pill and other hormonal methods should be one hundred percent reversible. I know a woman who was in her thirties and was on the pill for years. She decided she wanted to get pregnant. She took her last pill on December thirtieth and got pregnant on New Year's Eve!

But some women report that they had trouble getting pregnant after using hormonal birth control for years. It could be they would have had trouble getting pregnant anyway, but we don't know that because often these women started taking the pill when they were in their teens and took it for twenty years or more before trying to get pregnant. Because they had never been pregnant, we don't know how easy or hard it would have been for them to get pregnant. This unknown is something you should definitely consider if you are planning to use hormonal methods for an extended period of time before you try to get pregnant. That's why some doctors recommend taking a break from the pill every five years or so and using a different method for six months to a year.

If you are absolutely one hundred percent sure you never want kids or don't want any more, look into sterilization. It is the method with the best success rate, although even sterilization is not perfect. There is a very negligible failure rate due to surgical issues.

The male surgical sterilization operation is called a vasectomy. It is done under local anesthetic in a doctor's office. It involves making a small incision on both sides of the scrotum and gently pulling the vas deferens on each side through the opening. The vas deferens are the tubes that carry sperm from the testes to the body cavity. The tubes are either cut and tied off or cauterized.

I know a lot of men who have had a vasectomy and I won't lie to you. There appears to be some serious pain involved. After you have recovered sufficiently enough to masturbate, you have to have a sperm sample tested a couple of times to make sure the surgery worked. In some cases they have to do it again. This happened to my dad. (Before I was born—I kid). No, really, he had to have it redone, but he didn't really mind because he was a huge hypochondriac and was never happier than when there was something medically wrong with him.

You know how when you drive to Las Vegas, you see billboards that are just a little weirder than usual? For example, there are more ads for pawnshops, which is understandable. Anyway, I saw one on the way out of town advertising vasectomies. The phone number was 1-800-EZSNIP. No kidding. Of course, after you just spent a drunk night in Vegas, it's probably too late to do any good. What happens in Vegas!

Vasectomy surgery isn't very dangerous. It does carry the same minimal risk as any other surgery performed in a doctor's office. Some men refuse to get a vasectomy because they believe it will diminish their "manliness". "Nobody's going to cut into my balls!" Sperm makes up so little of the volume of semen that a vasectomy should not noticeably diminish the volume of your ejaculate. There was a rumor going around years ago that having a vasectomy was related to an increased risk of heart attack. I believe this was not supported.

Although vasectomies can sometimes be successfully reversed, depending on how long ago they were done, many doctors will only perform one if they believe you will not change your mind.

SAFE SEX RULE
Don't opt for sterilization unless you are really sure you don't want to have kids.

The operation that sterilizes a woman is called a tubal ligation. This is invasive surgery into the abdomen and requires general anesthesia so is riskier than a vasectomy. It is done laparoscopically, meaning there is no full incision, just a couple of punctures. No scars are visible. This is a huge improvement from how they used to do them when the surgery required a hipbone-to-hipbone incision.

In a tubal ligation, the Fallopian tubes, which carry an egg to the uterus, are cut on both sides. They may also be tied or clamped.

In today's climate, a tubal ligation is not that easy to obtain. Due to lawsuits, many gynecologists will not do them at all. Others will only do them on women who have reached a certain age or already have children. Fortunately that wasn't the case when I had my tubal ligation in 1979. Yes, the doctor was hesitant to tie the tubes of a twenty-two-year old woman who had no kids. But I used every argument I could think of. I think the one that won him over was "Insanity runs in my family. And if you need me to prove it, I can bring in the exhibits". I would like to take this opportunity to publicly thank my former gynecologist, Dr. William Jurewitz, for trusting me not to sue him. Best decision I ever made. Also, thanks to the United States Postal Service health plan, which paid for the whole thing (after a few nasty letters back and forth).

Tubal ligation carries the same risks as any other comparable minor abdominal laparoscopic surgery done under general anesthesia. I had some discomfort for about a week, but no pain.

You may think you don't want kids. But life circumstances change. If you decide to go through with sterilization, make sure you really don't want kids or more kids.

There's a relatively new non-surgical permanent alternative to tubal ligation. It's called Essure, and I can't believe it hasn't caught on more than it has because it sounds great. In this procedure, which is done in a doctor's office, the patient is lightly sedated. A small plug is inserted through the cervix and uterus and into the Fallopian tube. Once it is in there, it blocks the tube and over several months scar tissue forms in and around the tube and totally blocks it. Sterilization with no cutting! Amazing! If this option had been available in the 1970's I totally would have gone for it.

Since all contraceptives have a failure rate, even if you use them correctly, some women will experience an unintended pregnancy. Ending a pregnancy that has already begun is called abortion. There are several different methods that can be used depending on how early the procedure is done. In general, the earlier you end a pregnancy, the safer the abortion procedure is.

Medical (nonsurgical) abortion can be used up to about ten weeks. A medical abortion consists of a combination of the drugs mifepristone (formerly called RU-486) and methotrexate or prostaglandin. RU-486 used to be called the "French abortion pill". Some people think the Plan B emergency contraception pill is the same as a medical abortion, but it's not.

In a nonsurgical abortion, the woman receives the medication during a visit to the doctor. The combination of these two drugs causes the contents of the uterus to be expelled within two to three days.

The surgical abortion procedure that is most commonly used is called vacuum aspiration. In this procedure a syringe or vacuum is inserted through the cervix and suction is applied, drawing out the contents of the uterus. The procedure is done in a doctor's office under local anesthetic. Post-surgical complications can include cramping, pain, and bleeding.

Beyond the first trimester, a more dangerous procedure called dilation and evacuation may be used. It's not clear up to what point into the second trimester this can be used. It requires stronger anesthetic than vacuum aspiration. The cervix is dilated, suction is performed, and a surgical instrument called a curette may be used to scrape the lining of the uterus. This may cause infection or perforation of the uterus. In 1980, there were nine deaths in the United States from legal abortions. In 2010 there were eight deaths in the United States from legal abortions.

There's a form of abortion that's used in the third trimester called partial-birth abortion. This is only used when the fetus or the mother has a major medical problem.

I'm not trying to sidestep controversy here. That's beyond the scope of this book, although I certainly have my own opinions. Nobody wants to have an abortion. Nobody says, "Oh goody! I get to have an abortion!"

I just think it's sad that so many women who don't want to be pregnant may not have a choice, as the current trend is toward contraceptives and abortion becoming less available, when so many other women go through expensive and uncomfortable fertility treatments in order to try to become pregnant. I will say, reproductive technology is advancing at a rapid rate. There are procedures that allow women to be sterilized but freeze portions of their ovaries. Plans are underway for an artificial uterus. The use of egg donors and surrogate mothers has become quite common.

At this point, why don't we have a male hormonal contraceptive available? There have been many attempts to develop one, but the main problem is the anatomy of the testes. Remember that the cells that make sperm are surrounded by cells that make testosterone. Attempts at male hormonal contraceptives have failed because treatments that affected sperm production lowered male hormones and so decreased men's sex drive.

Having a child is probably the most serious long-range decision that you will ever make in your life. That's why it's not a decision you should make on the spur of the moment. Make sure you stay informed about ways to prevent unwanted pregnancy.

SAFE SEX RULE
Never have unprotected sex.

SAFE SEX RULE
Whichever contraceptive method you choose, use it correctly.

SAFE SEX RULE
Plan ahead and do a cost-benefit analysis to determine which contraceptive method is best for you. You don't want your body to end up as some kind of bad science experiment.

Next we turn to another cornerstone of safe sex—preventing sexually transmitted infections.

CHAPTER 7
SEXUALLY TRANSMITTED INFECTIONS

When I teach my human sexuality class, I'm old school. I write terms on a white board and I lecture. Sometimes students complain that I don't use PowerPoint or show illustrations on the large screen in the auditorium. When I talk about the subject of sexually transmitted infections, believe me, students are happy I'm too lazy to make slides. I tell them, "After you hear this lecture, you're going to want to go home and take a shower. When you come to class next week, you're going to want to bring a plastic trash bag with you and cover your seat with it because you don't know who's been sitting there before."

Preventing sexually transmitted infections (STI's) is one of the cornerstones of safe sex. The most common piece of advice for preventing STI's is to use a condom. This is good advice as far as it goes, but what most people don't realize is that condoms protect you from some STI's but not all of them. Condoms only protect you from STI's that are transmitted through intercourse by contact with penile or vaginal discharges. They protect you only from gonorrhea, chlamydia, and human immunodeficiency virus (HIV). They don't protect you from herpes, human papilloma virus (HPV), syphilis, or ectoparasites. Also, condoms tend to break or fall off. I also heard of a case in which a woman was performing oral sex on a man who was wearing a condom and inhaled the condom and choked to death on it.

SAFE SEX RULE
Sure, use a condom. But realize that there are many STI's that a condom won't prevent.

What follows is a description of the most common STI's currently diagnosed in the United States. It is not an exhaustive list of every STI in the world. Some of those can be really nasty, especially the ones found most often in tropical climates, where your balls swell up to the size of basketballs or your genitals disintegrate (seriously). As a sexually active person, it is vital for you to know at least the basics about the most common STI's—symptoms, diagnosis, prognosis, and treatment. Sadly, many sexually active people do not know these basic facts.

Information about STI's is usually organized by cause. Types of STI's include those caused by bacteria, viruses, and parasites. I also include a section on common vaginal infections which are not always sexually transmitted, but can be.

BACTERIAL STI'S
Gonorrhea can occur in both men and women. Symptoms in a man include a thick yellowish-greenish discharge

from the penis and pain or burning on urination. Women may have a vaginal discharge and burning, or no symptoms at all.

This is a huge problem with both gonorrhea and chlamydia—they may remain asymptomatic in women and the bacteria may travel into the Fallopian tubes and cause pelvic inflammatory disease (PID), a potentially life-threatening condition. PID can cause scar tissue in the tubes and result in infertility. Also, gonorrhea and chlamydia can be transferred to a newborn child. Diagnosis of gonorrhea is made by examination of the discharge under a microscope. Treatment for gonorrhea is antibiotics and it is curable. FYI, doctors don't routinely test for this during your well-woman visit. You have to ask for the test. Gonorrhea can be transferred to the penis, vagina, mouth, or anus.

Weird story. When I was working as a surrogate partner, the therapist I worked with called me into his office and told me that a client had accused me of giving him gonorrhea. I knew this didn't happen because we got tested all the time. It turned out that there is a very rare form of tongue cancer that looks almost identical to gonorrhea under the microscope, and he had it! The poor guy!

Chlamydia has similar symptoms to gonorrhea but the discharge is thinner and the symptoms are generally milder. Both men and women can be asymptomatic for chlamydia. This is a huge problem because a lot of people have it and don't know it and spread it around. Treatment is antibiotics. Chlamydia is curable, but it often takes time to cure because people stop taking the medication prematurely and couples keep passing it back and forth. Diagnosis is by slide under the microscope, and again, if you want to be tested, you have to ask for it.

SAFE SEX RULE
If you are prescribed antibiotics for an STI, take all of them.

A third bacterial STI, syphilis, is a bit different. It occurs in three stages. If it is contracted sexually, Stage 1 involves a genital sore called a chancre. This is a painless sore about the size of a penny that looks like a scab. Some people have contracted syphilis and didn't know it because the sore went away.

In Stage 2, the bacteria are still living in your body, and weeks or months after the initial exposure, you develop flu-like symptoms such as fever, sore throat, and joint aches. The telltale symptom at this stage is a red pinpoint rash on the back, legs, and arms. Syphilis might not be diagnosed at this stage, because most people don't connect an episode of unprotected sex with flu-like symptoms that occur months later.

If not treated at Stage 2, the bacteria burrow into your spinal cord and remain dormant. At some point years down the line, Stage 3 may develop. This is when the bacteria go into internal organs such as the heart and lungs and cause massive ulcers. Syphilis can also spread to your brain and cause movement problems and dementia. In the early 1900's before antibiotics were invented, the majority of people who were in mental hospitals were there due to syphilitic-related dementia.

Fortunately, most cases of syphilis today are identified and cured before they reach stage 3. The downside is syphilis can be spread not only by contact with a chancre, but by nonsexual blood-to-blood contact (as in sharing needles for drug use). In that case, the infection goes right to Stage 2.

Syphilis is diagnosed either with a scraping from the chancre or a blood test (called either the Wasserman or a VDRL panel). Syphilis is curable and treated with antibiotics.

VIRAL SEXUALLY TRANSMITTED INFECTIONS— THE GIFTS THAT KEEP ON GIVING

Human Papilloma Virus (HPV) is the virus that causes genital warts. Warts that appear on the genitals can be flat, smooth, round, or cauliflower-shaped. Technically, HPV is not curable, although there have been cases in which a person tested positive for it and then tested negative years later. Outbreaks of warts can be treated by freezing them off with liquid nitrogen, cauterizing them, applying topical medication, or removing them surgically.

Genital warts can appear on the cervix. The danger is that this warty tissue may turn pre-cancerous or cancerous. HPV is most often sexually transmitted, but there have been cases in which genital warts spontaneously arose with no sexual contact.

Many people (especially women) who have HPV don't know it because they have never had an outbreak of warts. There are different patterns of outbreaks. Some people only have one outbreak in their life, and other people have fairly constant outbreaks.

There is a vaccine available for several strains of genital warts. It is usually administered to children after age nine and to be effective it must be administered before age twenty-six. It works for boys too.

There is another type of warts that may appear near the genital area, usually on the lower abdomen. These are called molluscum warts and occur in clusters. They usually appear and disappear spontaneously.

There are many types of herpes viruses. Chicken pox, shingles, and cold sores are all caused by herpes viruses. When sexually transmitted, herpes sores most commonly occur on the mouth or genitals.

If you catch genital herpes, here's what happens. A few days after sexual contact with an infected person, you will feel a sense of pulling, tugging, or itching on your genitals as if you have a pimple or a clothing seam is rubbing. A red raised mound will surface and in a few days it will divide into a few separate pinkish yellowish blisters which will break and ooze fluid. Because herpes is an inflammation of a nerve, at this point you will be in serious pain. In men, genital herpes sores usually occur on the shaft of the penis or on the scrotum. In women, they occur on the vaginal lips or inside the vagina. In a few days, the blisters heal, leaving no scar.

When herpes blisters are present and oozing fluid, herpes is highly contagious. You won't want to have sex at this point anyway because it would be too painful. How contagious it

may be at other times is controversial. It is suspected that herpes may be contagious in between outbreaks. This is called asymptomatic viral shedding. Herpes can arise spontaneously with no sexual contact.

The incidence of the herpes virus in the population is highly underestimated. In my opinion, pretty much everybody who had unprotected sex with multiple partners in the 1970's probably has it. Many people have the virus and never have an outbreak. Others have only one outbreak in their lives. Others have a couple outbreaks a year. Some unlucky people have continuous outbreaks. The most common pattern is a few outbreaks a year triggered by stress or sexual contact. Anything that depresses your immune system can trigger an outbreak.

There are a number of medications that can lengthen the time between outbreaks and shorten the duration of the outbreaks. Once you are aware that you have the virus and have had an outbreak, you learn to recognize when one is about to happen. People who are experiencing the preliminary stages of an outbreak (called the prodrome) may feel flu-like symptoms such as fever and swelling of the lymph nodes in the groin.

Living with herpes means living with a chronic condition. Support groups, whether online or in person, may be helpful. There is a stigma attached to herpes because of possible sexual transmission. Let's get over it. It's a skin disease that can be managed, and it is not the end of your sex life in all but the most extreme cases.

You are not alone. So many people have herpes that you will be able to find an accepting partner.

HIV/AIDS

Obviously, one could write volumes about human immunodeficiency virus (HIV) and Acquired Immune Deficiency Syndrome (AIDS). You'd have to be living under a rock to not know anything about it. I'm not trying to be flip. HIV and AIDS have been devastating on both an individual and global economic basis. The most basic fact is that it is a virus that can be sexually transmitted. It weakens the immune system, allowing opportunistic infections to develop. If the immune system is totally compromised, AIDS can be fatal.

AIDS is not curable, although I have read documented cases in which a person tested positive for the virus and years later did not. I have also read two cases of women who were in the advanced stages of AIDS and recovered. There are a number of new treatments that are available now or will become available shortly.

From a safe sex standpoint, you can't tell if someone is HIV positive or has AIDS just by looking at them. So the only things you can do are get tested with anyone before you have sexual contact, use a condom, and know your partner's sexual history (more on that later). Also, educate yourself! Read about the nature of retroviruses and how they are transmitted. Combinations of the medications that are available now are allowing more and more people who are HIV positive to live a normal lifespan.

It's now possible to measure how much of the virus is present in body fluids. This is called the viral load. In most cases, the body fluids that contain the highest viral load are blood, semen, and vaginal secretions. So one way to protect yourself would be to avoid those fluids in particular.

VAGINAL INFECTIONS

Here's a question. Suppose you are a married woman who believes she is in a monogamous relationship. You experience an unusual vaginal discharge and pain on urination. Your gynecologist diagnoses you with gonorrhea. Are you justified in going home and saying to your husband, "You cheating son of a bitch. You fooled around with someone else and you gave me gonorrhea."

I believe you are justified in this accusation. Symptoms of bacterial diseases tend to show up quickly and are fairly straightforward. If you know you haven't had sexual contact with anyone else, I think you can be pretty sure your husband gave it to you in this case.

Now, imagine the same scenario, but with a viral disease such as herpes. You are diagnosed and blame your husband. He swears on his life that he has not had sex with anyone else. Could he be telling the truth?

Yes. As I discussed before, people can have the herpes virus and not know it because they never had an outbreak. Either the husband or wife in this case could have contracted the herpes virus years ago in a previous relationship, so there's no use blaming the current partner.

The same thing is true for vaginal infections which include bacterial vaginosis and yeast infections. The name implies that these are female problems, but men can transmit them.

Let's say that you, as a woman, start experiencing symptoms such as vaginal itching and a fishy, musty-smelling gray discharge. You go to your gynecologist and are diagnosed with bacterial vaginosis. You go home and blame your husband for screwing around, which may not be the case. Vaginal infections can be spread through sexual contact, but can often arise spontaneously due to a change in the chemistry of the vagina, which requires a very delicate pH balance.

Bacterial vaginosis is a catchall term for a number of conditions including gardnerella, non-specific vaginitis, and non-gonococcal urethritis. In men it would be called non-specific urethritis (NSU). In women, the symptom is the above-mentioned discharge. It's diagnosed just by the odor, which smells like somebody left a dead fish in a library book. (Students love this lecture). Seriously, it smells like something crawled up there and died. In men the symptoms are itching or burning on urination. Treatment is a drug called Flagyl, which is difficult to take as it causes severe side effects such as skin flushing and nausea, and you can't drink alcohol while you're taking it.

Yeast infections (also called candida or candidiasis) affect so many women that the treatments are now available over the counter. Symptoms of a yeast infection include intense itching, painful red scaly patches on the vulva, and a copious white discharge called a cottage cheese discharge. In men, symptoms would be red scaly patches on the penis. Yeast infections can be transmitted sexually, but often are caused by an imbalance in the vagina's chemistry that causes normal yeast to overgrow. This can be triggered by wearing tight pants, sitting around in a wet bathing suit, or taking birth control pills. Treatments (sold over the counter as mentioned) include creams or suppositories which are inserted in the vagina.

Trichomoniasis is sometimes considered a vaginal infection and sometimes considered a parasite called a protozoan. Symptoms in women include a yellowish green foaming discharge with an unpleasant odor. Men may have no symptoms. Treatments are either antibiotics or Flagyl.

PARASITES

Parasites are creatures that live on your body. You're the host and they're the guests. The most common type of sexually transmitted parasites are pubic lice, also called crabs. They can be seen with the naked eye unlike other STI's. Lice can be transmitted through contact with clothing, sheets, towels and toilet seats in addition to people. They are highly contagious. The symptom of crabs is intense itching.

When people discover that they have crabs, they freak out and do stupid things like shaving off all their pubic hair. This doesn't really help, as the parasites were your guests and now you've left them homeless and pissed off. Some people have even poured pesticides or kerosene on their genital area (definitely not a good idea).

Treatment is a special shampoo, cream or ointment that kills the lice. You just know when you go to the drugstore to buy the treatment, it's not going to be on the shelf where you can easily find it, and you're going to have to ask someone. Or, even worse case scenario, you find the medication and go to the checkstand and the cashier says, "What's this? I've never seen it before. Oh, lice medicine. Price check on lice medicine in aisle three!" You should make the dirty dog who gave you this get the medicine for you. Yes, that's right. You catch lice from somebody who's a total slob and never washes their clothes, sheets, and towels. I believe crabs deserve a couple of safe sex rules of their own.

SAFE SEX RULE
Don't sleep with somebody who is a complete pig. (That's probably an insult to pigs everywhere).

SAFE SEX RULE
If you find you have crabs, stay calm. Take a few deep breaths and don't panic. Don't do anything stupid. Just go buy the medicine.

PREVENTION
Safe sex is all about preventing STI's in the first place. In addition to abstinence, education, and using a condom, there are a couple of other safe sex rules.

SAFE SEX RULE
Inspect your partner's genitals. Do not have sex with anybody who has unusual sores, growths, odors, or discharges in the genital area.

Have sex with the lights on so you can see your partner's genitals. If necessary, use a miner's headlamp. (I was kidding on that last one).

There are some STI's that cannot be identified by visual inspection. For example, herpes sores could be inside the vagina and you would not be able to see them, or someone could have gonorrhea but be asymptomatic. That's why this last safe sex rule is so important.

SAFE SEX RULE
Know your partner's sexual history.

In addition to inspecting your partner's genitals, it is imperative to discuss your respective sexual histories before embarking on a sexual relationship. It sounds easy enough, but most people don't do it, or they only share a partial history or lie about their past. Why?

They might be embarrassed about how many partners they've had. In general, men and women use different strategies to count the number of sexual partners. Women enumerate—they actually count off the names. Men estimate—they tend to take credit for a close call. "She agreed to sex and changed her mind at the last minute, but I'm counting it." People want so much to believe that a new relationship will succeed that they want to forget what happened before and make a fresh start.

Joke:
Man (to woman, after sex). "So, am I your first?"
Woman: "I don't know, were you in a Holiday Inn in Cleveland in 1974?"

My policy before I start a new relationship is to disclose everything, including marriages (past or current!), types of partners, and any history of problems in the genital area. If that turns off a potential partner, then I feel it's good to find that out now, instead of having it thrown in my face years down the line.

I expect a potential partner to share the same level of detail with me. My sexual past has been so bizarre that I'm not in a position to judge.

Here's a story about the consequences of not being candid about your sexual past upfront. I worked with a guy who was bisexual. This is before awareness of HIV and AIDS. He was in his forties and went back to his hometown in the Midwest for a high school reunion. He met an old girlfriend. They were both divorced so they decided to start a relationship and they ended up getting married. A few years later they were talking about AIDS and he told her that in the past he had sex with men, but that of course he had been tested and was negative. Well, the shit hit the fan and she left him the next day! He had never mentioned this before because it literally no longer meant anything to him and he didn't think she would care.

I don't get upset when I hear about a partner's past sexual relationships. Apparently, I was born without sexual jealousy. In fact, it's just the opposite. If I am attracted to a person enough to have sex, I get turned on thinking about that person having sex with somebody else. It's probably a character flaw. Oh well.

In addition to knowing a partner's sexual history, I also like to request financial documents, such as income tax returns for the past ten years or so. I guess this requirement will prevent me from having sex with Donald Trump. Whatever—it's not like there would be anything in it for him anyway.

Here are a few other final facts about sexually transmitted infections. All other things being equal, women are more likely to catch an STI from an infected man than men are to catch an STI from an infected woman. Just another example of women getting screwed! Also women are more likely to catch an STI from an infected male partner when they are on their period than when they are not. We can't win for losing! This is why it's important not only for women to inspect their partner's genitals, but to inspect their own genitals also. Women have to be extra careful. You can't see inside your own vagina, unless you use a speculum and a mirror, but it's important for women to be extremely familiar with their vulva and notice any changes such as growths, moles, or discoloration.

CHAPTER 8
PARAPHILIAS

This chapter and the following two will deal with the paraphilias. Paraphilias have several definitions. The word itself means abnormal love. In my view it also means strange love or almost like love. Formerly, when people were less accepting of unusual sexual behaviors, these practices were called sexual deviations or perversions. I include two chapters on the paraphilias. This one covers an overview of the most common paraphilias, at least in the United States. The following chapter delves into more detail on extreme forms of masochism—self-harm.

The difference between what's considered normal and abnormal sexual behavior has changed dramatically over the decades. One of the first systematic accounts of paraphilias was "Psychopathia Sexualis", written in the 1880's by Richard von Krafft-Ebing. In this book he describes practices that would still be considered unusual today, such as having sex with chickens, but you have to keep in mind that back in Krafft-

Ebing's day, behaviors such as oral sex and masturbation were also considered abnormal and perverted.

There are a number of criteria that can be used to determine whether behaviors are abnormal or not. In a statistical sense, do most people do the behavior? In that case, the behavior would probably be considered normal. However, we don't really have any good data about how many people engage in the behaviors that will be described in this chapter and the following two. Also, I'm sure that many more people fantasize about these behaviors or look at pictures of them online than actually do them, and we don't have any good data about that either.

Is the behavior compulsive? That is, do you have control over your behavior or does the behavior have control over you? Even behaviors that we consider perfectly normal such as masturbation can become compulsive. Paraphilic desires are often characterized as compulsive, recurrent, persistent, or uncontrollable.

There are some other issues to consider. Is the paraphilic behavior the only way you can get aroused and have an orgasm even when other outlets (such as a human partner) are available to you?

Is the behavior illegal? Some paraphilic behaviors are illegal and some are not.

Paraphilias are one of three types of sexual problems that may become so troublesome that they may assume the status of mental disorders. The others are sexual dysfunctions and gender identity disorders. Remember in Chapter 4 I introduced you to the DSM? The two criteria the DSM uses are "does the behavior cause personal distress", and "does the behavior impair functioning"? If both of these are true, the behavior may qualify as a paraphilic disorder.

Another factor to consider when we look at the paraphilias is whether they are coercive or not. That is, whether they are victimizing or victimless.

Mental health practitioners who deal with the paraphilias recognize that they differ from normal sexual behaviors in quantity, not quality. They are extreme versions of normal sexual curiosity and behavior. Here's an example. My mom told me this one.

She lives in a multi-story senior apartment building next to the Department of Motor Vehicles. Apparently there are a lot of homeless people living in the parking lot of the DMV. (Maybe they're just people waiting all night in line for the DMV, who knows?). Anyway, my mom overheard the following conversation between two old ladies in her building.

> *First old lady*: "There are people living in the DMV parking lot having sex at night."
> *Second old lady*: "You mean you can look out your window and see people in the DMV parking lot having sex?"
> *First old lady*: "Well, with the binoculars".

True story, not a joke. The point is, we all have had natural sexual curiosity ever since we were kids. It doesn't stop just because you grow up. Let's face it—if you were walking down the street on a public sidewalk and saw a naked woman standing in front of a window, you'd look. It's normal! It doesn't mean you're a pervert. You're not doing anything wrong.

The following is a list of the paraphilias that will be covered in this chapter, along with a one-sentence definition of each. I'll follow that with a more in-depth examination of each one. As always, I'll focus on the safety aspects of each of these practices.

Sadism
Sexual arousal from hurting or humiliating another person.

Masochism
Sexual arousal from being hurt or humiliated.

Fetishism
Sexual arousal from an inanimate object.

Partialism
Sexual arousal from unusual body shapes or parts of the body we don't normally think of as sexual.

Transvestism
A particular form of fetishism in which a man gets sexually aroused from women's clothing.

Exhibitionism
Sexual arousal from exposing your genitals to an unsuspecting person.

Voyeurism
Sexual arousal from peeping on unsuspecting people.

Zoophila/Bestiality
Bestiality is sex with animals. A zoophile considers an animal his romantic or sexual partner.

Necrophilia
Sexual arousal from having sex with a corpse.

Pedophilia
The compulsion to have sex with children before the age of puberty.

Frotteurism
The compulsion to rub up against or grope unsuspecting people in crowded public places such as public transportation.

Necrophilia, partialism, and zoophilia/bestiality are not specifically included in the DSM. They can still be written in as part of a diagnosis.

Most people with paraphilic interests are men, although many women are masochists and zoophiles. Can we conclude from this that men are perverts? I believe we can. Also, paraphilias are generally found in Western/European cultures. Can we conclude from this that Europeans are perverts? Absolutely! (I hope you know I'm kidding).

SADISM

Sadism is named after a fake French nobleman, the Marquis de Sade. While imprisoned in the Bastille, he wrote stories in which the characters became sexually aroused by hurting or humiliating other people. Sexual sadism can take a number of forms.

In one form, nonconsensual sexual sadism, two partners hook up, and unbeknownst to partner number one, partner number two is a sadist. Here's how this could play out. You as a woman have just started seeing a man and it is your first time in bed together. Without warning or asking permission, he starts slapping you or pulling your hair or otherwise hurting you during sex, and not in a playful way. This is not what you signed up for. Insist he stop now, and leave the scene. How could you have prevented this?

SAFE SEX RULE
The only way I know of to ask whether your partner is a sexual sadist is to ask, and he'll probably lie. If you can think of another way to find out, I'm open to hearing it.

This is why it's important to ask about a partner's sexual history, as I explained in the chapter on sexually transmitted infections. You could ask an ex-wife or girlfriend about him. Insulting or dirty talk as a prelude to sex could be another clue. However, keep in mind that when you're really turned on, your brain is producing endorphins so that you don't feel pain the way you usually would. In that case, you might not notice there's a problem until there's really a problem.

A truly terrifying example of this occurs in a memoir by Dr. Pepper Schwartz, a famous sex researcher, entitled "Prime". In this book she recounts an incident that happened to her with a man she met in Beirut, in which she agreed to ride with him in his car, he pulled over, started kissing her violently, and slapped her in the face when she did not respond. Fortunately, she was able to talk him into driving her back to her hotel.

The genders could be reversed. It's not only men who can be sexual sadists.

Another form of sexual sadism is really scary. This is a sexually sadistic psychopath—someone who is not only sadistic but does not have a conscience and has a pattern of assaulting multiple victims. Research estimates that about five percent of rapes are committed by sexually sadistic predators. Many famous serial killers such as the Hillside Stranglers and Ted Bundy were sexually sadistic psychopaths who tortured and killed their victims. They often used elaborate ruses to kidnap their victims. Bundy in some cases put a fake cast on his arm to get a victim to help him. I believe that one of the Hillside Stranglers, Kenneth Bianchi, impersonated a law enforcement officer.

There will be more about protecting yourself from this type of assault in the chapter on Sexual Coercion. All of the safe sex rules in that chapter apply here. They all have to do with basic personal safety, such as locking doors and windows, not driving alone on isolated roads, and other such self-protective measures.

The most common form of sexual sadism is practiced in the context of a consensual encounter with a masochist that is called an S and M "scene". In this practice, a person with sadistic interests and a person with masochistic interests hook up and do an agreed-upon role-play involving the sadist punishing the masochist in some way. Costumes are often used, such as nurse and patient, or pirate and wench. Other paraphernalia may be used such as whips, ropes, or paddles. Consensual S-M scenes are mostly safe, with a couple of exceptions, when practiced by experienced people.

SAFE SEX RULE
During a consensual S-M encounter, don't do any activities that break the skin or draw blood.

Some S-M practitioners specialize in "edge play". These are extreme S-M practices that can be dangerous. These are described in the next chapter.

SAFE SEX RULE
During consensual S-M encounters, always agree beforehand on a safe word. This is a word that the submissive partner uses if he or she wants to stop the interaction.

Consensual S-M scenes often take place on a paid basis. Commonly, a male client will pay a mistress (also called a dominatrix) to hurt or humiliate him. Most S-M mistresses do not consider themselves to be prostitutes. For the most part they don't touch their clients' genitals or have oral sex or intercourse with their clients.

Here are a couple of examples where consensual S-M scenes went bad and someone got hurt. This first one occurred in Southern California near where I live.

An older S-M mistress had a client who was in his fifties. She had him strapped to a device called a wheel. The client's hands and feet are hooked onto a large wheel that looks kind of like a ship's wheel, and the client is turned upside down and held there for periods of time. In this case, the mistress didn't know that the client had a heart condition and he had a heart attack and suddenly died while hanging upside down.

This is bad enough, but instead of calling the paramedics, (she wasn't doing anything wrong, the scene was consensual and it was an accident) she panicked and called her boyfriend and they tried to get rid of the body. Of course they were eventually caught and by then it was a case of trying to cover this up. In a case such as this, I'm thinking a doctor's note or a signed waiver might not have been a bad idea.

Another example has a more humorous aspect to it. I have a male friend I've known for over thirty-five years, and he was always into consensual S-M scenes (not with me, I'm not into this) in which he was the sadistic partner and got aroused by whipping his female partner. He had a dungeon in his house with a whipping post in the middle of it. When he was in his seventies, he had a girlfriend about thirty years younger and she was really into being whipped. I saw him at a party and he was really out of it. I asked him what was wrong and he said he was totally stoned on Vicodin because he was whipping his girlfriend so hard he threw his back out. Somehow I couldn't feel sorry for him. Maybe that sounds unsympathetic.

MASOCHISM

Masochism is getting sexually aroused by being hurt or humiliated. It was named after an Austrian, Leopold von Sacher-Masoch, who lived in the 1800's. He wrote stories in which the main characters got sexually aroused by being hurt or humiliated. The same safe sex rules apply to masochism that apply to sadism since many masochistic activities take place in the context of a consensual S-M scene. An exception is solitary masochistic activities and edgeplay which can be quite dangerous. These are discussed in the following chapter.

Remember when I said that paraphilias are extensions of normal desires and behaviors? A lot of people enjoy some mild restraint during sex. This could take the form of a blindfold, fur handcuffs, or holding your partner's hands over his or her head while having sex.

FETISHISM

Fetishism is sexual arousal to inanimate objects. Most fetishists are men and the most common fetishes for men are women's clothing and shoes.

Let's take the case of shoes. Shoe fetishes can take a number of forms. Most commonly, a man will collect women's shoes in women's sizes and keep them in a special closet and use them to masturbate. Some men can't get turned on unless they've seen the shoes being worn by a woman and so they steal shoes from women who take them off in semi-public places such as dark movie theaters or airplanes. My stepmother told me that she took off her shoes and fell asleep on a flight to Hungary and when she woke up she found that someone had stolen her shoes. A student told me that she was supposed to participate in a wedding in Hawaii and had packed four pairs of shoes in her checked luggage. When she opened her suitcase at the hotel, she found that someone, obviously an airline employee, had stolen the left shoe of each pair.

In the transvestic version of a shoe fetish, a man buys women's-style shoes in custom-made large sizes and gets turned on by wearing them. Some men have a shoe fetish that involves being walked on by a woman wearing high heels. This is obviously a combination of a shoe fetish and masochism.

Some men are only turned on by a particular type of shoe, such as a black pump with a stiletto heel. Some men get turned on by a shoe with a "deep throat". This is when the top part of the shoe (the throat) is low enough that it exposes toe cleavage. Some men are turned on by the odor of shoes.

One time I was in my classroom and I was lecturing about shoe fetishes. I looked over and lying on a side table was a Victoria's Secret bag. (People leave unbelievable stuff in classrooms—coats, umbrellas, sunglasses, food, etc.). I said, "I wonder what's in this?" and I reached over and opened it. Inside was a pair of stinky women's athletic shoes! Totally unplanned!

Wearing women's shoes or buying them and masturbating with them is safe sex. Stealing shoes is dangerous. It leaves you open to the possibility of being arrested.

There was a case back in the 1950's in San Diego in which a man accosted several women, knocked them down, and stole one of their shoes. He also broke into houses and stole shoes. The perpetrator was a navy pilot whose name was Wayne McFarland. He was sent to Atascadero State Hospital and then sentenced to prison. He was released and died in 1999.

SAFE SEX RULE
If it's illegal, it's not safe.

PARTIALISM

Partialism is when you can only get turned on by body parts that we don't normally think of as sexual or as erogenous zones. Examples are feet, hands, or ears. Partialism also includes the attraction to particular body shapes. Some partialists are attracted to women who are extremely tall, short, or overweight.

In the case of feet, some partialists want to have sex that involves feet. Some men want to insert their penis between a woman's toes. Others want to insert their big toe into a woman's vagina. I would say that the former is safe but the latter is probably not due to potential toenail fungus and the delicate pH balance of the vagina.

SAFE SEX RULE
If you are going to engage in foot-related sex practices, your feet don't just have to be clean. They have to be free of fungus conditions such as athlete's foot.

TRANSVESTISM

Transvestism (also called transvestic fetishism or cross-dressing) is getting turned on by wearing women's clothing. The range includes someone who is highly closeted and has a small collection of women's lingerie and only wears it to masturbate for special occasions. Men who are this highly secretive about their practices would usually be mortified if someone found out about this.

On the other extreme, some transvestites dress in a full outfit of women's clothing including make-up, wigs, and high heels. Contrary to popular belief, most transvestites are not gay. Most are married heterosexual men. Some men's wives are accepting of their practices and some are not. I can't see anything unsafe about these practices as long as they are solitary or consensual. They may be unsafe in a relationship sense if they are secretive. I guess the biggest danger here is you might sprain your ankle while walking in high heels!

A gay friend once told me about a festival that takes place in Provincetown, Massachusetts, a noted gay enclave. It's called "Fantasia Week". Provincetown is famous for its acceptance of alternative lifestyles. During Fantasia Week, crossdressers converge on the town and bring all of their women's outfits that they cannot wear in their conservative hometowns. Unfortunately, Provincetown, being a historic whaling village, has cobblestone streets. So here we have men who are not used to wearing high heels on a regular basis stumbling on cobblestones while wearing elaborate outfits which they change several times a day.

EXHIBITIONISM

Exhibitionism is sexual arousal from exposing your genitals to an unsuspecting victim. The turn-on here is the shock on the face of the victim, so exhibitionists often pick the most helpless victims, such as older women or children. Exhibitionism on the part of the perpetrator is extremely dangerous, as a conviction could get you a sex offender label for life which could result in loss of civil rights such as mobility and freedom to live where you choose.

Exhibitionism is probably more common than we think. A study cited in my Human Sexuality textbook claimed that one-third of female college students had been the victims of exhibitionists. The author of the study was named Cox. I wondered if the author had included this just to see if students were paying attention.

EXHIBITIONISTS SEEM TO LIKE ME

I was going to call this section Exhibitionists Like Me, but it made me sound like I was one of them. When you are a female mail carrier, men expose themselves to you all the time. You can't believe how brazen they are. I could walk up to someone's front door and stand there putting mail in the mailbox and the door would open and the resident would be standing there naked stroking himself. Really. Come on, I know this guy's name and where he lives and he's risking a lifelong sex offender designation? All we could do was report it to the supervisor and the supervisor would report it to the Postal Inspectors. If it happened more than once the Postal Inspectors would pay a visit to the man and inform him that he would no longer receive home delivery—he would have to pay for a P. O. box.

It got to be such a problem that we asked the supervisor what we were supposed to do. This wasn't covered in the Postal Manual or the postal motto ("neither rain nor snow nor someone wagging his wienie at me…"). The supervisor of course said, "Why don't you just look at the guy and say, 'Looks just like a penis, only smaller.'" His own wit caused him to go into a coughing fit and almost have a heart attack.

I'm guessing our postmaster didn't take these cases too seriously and here's why. One time a carrier (male) had to deliver some paperwork to the postmaster's house on a Saturday. The postmaster came to the door naked. The guy got back to the office totally traumatized. "You look like you just saw a ghost." "Worse!"

Someone exposed himself to me the very first week I worked. The trainee would do the route and the trainer would follow about half a house back. When you're a mail carrier of either gender, people understandably ask you for directions all the time. Sometimes they even ask, "Do you know where the post office is?" Seriously. So this guy pulled up to the curb and was waving a map out the window. He yelled, "Mail lady! Come over here! I need some directions." So I walked up to his window and looked in and he moved the map and his penis was sticking out. I said, "You need some directions? Why don't you put your hand around it and move it up and down?" He screeched away in his car. My trainer was standing behind a hedge and heard the whole thing and laughed so hard he started coughing and almost gave himself a heart attack. (Lots of people at the post office smoked.)

Again, here's a guy driving a car with a license plate on it. He probably figured his victims would be so freaked out that they wouldn't think to look at the license plate. I didn't think to look at the license plate, not because I was freaked out, but because I was laughing so hard. Some people who hire on at the post office don't pass their training period or their probation period. The trainer told the supervisor that I was definitely a keeper.

One of my weirdest exhibitionist stories doesn't have anything to do with the post office. I was driving down the freeway and a guy pulled up beside me and started making obscene hand and mouth gestures. Big surprise, right? I looked over again and he was now squatting on the driver's seat with his penis sticking out the window. He started following me, but I wasn't freaked out because I was headed to a semi-public place—a hotel with outdoor parking. I parked, he parked, and he walked to my car with his penis hanging out. The parking lot was full of people, but no one noticed him. Not a good advertisement, hunh?

I had no idea what was going to happen. He threw open my passenger door and said, "I have to jack off right now." I said, "Don't get it on the sheepskin seat covers—they're new." He said, "Don't worry. I brought a Kleenex."

He pulled a tissue out of his pocket and ejaculated in one stroke. It gets even weirder, if that's possible. He thanked me, reached into his other pocket, pulled out a twenty-dollar bill, and threw it at me! He walked back to his car and drove off, his license plate covered with mud so I couldn't read it.

The next day I read in the paper that the police were looking for this guy. Apparently they were getting up to twenty complaints a day about him. I know this sounds unbelievable but I am not making this up. It didn't say anything about him paying his victims. I like to think I was special. I don't know if they ever caught the guy, but dude, if you're still out there, make it fifty and here's my address. Stop by every day.

In the city in which I live now, exhibitionism occurs quite frequently. One man, a serial offender, was arrested for dropping his pants in front of some women in a park called Moon Park (really). In another case, a man was masturbating naked on the roof of a two-story building.

VOYEURISM

Voyeurism is the sexual turn-on from peeping in windows hoping to see people naked or having sex. Where voyeurs get into trouble is they sneak around peoples' houses and into back yards. They trespass on private property. This is usually what they get arrested for—that, or loitering, because it's pretty impossible to prove what a person was staring at. Voyeurism is dangerous because of the possibility of getting arrested. Men with voyeuristic interests often get jobs where they have to go into peoples' yards, such as meter reader or telephone lineman. Contrary to popular opinion, exhibitionists and voyeurs are not usually dirty old men. They are mostly young men with low social skills and little to no experience of partner sex.

Are exhibitionists and voyeurs dangerous to their victims?

These are coercive paraphilias and they have victims. Victims are often psychologically freaked out or even traumatized. Most exhibitionists and voyeurs do not touch or otherwise physically assault their victims but there are exceptions. The estimate is that about ten percent of exhibitionists and voyeurs will go on to commit sexual assault, but unfortunately we are unable to predict who those ten percent are. A couple of rules of thumb are if a person is a serial offender, he is likely to escalate in terms of the risks he is willing to take. The other is that most offenders stay within their preferred category. If you have someone who is both an exhibitionist and a voyeur, then he is more likely to escalate.

Let's face it. Pretty soon a voyeur is going to get tired of just looking in windows and masturbating. At some point he's going to see if that window is unlocked. The ultimate turn-on for a voyeur is to masturbate at the foot of the bed while a woman is asleep naked. This is what gets them caught. The woman hears something and wakes up and screams. I'll tell you, if I woke up and saw an unknown man at the foot of my bed masturbating, I'd still be screaming.

SAFE SEX RULE
Lock your doors and windows and close your curtains.

Several years ago, I had quite a disturbing experience. I used to live in a condominium complex with a pool, and I was pretty much the only person who ever used the pool. I used to sit out there and write. One Sunday morning I was sitting by the pool, which was surrounded by a metal fence. I heard something in the bushes next to the outside of the fence, and I looked up and saw a guy standing there masturbating. I was freaked out because not only was he masturbating but he had obviously been staring at me for some time and I didn't realize it. He was wearing one of those Mexican wrestling-type masks so I couldn't see his face. Just even writing this now is grossing me out. I yelled at him to get lost and I called the police. The police wanted to know a lot of details but they seemed to be too embarrassed to ask the questions. I tried to reassure them that I was used to talking about these topics. Hopefully they caught the guy because he clearly (to me) was somebody who had the potential to escalate to sexual assault.

ZOOPHILIA/BESTIALITY

Zoophilia and bestiality are having sex with animals. Bestiality, in contrast with the other paraphilias, is a cultural and historical universal. It is the oldest paraphilia. In Greek mythology, it was believed that gods could come to earth in the disguise of animals and have sex with humans. The outcome of this union would either be a beautiful woman or a demigod.

Christian mythology painted a darker picture. The belief was that Satan could come to earth in the guise of an animal and have sex with a human woman. The outcome of this union would either be an extremely ugly or evil person.

According to historical records as cited in the book "Understanding Bestiality & Zoophilia" by Hani Miletski, here are some of the types of animals that people have tried to have sex with—bulls, cows, horses, cats, dogs, pigs, sheep, rabbits, goats, fowl, snakes, donkeys, bears, crocodiles, wolves, and baboons. I know you're thinking, "Crocodiles? Really?"

SAFE SEX RULE

To have sex with a crocodile, pick a small one that's asleep next to a river. Run behind it and flip it over on its back. That way it won't be able to open its jaws. When you are done, flip it back over and run!

Sex with animals can take many forms. Adult entertainment could consist of a show involving people having sex with animals. Some people get turned on by watching animals have sex. Some people use animals to masturbate with, and others actually have oral sex or intercourse with animals. Others have animals lick their genitals after sex. Many people who have had sex with animals did it because they grew up in a rural area and there were no people to have sex with.

Another aspect of sex with animals is zoophilia. This is a case in which a person believes that an animal is their romantic partner and has an emotional relationship with the animal, or obtains an animal that has been trained to have sex with people.

Take the case of dogs. You can only train an animal to do a behavior that's already part of its instinctual responses. In the case of dogs, this is licking. Dogs already do it, so all you have to do is pair the licking response with some kind of reward for the dog. In most cases peanut butter is used to train a dog to lick a woman's vagina.

I once asked a friend, "Guess what I'm doing for my fiftieth birthday?" And he said, "I don't know. Getting a jar of peanut butter and going down to the dog pound?" (Why am I friends with you? Tell me again, please).

The most common reason people report for having sex with animals is to express love or affection to the animal. Other reasons are curiosity, attraction to the animal, lack of social/interpersonal skills, I was horny, the animal was available, and "the dog started it".

Is having sex with animals safe? First of all, it's illegal, so you can get arrested for it. I believe the laws against bestiality are the last remnants of the old sodomy laws that forbade anything but heterosexual intercourse. The reason it's illegal is that dogs, like children, cannot consent to sexual activity.

Beyond that, you could probably catch a disease from an animal (worms?) but that would depend on the species. Also, a large animal could bite, kick, or otherwise injure you.

A man who had sex with his dog was interviewed and he claimed that it wasn't true that animals couldn't consent to sex. His reasoning was that if his dog didn't want to have sex, it would bite him.

Another man in Florida was arrested for having sex with a dog and he claimed he didn't know it was wrong because the dog was female and weighed over forty pounds. (No, there really is no weight limit for the dog age of consent).

This occurred when I worked for the post office. A bunch of us were sitting around having breakfast in a greasy spoon and somebody asked this one woman about her new apartment. He said, "Don't you have a dog? Doesn't it upset the dog to be cooped up in the apartment all day when you're at work?"

And she replied, "I know. I feel so bad about the dog being in the apartment alone that whichever one of us gets home from work first masturbates the dog." (!) We all finished our breakfast quickly and left.

Here's one of the more bizarre (true) zoophilia stories I ever heard. This female professor's graduate student wanted to give her a surprise birthday party. The student had a key to the professor's house and went over there with a bunch of people and hid in the kitchen. She didn't realize the professor had a dog and put it outside the kitchen door.

The professor came home and the crowd didn't even have a chance to come out of the kitchen and yell "Happy Birthday!" because she took off running up the stairs. The dog was going crazy barking so they let him back in the house. The guests all watched as the professor came down the stairs naked covered with peanut butter, and the dog ran up and started licking her.

SAFE SEX RULE
If you're having a sexual relationship with an animal, don't give anyone a key to your house.

SAFE SEX RULE
Surprise parties are never a good idea.

I heard that story from a professor in the context of a class in which I was a student. Everybody else in the class was horrified by this story. My response, if I was the professor with the relationship with the dog, would have been, "You are invading my privacy!"

As I was finishing this manuscript, a story came over the Fox News feed. A man in Arkansas was arrested because a security camera caught him putting a bag over the head of his neighbor's donkey and having sex with the donkey. My question is, why the bag? He was afraid the donkey could identify him in a lineup? The donkey was into autoerotic asphyxiation? (See the following chapter).

Another case reported a man dying from having sex with the horse. He was the receiver, not the inserter, and died of a perforated colon.

I once read a book written by a well-known counselor. The book was a compilation of therapists' weirdest cases. A man came to the counselor's office and kept asking, "Do you smell cows?" It turned out he was having a sexual affair with a cow and was afraid he smelled like cows. The counselor asked him how that happened. The guy said, "I use a stepladder".

That was obviously not what the counselor meant. He meant, how do you fall in love with a cow? It's such a good thing I am not a therapist, because I probably would have said, "So, what was it about the cow that attracted you? Something in the way she mooes?" (It is such a good thing that I'm not a therapist).

NECROPHILIA

Necrophilia is the sexual compulsion to have sex with corpses. There are three forms.

In fantasy necrophilia, a person acts out the fantasy by having a partner "play dead." In regular (!) necrophilia, a person gets a job at a morgue or funeral home and actually has sex with dead bodies. In homicidal necrophilia, a person wants to have sex with a corpse so badly that he kills someone in order to have a sexual partner. The most famous homicidal necrophiliac of modern times was Jeffrey Dahmer.

I also heard of a case in Europe in which somebody went online looking for somebody to kill him and eat his body. He actually found somebody to do it, but the guy was found not guilty because he had the proof that the guy asked him to do it. Not sure if that was a sex thing, or on whose part it was.

Another famous homicidal necrophiliac was Edmund Kemper, who picked up hitchhikers and killed them in the Santa Cruz area in the 1970's. He also killed his mother, cut off her head, kept it in the refrigerator, and had oral sex with it until it fell apart. The Russian serial killer Andrei Chikatilo murdered people, cannibalized them, and had sex with their body parts.

Obviously, fantasy necrophilia is physically safe, but who knows about emotionally, particularly for the person who is being asked to play dead. The other two practices are illegal.

There is apparently some overlap between fantasy necrophilia and disabling a victim with date rape drugs and having sex with the unconscious person. The comedian Bill Cosby has been accused of this. As of this writing only one trial has taken place and he was found not guilty.

As I was completing this manuscript, a story came over Fox News feed. In Connecticut, a man was sentenced for sexual assault on a corpse. Apparently his girlfriend had overdosed on heroin and he had sex with her in an attempt to revive her.

The theme of necrophilia is graphically illustrated in a 1987 German horror/exploitation film called "Nekromantik". This film also depicts other paraphilias such as sadism.

PEDOPHILIA

Pedophilia is the compulsion to have sex with children before the age of puberty. Not much is really known about this, as we only know about the ones who got caught. We do know that most pedophiles were sexually abused themselves as children. They often use illegal child pornography to fuel their behavior.

It might surprise you to know that there is no hard experimental evidence that shows that being forced to have sex when you are a kid is bad for you. Most non-pedophiles believe it is bad, but all we have to go on is retrospective accounts of people in therapy in adulthood who have mental problems such as anxiety, depression, eating disorders, and many other issues. Many of them report that they were sexually molested as children.

Pedophilic behavior is a sex crime. Punishments are severe, including jail time and restriction of civil rights after release. Pedophilia is not curable. Pedophiles will apparently always have the attraction to underage children. In some cases they can be induced to change their behavior through chemical castration, or can be forced to change their behavior due to legal interventions such as Megan's Law or restrictions on where convicted sex offenders can live. Parents must be vigilant in protecting their children from people who are likely to sexually abuse them. Child sexual abuse will be discussed in more depth in a future chapter.

SAFE SEX RULE
When it comes to protecting your child from sexual abuse, it's not the creepy stranger hanging around outside the schoolyard that you have to be afraid of. Most children are sexually abused by people who know them or their family.

FROTTEURISM
Frotteurism is rubbing up against or groping an unsuspecting person in public. This usually occurs on public transportation. It's not very common in Southern California where I live, since people there have a well-known aversion to public transportation. This also includes the compulsion to grope in the context of a sexual harassment situation. It appears that many of our elected public officials have suffered from this.

Back in the 1980's there was a Charles Bronson movie that dealt with frotteurism. It was called "Kinjite—Forbidden Subjects". In the film, a man in Japan sees a woman on a train being groped by an unknown assailant and she appears to have an orgasm. He can't get this scene out of his mind and he becomes obsessed with it. He is transferred to the United States for work and he gropes a teenage girl on a bus with tragic results. No spoiler alert—I'm not going to tell you what happens, but basically this isolated act unleashes a shitstorm that has a negative impact on many lives.

OTHER PARAPHILIAS
There are some relatively new paraphilias that I'm not sure how to classify. They're not really masochistic, and most of them seem to be relatively harmless. Many of them involve behaviors that we would think of as regressive; that is, behaviors that are typical of children, but the practitioners use them for sexual

arousal. They have a fetishistic component to them but they more likely involve role play or character play.

Furries are people who dress in animal or character costumes for sexual purposes. The costumes are full body costumes often made of fur and they have heads. They are similar to costumes worn by performers at theme parks. People get turned on just by wearing the suits or seeing others in the suits or having sex while in the suits. This seems harmless enough to me as long as it involves consenting adults. I was trying to explain this practice to my class one time, and of course, living in Orange County, I said, "Well, it's like the people in the outfits at Disneyland." This student just looked at me with this dumbfounded look on her face and said, Why…would…anyone…do this?" And I said, "I don't know. I guess you'd have to be fucking Goofy to do that." I couldn't resist. How many times in your life do you get an opening like that? If the Grand Canyon opens in front of me, I'm going to step into it.

Plushies are people who have sex with stuffed toy animals. (I always get furries and plushies confused but I think I have it straight here). Again this seems regressive, back to the time when you were a kid and you slept with stuffed animals. These people take it a step farther. Sometimes they use puppets that already have an opening and they use a condom. In stuffed animals that aren't puppets, they cut an opening in the animal and line it with plastic or rubber. I read somewhere that one of the most popular stuffed animals for plushies is Meeko, the raccoon from the movie "Pocahontas". Please don't ask me how I know this.

Messy fun, also known as sploshing, involves getting turned on by seeing messy substances poured on women, or poured on yourself, or doing the pouring. Substances include mud or foods such as baked beans, chili or spaghetti. I had a client once who was into this. That's not what he was seeing me for—he also had issues with voyeurism and lack of peer sexual relationships. He subscribed to messy fun newsletters that had pictures of women with all of this stuff poured all over them. These are not considered pornographic and so can be disseminated in the form of newsletters. Sploshers either prefer to see clothed women or nude women with stuff poured all over them.

My client told me that when he was a kid, he used to get turned on and ejaculate when he would watch an old movie that included a pie fight, but only if a woman was hit by the pie and had it on her face. Do you think this could have something to do with wanting to come on a woman's face and see it dripping down? Food for thought. (Pun intended). When I think about this, I picture that scene in the movie "Tommy" near the end when his mother (played by Ann-Margret) is sitting in front of the television and throws a champagne bottle at the screen. The screen breaks and baked beans and dish soap go all over her and she's rolling around in them . This is probably a splosher's favorite movie.

Some people get turned on by pony play. This is dressing up in horse costumes complete with horse heads and prancing around. This appears to be popular in England. Sometimes the people dressed as horses pull carriages. Is this some kind of "Black Beauty" fetish? That was my favorite book when I was a kid, please don't ruin it for me. I remember when I was a kid, one of our favorite games was "horses", in which one person was tied up with ropes like reins and the "rider" held the ropes and ran behind. (We must not have had a lot of toys when I was a kid). There is an S-M undertone to pony play as it sometimes involves the person dressed as a horse being beaten.

A digression—A few years ago I attended a sexuality convention with a group I belonged to called Quad S. I know

I mentioned them earlier. Sex conferences are not half as exciting as they sound, by the way. I attended a presentation on some of the fetishistic and masochistic practices described above. When the presentation was over I asked the presenter why he thought so many of the current fetish practices seemed to tap into stuff we did when we were kids. He really didn't have an answer for that. Why do you think it is? I don't know, but I have a feeling that this implies that sexual feelings could be starting in kids a long time before we think they do. This kind of goes against modern thinking, which is that sexual impulses start at puberty due to hormones. Paging Dr. Freud!

I've written elsewhere ("Men In Bed") about possible explanations for paraphilias (especially masochism) that have been put forth by various experts so I won't repeat that. But Dr. David Reuben, a psychiatrist and the author of "Everything You Always Wanted to Know About Sex", a book I really like, thinks these people never grew up sexually.

Here's another example—balloons. Remember when you were a kid and went to birthday parties and one of the games was the room was filled up with balloons and the kids ran around sitting on them and whoever broke the most balloons won? I know I'm dating myself. If they even still have birthday parties, kids probably just sit around and look at their phones. But there are some people who get turned on by watching naked adult women sitting on balloons and popping them, or by sitting on balloons and popping them themselves.

A final fetish involves wearing outfits other than animal costumes. These include rubber clothing, wetsuits (like surfer wetsuits) and inflatable suits. Rubber fetishes are common. You can go online and order rubber clothing, even evening gowns and tuxedos. Some people wear surfer-type wetsuits and cut a hole in the crotch so they can have sex. Some people get turned on just by seeing people in wetsuits. As a person who lives near a beach, I find this somewhat disturbing. When I ride my bike at the beach I frequently see surfers changing from wetsuits into regular clothing at their cars. Are other bike riders getting turned on by this sight? I'm not.

Inflatable suits are just what they sound like—special custom made suits that are equipped with air pockets that can be inflated. They include openings for the genitals and people have sex with the suits on.

I've read about people being arrested for having sex with a bicycle, a car, and pavement. As far as I know there are no terms for those specific fetishes.

In conclusion, I think we have a final safe sex rule here. Paraphilias that only involve dressing in costumes are safe. If paraphilic behavior causes personal distress or impairs functioning or is illegal or coercive, it's a problem. The next chapter deals with more extreme paraphilias that are forms of masochism.

CHAPTER 9
EXTREME MASOCHISM

Recall that sexual masochism involves becoming sexually aroused by being hurt or humiliated. All of the paraphilias have increased in popularity due to the Sexual Revolution and other factors. However, masochistic sexual practices have skyrocketed, probably due to the Internet.

In the past, if people had unusual sexual tastes, it was not always easy to find reading material or pictures to cater to those tastes. Books about S and M that were banned in the United States for decades such as novels by the Marquis de Sade or Leopold von Sacher-Masoch now seem not only dated but very tame in comparison with the information that is available with a couple of mouse clicks today. If people today want to find out about masochistic practices, all they have to do is log on and put in some key words.

I'll cover classic masochistic specialties and some of the newer ones. Most of this chapter concerns autoerotic (self-practiced) masochistic behaviors that are extremely dangerous and can result in death. Here is a list of a few classic masochistic specialties, with an eye toward whether they are risky or not.

Flagellation is a masochistic specialty that involves being whipped. Whips could be serious cat o' nine tails with metal tips or they could be fake whips made of fur. Obviously the risk here depends on the type of whip that is used and how hard the masochist is whipped. Flagellation usually requires a sadistic partner to do the whipping. I suppose you could whip yourself a la the old saints in the Catholic Church who used a rope whip called a "discipline" to punish themselves for their sins.

Bondage is a practice that involves getting turned on by being tied up or restrained. Ropes could be used, as well as handcuffs, chains, or hospital restraints. With the use of ropes, special kinds are used as well as special quick-release knots. People who are into bondage often order custom-made furniture such as chairs and beds that have openings and hooks so it's easier to tie someone to them. If you are going to practice serious bondage, be sure the sadistic partner is trained in sexual knot tying. You can see demonstrations in magazines or on the Internet. Tying a knot around a body part with the wrong type of rope or the wrong type of knot could result in loss of circulation.

SAFE SEX RULE
Don't lose the key to your handcuffs.

Remember in the previous chapter when I said that paraphilias are extensions of normal desires, curiosity and behavior? A lot of people enjoy some mild restraint during sex. As I said before, this could take the form of a blindfold, fur handcuffs, or holding your partner's hands over his or her head while having sex.

Most people who like bondage like a little discipline along with it. In addition to being tied up, they like to be hit or spanked. Hands, paddles, hairbrushes, or other items could be used to spank. Canes are especially popular in England, I read somewhere. Being hit hurts (that's the point) and can leave bruises or other marks.

Discipline can also include humiliating verbal patter. "Have you been a bad boy? Am I going to have to discipline you?" Verbal discipline creates a lot of psychological arousal for masochists and isn't physically harmful because, let's face it, "Names can never hurt me."

I talked a little about piercing in the chapters about penises and vaginas, but that mostly had to do with people who have their genitals pierced in order to wear jewelry or because the tugging and pulling on the jewelry feels good during sex. In masochistic piercing practices, the nipples or genitals are repeatedly pierced for purposes of sexual arousal. It's about the pain, not about what you are using to pierce with or leaving the piercing in. This is sometimes called nipple or scrotum torture.

I knew a guy who was into this, back in the 1980's before it was as popular as it is today. For sexual arousal purposes, he would stretch his scrotum over a kitchen cutting board and pin it down. Then depending on his mood he would insert various objects into his scrotum and take pictures of it. I saw one of these pictures and it looked like he had taken everything sharp out of his kitchen junk drawer and stuck it into his scrotum. There were corn on the cob holders in there! I haven't been able to eat corn on the cob since.

People who pierce their genitals (and nipples, and tongues) may develop the following complications—nerve damage, infection, formation of scar tissue, and blood poisoning. There is also the danger of piercing into a testis or the erectile tissue of the penis. In addition, if you have jewelry pierced into your genitals you have to remove it if you have an x-ray or MRI exam.

When doing research for this book, I found many articles on the dangers of piercing. I tried to find a medical article about the dangers of repeatedly piercing the genitals and nipples and then removing the piercing object but couldn't find anything. I believe we will have to go with the dangers listed above, realizing that the dangers are multiplied if you pierce repeatedly.

Suspension sometimes goes along with piercing. Suspension involves a couple of practices. One is piercing the nipples or genitals and hanging weights or other objects from the piercing. This could result in the problems mentioned above, as well as potential tearing of the skin or other tissue.

Another form of suspension is having piercings done all the way up and down your body, putting rings in those piercings, and partially or completely suspending your body from wires and hooks connected to the rings. One of the weirdest pictures I ever saw was of a man who appeared to be flying with a tree in the background. He was actually suspended from a tree branch with wires clipped into piercings all along his back from his head to his feet.

Infantilism is a masochistic practice in which a person gets sexually turned on by being dressed or treated as an infant. Infantilists may wear baby clothing in adult sizes. They wear diapers and baby bonnets and suck on pacifiers and drink from baby bottles. They may have a nursery set up in their house with baby furniture made to fit adults, such as a crib or changing table.

I had a therapist consult me on a case of a client who had infantilist fantasies and wanted to act them out in the context of a relationship. He wanted to wear a diaper and soil it and have a woman change him. He was having a difficult time with relationships, because when he would get interested enough in a woman to feel comfortable sharing that fantasy, it was a deal-breaker for the woman. He's not the only one out there with that fantasy. I'm sure if he looks long enough, he'll find a woman who not only agrees to do this, but also gets turned on by it. I can't see where infantilist sexual practices would be physically unsafe in any way.

There are body fluid fetishes involving urine, feces, vomit, and menstrual blood. I'm sure there are other body fluid fetishes I'm not familiar with. I'll deal with feces fetishes and anal sex practices in the next chapter on anal eroticism. The other three fetishes I've mentioned have several aspects.

In the body fluid fetish for urine (urophilia, also called "golden showers"), in the masochistic version you want someone to urinate on you. In the sadistic version you want to urinate on someone, and in the fetishistic version you get turned on by seeing someone urinate.

In a fetish for vomit it's the same thing. In the masochistic version you want someone to vomit on you. In the sadistic version you want to vomit on someone, and in the fetishistic version, you get turned on just by seeing someone vomit.

Menstrual fetishes are a bit different. Mostly they involve a man wanting to have sex with a woman when she is on her period, or wanting to perform oral sex with a woman when she's on her period.

I once ran into one of these people. I was having an affair with him and we were trying to plan an assignation. I ruled out a certain weekend because I would be having my period. It turned out this was not only not a problem for him, he preferred it. I was a little surprised when he dove right in to perform oral sex but I went with it.

I should mention that many people who have body fluid fetishes do not act on them in real life. They watch these scenes on the Internet and get turned on. As for the safety issues, people have consumed urine, vomit, and menstrual blood with no ill effects. Problems could occur if a partner had a bladder or kidney infection, a gastrointestinal infection, or an STI.

One of the weirder body fluid fetishes is vampirism—the compulsion to drink blood for sexual arousal purposes. As with the other body fluid fetishes this can take several forms. In the voyeuristic version, the person gets turned on by the sight of blood. In the homicidal version, the person kills somebody so he can drink their blood. In that case it's related to necrophilia.

Vampirists sometimes build up to more extreme versions of the behavior. They may start by drinking their own blood and then drink animal blood before they move on to drinking blood from other people. Sometimes the turn-on is more about biting and sucking the blood from a wound than it is about drinking a cup of blood. You can actually die from drinking too much blood due to the iron content.

Sometimes vampirism is the result of mental illness such as schizophrenia. This is called Renfield Syndrome after the character in Bram Stoker's novel "Dracula". People with this issue believe they can become more powerful by drinking the blood of other people.

It's tempting to think that sexual vampirism got started because of the influence of the book "Dracula" or even the Bela Lugosi movie from the 1930's. But it predates those. It was identified by Richard von Krafft-Ebing in the 1880's in his book "Psychopathia Sexualis".

The two most famous sexual vampirists were John George Haigh and Richard Trenton Chase. Haigh, an Englishman, was known as the "Acid Bath Murderer". He killed several people in the 1940's. He pleaded insanity and claimed that he drank his victims' blood.

Chase killed six people in the Sacramento area between 1977 and 1978. He cannibalized the remains of his victims and drank their blood. He apparently suffered from paranoid schizophrenia.

Now we're getting into the more dangerous stuff. These practices include autoerotic asphyxiation (choking yourself when you get close to orgasm), electricity, overdressing/body wrapping, foreign body insertion, and immersion in water. Sometimes people use combinations of these.

Autoerotic asphyxiation (also called hypoxyphilia) is a sexual practice involving choking yourself with a noose or plastic bag as you are getting close to orgasm. People do this because they have heard that it intensifies your orgasm and creates unusually pleasurable sensations. The sad thing about this is that it's apparently true, and unfortunately kids read this stuff on the Internet and try to do it. It is said to create sensations similar to using amyl nitrite (poppers) at the moment of orgasm.

As the name implies, this is usually done as a solitary practice during masturbation and that's where the danger comes in. People have died of asphyxiation because they passed out while masturbating with a plastic bag over their head. In other cases, people attempted to masturbate with a noose around their neck while hanging from a closet pole and accidentally hanged themselves. If another person had been present, they wouldn't have died.

There have supposedly been a couple of famous cases of this. The actor David Carradine and the lead singer of the band INXS were both found hanging in suspicious circumstances.

Much of the following material I got from an article published in the Journal of Forensic Sciences in 2006. The title of the article is "Autoerotic Deaths in the Literature from 1954 to 2004: A Review." It was written by Anny Sauvageau, M.D., and Stephanie Racette. Brief descriptions of cases in this section come from that article.

Some people have died while trying to use electricity to stimulate their genitals.

- A 36-year-old man connected wires to a television and to his scrotum and anus. One of the wires broke and he was electrocuted when he looked into the back of the TV to see what was wrong.
- A 27-year-old man inserted a homemade electrode into his anus and was electrocuted when he tried to attach another one to his penis.

SAFE SEX RULE
Unless your last name is Edison, do not use electrical devices for sexual stimulation.

SAFE SEX RULE
The words "homemade" and "electrode" do not belong in the same sentence.

You can die of hyperthermia from wearing too many clothes or wrapping your body in other materials.

- A 34-year-old nude man wrapped himself in plastic at his workplace and put a snorkel in his mouth to breathe. The snorkel fell out and he was too tightly wrapped in the plastic to retrieve it, so he died of asphyxiation.
- A 60-year-old man wrapped himself in fourteen blankets and put a plastic bag over his penis. He died of combined asphyxia and hyperthermia.

- A 56-year-old man tied a plastic bag to a board and put the bag on himself. He fell off a stack of chairs and ended up upside down and died.

The journal article described this last one as a "mishap". To me a mishap means stubbing your toe, not hanging upside down from a stack of chairs with a plastic bag on you.

SAFE SEX RULE
Masturbate naked.

People often insert foreign objects into their body orifices for sexual pleasure. I already talked a little bit about this in the chapter on the "Perils of the Penis", and I'll deal with objects inserted into the anus in the next chapter, but here are some other examples.

- A 29-year-old man performed oral sex on a zucchini and choked to death on it.
- A 40-year-old woman inserted a carrot into her vagina and died of an embolism.
- A 40-year-old man died of a perforated bladder from inserting a pencil into his urethra.

Some people combine cross-dressing, ligature, hanging upside down, masturbation, and immersion in water.

- A 62-year-old man, nude but wearing women's shoes, hung himself upside down from a tractor and accidentally ran over himself with the tractor.
- A man tied a large rock around his ankle, dressed in women's clothes, jumped in a river and tried to masturbate. He drowned.

Other people have drowned in their bathtubs while trying to choke themselves and masturbate under water.

SAFE SEX RULE
You only have two hands.

Here are a couple more accidental autoerotic deaths (AAD's) that I found interesting.

- A 28-year-old man wearing three layers of plastic as well as female lingerie, hung himself from a bridge using a type of belt contraption usually used by mountaineers. The cause of death was asphyxia combined with chest compression.
- A teenaged boy wearing a dress tied himself into a hogtie position and asphyxiated himself by rocking back and forth while masturbating.
- A 28-year-old man suffered from muscular dystrophy. He convinced his caregiver, a 20-year-old male nurse, to wrap him in plastic garbage bags and throw him in a trash dumpster, where he died of suffocation.

A couple of things struck me while I was writing this. One is that these people are old enough to know better. Another is that these aren't the only people who did these practices, these are just the ones who died from it. A third insight is that some of these deaths go back to the 1950's, so we can't really blame the Internet for this.

Have you ever heard of the movie "In the Realm of the Senses"? It is a Japanese movie that was released in 1976. It is supposedly based on a true story. It was famous because apparently some of the sex scenes were not simulated.

In this movie, a man and a motel maid who is a part-time prostitute check into a hotel and basically try to screw each other to death. One of them succeeds. The woman supposedly inadvertently strangles the man to death while they are having sex. (I hope this was the simulated part.) Then she cuts off his penis and vows to keep it inside of her as long as she can. If you have a voyeuristic interest in the extreme paraphilias, this movie might be a good choice for you. I'm a regular Siskel and Ebert here, hunh?

Another issue with autoerotic deaths is a legal one—whether they can be considered suicide or an accident. Some insurance companies have refused to pay in the cases of autoerotic deaths because it was deemed that the victim caused his or her own death.

I've covered possible psychological reasons for masochism in another book, so I won't repeat that here. Many masochists believe that external pain wipes out internal pain; in other words, they are suffering in some way and creating physical pain gives them something else on which to focus.

The next chapter deals with sexual practices involving the anus and rectum. These include relatively safe practices such as anal touching practiced with a partner to more extreme degrees of anal erotic activities.

CHAPTER 10
ANAL EROTICISM

Here's another chapter where you're lucky I don't have slides. When I first began studying human sexuality back in the 1970's, many textbooks did not even include material on anal sex. If they did, it was usually in a short section in the chapter on sexual orientation, as it was assumed it was practiced exclusively by gay men.

Since then, anal sex practices have become much more mainstream. It is recognized that the anus can be an erogenous zone for people of all sexual orientations. Current estimates report that between twenty and forty percent of heterosexual couples have engaged in anal sex practices.

Anal sex practices are not limited to anal intercourse. Anal sex practices can include touching the anus or penetrating it with a finger, anilingus (licking the anus), or inserting objects into the anus.

There are a number of sex toys that are specifically designed for anal stimulation. Anal beads look like a string of large pearls separated by string. The beads are successively pushed into the anus and then the string is slowly pulled to create stimulation. Scarves can be oiled up and used in the same way. It's all about how slowly the scarf is pulled out, not how it's inserted.

What about the safe sex aspect? Anal sex practices are not inherently unsafe. However, because the anus is quite different anatomically from the vagina, certain precautions should be taken. Let's take the issue of anal intercourse (penis in anus) first.

Unlike the vagina, the anus contains two sphincter muscles, an outer one and an inner one. For penetration to occur, both sphincters must be relaxed. For this to happen, before penetration begins, make sure to gently massage the anus with a lot of lube. If pain occurs, you are not being gentle enough, the receptive partner is not relaxed enough, or you are not using enough lube. The myth is that anal sex hurts at first and then it will feel okay. That's not okay—nothing should hurt.

SAFE SEX RULE

Do not do anything that causes you pain, unless, in the case of the previous chapter, that's your goal.

If you are having both anal intercourse and vaginal intercourse in the same sexual session, be sure to thoroughly wash the penis in between switching from the anus to the vagina. Otherwise, e. coli bacteria can be transferred from the anus to the penis and then to the vagina, causing a nasty vaginal infection.

It's always a good idea for the passive partner in anal intercourse to take an enema in order to avoid contact with feces. (There are some people who like to have contact with feces in a sexual situation—more on that later).

Most authors recommend that you use a condom for anal sex even if you're in a monogamous relationship. It just minimizes any potential problems. Be sure to follow instructions for use of a condom the same way you would for vaginal intercourse. This is tricky, because as we saw in an earlier chapter, a condom could break or fall off. If that happens during vaginal intercourse, the condom could easily be retrieved, but that's not the case if a condom gets lost in the rectum. Medical treatment may be required to remove it.

Given that vaginal sex is such a no-brainer (I mean, I could do it with both hands tied behind my back, and have!), why would people take the extra time and make the effort to engage in anal sex?

The answer to this question comes from Jack Morin, Ph.D., a sex therapist in the San Francisco area and the author of "Anal Pleasure and Health". Back in the 1990's, I used to do a radio show on KUCI, the radio station at the University of California, Irvine. Dr. Morin was the first guest I interviewed. According to him, people like anal sex for the following reasons. There is no concern about pregnancy. The anus feels different from the vagina and is often tighter. Fans cite the "anal taboo"—the idea that the anus is forbidden, which makes it all the more exciting. There are a lot of people who get turned on just because you tell them they are not allowed to do something.

For many people, the anus is an area of great sensitivity, as it is located so close to the genitals. Apparently this is what Freud meant when he said, "Anatomy is destiny". Most people interpret that remark to be about the difference between men and women, but I think in context he was actually talking about the anal stage of psychosexual development, when the anus is the source of a child's unconscious sexual gratification. Anal sex often brings to mind prison fantasies. For many people, anal sex is the ultimate psychological dominant or submissive act.

Dr. Morin's suggestions for anal intercourse include the following. Before having any kind of anal sex with a partner, learn as much as you can about the structure of the anus. Take a mirror and look at your anus. Relax and explore the area with your fingers. It's important to be comfortable yourself before allowing someone to "boldly go where no man has gone before".

Oral-anal practices can be safe with a couple of precautions. Have the passive partner use an enema and clean the anal area thoroughly, to avoid an e. coli infection. Make sure your partner does not have hepatitis, as it can be transmitted through anilingus.

Because of the sensitivity of the anal area, a lot of people like to use dildos or vibrators on or in the anal area. Here's where you can really get into trouble if you're not informed. Never use a dildo that's meant for a vagina in the anus. Special dildos (called butt plugs, nice, right?) are made for use in the anus. They have a handle or a base on them.

The reason you should not use a vaginal dildo in the anus is you will have to use a lot of lube to insert it, and it's easy to lose your grip. If you lost your grip on a dildo in the vagina, you would just reach in and get it. But the anus has two sphincters—an outer one and an inner one. If you insert a dildo past the inner second sphincter, contractions may suck the dildo or any other object so far into the rectal area that you won't be able to reach it and you will need to seek medical help.

SAFE SEX RULE
Never insert anything in your anus unless it has a handle or a base on it.

TRUE STORY

An old client of mine told me this one. He had a girlfriend who was really into anal stimulation. He was using one of those pocket-rocket-type vibrators on her. They weren't aware of all the safety stuff I've just told you about. His girlfriend kept urging him to stick the vibrator in faster and deeper. Of course he lost his grip on it. He had to take her to the emergency room and the whole time she was waiting, the thing was still vibrating! People kept staring at her and/or checking their phones.

When we think of heterosexual anal sex, we usually think in terms of the man inserting his penis into the woman's anus. But a woman could wear a strap-on dildo and insert it into a man's anus. This is called "pegging".Some men enjoy an object inserted into their anus because it massages the prostate. This often causes an involuntary ejaculation. There is some evidence that prostate massage may be a good thing, especially for older men, in order to increase ejaculatory frequency and volume.

BACK TO THE PARAPHILIAS

As we saw in the previous chapter some people have died from, for example, using electricity in their anal area. I want to expand on that topic in this chapter. There is a form of masochism called anal eroticism for lack of a better name. People who do these practices get extremely sexually turned on by inserting larger and more unusual objects in their anus. Doing this can cause medical complications such as rectal bleeding, hemorrhoids, anal fissures, perforation of the intestine, or rectal prolapse.

Some of the objects that have been found in the rectums of emergency room patients include the following. The list is so numerous and varied that it's arranged according to category.

Food—onion, zucchini, potato, apple, banana, carrot, bottle of maple syrup, jar of peanut butter, lemon, hard-boiled egg, turnip, salami, cucumber, pieces of frozen chicken.

Cosmetic Products—deodorant, jar of Vaseline, bar soap, container of baby powder, toothbrush holder, perfume bottle, shoe horn.

Kitchenware—spatula, tin cup, measuring cup, drinking glass, ice pick.

Tools—broom handle, light bulb, axe handle, antenna, screwdriver, flashlight, knife-sharpening steel, candle.

Miscellaneous—rolled-up magazine (hope it wasn't the September issue of Vogue), curtain rod, steer horn, vibrator, dildo, soft drink bottle, table leg.

SAFE SEX RULE
To defrost chicken, take it out of the freezer and put it in the refrigerator for a day. If it's not totally defrosted, put it in the microwave for a few minutes.

Obviously, some of these objects are more dangerous than others. A soda bottle could break or cause an embolism. A light bulb could break and perforate the intestine. These conditions could be life-threatening.

In addition to objects, some men have tried to insert their penis into their own anus. Obviously this has to be done when the penis is flaccid. I don't see anything inherently unsafe in this practice. Plus, it kind of makes sense because it eliminates the middle man, you know what I'm saying?

I know you're probably asking yourself right now, "Okay, I know how the object got in there, but how would a doctor get it out?" In some cases the patient can be sedated and the doctor can reach in and pull the object out by hand. In the case of multiple or broken objects, fast-drying dental cement is shot into the anus. It surrounds the objects and dries and the doctor pulls the whole thing out in one piece. In some cases, abdominal surgery is required to remove all traces of foreign bodies from the intestinal tract.

THREE CAUTIONARY TALES

My sister told me this one. She used to be an ER nurse. (I know a lot of nurses). A man came into the ER complaining of abdominal pain. Along with headaches and chest pain, this is taken very seriously as it could be a sign of a life-threatening condition, such as a burst appendix. The patient was asked if he knew of anything that could be causing his pain and he said no.

The patient was x-rayed and the x-ray film was put up on the light box. The ER doctors and nurses were all standing around scratching their heads. They couldn't figure out what the heck was in there.

There were three objects. Closest to the anal opening was a large cylindrical object about ten inches long. Then there was a triangular-shaped object and a small flattened mass.

They sedated the patient and removed the objects. They turned out to be a large deodorant can, with the cap on, the top of a Halston perfume bottle, and a deflated balloon. As my sister was wheeling the patient out of surgery, she told him what they had found. She asked him how all of those objects had gotten into his rectum, and he said, "I slipped in the shower."

Here's what really happened. He tried to insert the large deodorant can into his rectum but it was too blunt. So he took the tapered top of a perfume bottle and tried to make a dildo out of the whole thing by putting a condom on it. But the condom wouldn't fit. So he took a kid's balloon (the kind they make animals out of at a birthday party) and used that instead of a condom. Unfortunately, when he tied the balloon at the base of the deodorant can, he didn't tie it tight enough. When he inserted the whole rig, he not only lost his grip on it but the knot came untied and all the pieces separated. In the x-ray it did kind of look like a rocket ship that lost its nose cone.

Here's another case. I heard this one from one of my students who was an ER nurse. A man was masturbating while inserting a full can of spray paint into his anus. Of course he lost his grip on it. Instead of going to the ER (because that would be too embarrassing) he called his friend who was a plumber. The plumber brought over a small snake, the size you would use to unclog a bathroom sink. The plumber stuck the snake into his friend's anus and turned it on. The snake punctured the spray paint can and paint went all over the guy's intestines. He was taken to the ER and almost died of peritonitis.

I heard this next one from one of my students whose brother was a police officer. Apparently, this guy's wife left for work and he decided to masturbate while choking himself with a rope (see the previous chapter). He also wanted to insert something into his anus at the same time. So he went into the garage and rigged up a thing where he was standing on a chair that had an opening in the back. He threw the rope with a noose over a rafter and put the noose around his neck. He stuck a broom handle into his rectum with the rest of the handle through the opening in the back of the chair with the broom balanced on the ground. Then he started masturbating. Somehow, he kicked the chair over and managed to hang himself with the broom stuck in him.

When his wife came home from work and used her garage door opener that is what she saw—her husband hanging in the garage (dead) with a noose around his neck and a broom handle up his butt.

Whenever I hear of cases like this, I have to ask myself, how bored would I have to be to start looking around my house and thinking, hmm, I wonder if that would fit up my butt. Pretty darned bored, I'm guessing.

SAFE SEX RULE
Get another hobby. No, really. As we saw in the previous chapter, if you are going to combine two or three different activities with masturbation, don't do the solitary version. Bring a friend with you.

Here's one of my favorite stories about people putting objects in their anus. An airplane was delayed leaving LAX because a passenger was called for a secondary screening. He had set off the metal detector. When he was taken to the private room, he told TSA he knew what had set off the metal detector and proceeded to pull several objects out of his rectum—chewing gum, wire filament, and a rock. It was obviously the wire that set off the metal detector. He told TSA that he had inserted these objects into his anus in order to relieve stress. He also told them the rock was from another planet. If you guessed "Uranus" you win a prize. This newspaper article left many questions unanswered as usual. For example, was the gum already chewed or still in the package?

SAFE SEX RULE
If you're a nervous flyer, have a few drinks, or take a Xanax or something.

Another anal practice that can be dangerous is fisting. In this practice, the entire hand and part of the arm is inserted into the anus. According to "Trust: The Handbook" one in every two thousand acts of anal fisting results in serious injury to the passive partner. That seems like a low estimate to me, but what do I know? If done properly (wrong word) anal fisting takes a long time. You don't just slam your fist in there. Also, be sure to trim your nails.

When I belonged to Quad S, the sex research society, I attended a presentation on what was called "brachioproctic sex". If you understand medical terminology, you will know that this means anal fisting. A member of the audience asked the presenter why he used the longer term. Studies that take place in universities have to pass the Institutional Review Board (IRB) to make sure that no harm will come to people who participate. The author figured that a survey about anal fisting would never pass the IRB. He also figured correctly that the members of the IRB would have no clue what brachioproctic sex meant.

COPROPHILIA AND COPROPHAGY

In the previous chapter I talked about body fluid fetishes such as urophilia. Coprophilia is a fetish for feces. In the sadistic version, you get sexually turned on by defecating on another person. In the masochistic version, you get sexually turned on by having another person defecate on you. In the fetishistic version, you get turned on by the sight of feces.

A version of this is klismaphilia, which is a fetish for either giving or receiving an enema. Enemas using anything other than water can be dangerous. Sometimes people use soap suds or intoxicants. Even too much water could cause a rupture.

I was reading a magazine the other month and there was an

article about the growing popularity of high colonics. People who have their colon cleansed do not usually do it for sexual reasons. A woman who owned a colonics parlor in Santa Monica was quoted as saying that colonics had become so popular that she had to open a second location to handle the overflow. I'm not kidding; she really said that. And this was a legitimate magazine, not some unedited internet rag. Maybe she meant it tongue in cheek. Really, I expect more of myself than this. To quote Triumph the insult comic dog, this is a very nice book. "For me to poop on!"

Coprophagy (or coprophagia) is the practice of eating feces. This could be done for sexual or nonsexual reasons. In terms of nonsexual reasons, in ancient history before the rise of modern medicine, eating the feces of various animals was prescribed for medical problems. Keep in mind in this era, people who showed symptoms of mental illness had holes drilled in their heads to let out the evil spirits. Saints in the Middle Ages sometimes ate feces to punish themselves for their sins. People in some parts of the world use animal dung as cooking fuel.

There is a medical condition called clostridium, which is a bacterial infection in the intestines. In severe cases, the treatment consists of a fecal transplant. Basically they put someone else's poop in your intestines, and it cures you.

People who eat feces for sexual purposes risk a number of medical issues—hepatitis, giardia, dysentery, cholera, shigella, and other parasites. According to Brenda Love, the author of "The Encyclopedia of Unusual Sexual Practices", eating feces is the most dangerous kind of unsafe sex. I have to say I disagree with her. I think the autoerotic asphyxiation practices described in the previous chapter are more dangerous. Also, I think it's more dangerous to have unprotected sex with someone with HIV and exchange body fluids such as blood and semen.

I read about cases in Japan in World War II in which girls who were held prisoner by the Japanese were forced to take an enema and eat a controlled diet and then defecate on a plate. High ranking Japanese officers then ate the result. I don't know if this was a sex thing or not. There's also a practice in which someone takes an enema and spews the result into a goblet. Someone else then drinks it. This is called an enema cocktail. I also read a case in which a dominatrix in the context of an S and M scene put corned beef hash into her rectum, disgorged it on a plate, and told her client to eat it. (As of this writing, I have a very nice large corned beef in my freezer that I was going to use to make hash. After writing this, I'm guessing that that corned beef will not be used for quite some time, if ever).

There's another sexual practice called fellching, which means sucking semen out of an anus. In terms of safety, the semen part is probably safe as long as the person who contributed it did not have an STI. However, the anal aspect of it would have the same dangers as noted above with eating feces or performing anilingus.

You have probably heard stories about people inserting small animals into their rectum for sexual pleasure. Gerbils are usually cited here. None of these stories have held up under scrutiny. The only examples I know of in which animals were inserted into the rectum involved torture. According to Dan Savage, author of the syndicated relationship and sex advice column "Savage Love", gerbiling is an urban myth. (I wasn't really that familiar with Dan Savage before I wrote this chapter, but now he's my favorite person for coining the term "saddlebacking", which means Christian teens having anal sex to preserve their virginity. It's named after a large conservative mega-church in Orange County).

SAFE SEX RULE

"This is what happens when you fuck a stranger in the ass!" (Sorry, I couldn't resist. That's a quote from The Big Lebowski when John Goodman is beating the crap out of the wrong car).

The bottom line (I know, I know)—anal sex practices are not inherently dangerous. Many of these practices can be safe if you take care and use common sense. People practice unsafe acts either because they don't know any better or they are so sexually turned on they're not thinking clearly.

Some authors think that the urge to stick unusual objects in your anus (or vagina, or urethra) is a holdover from childhood. Kids learn about their world through touch and so often stick food or other objects into their ears, noses, and other body openings. I guess when you combine those primitive urges with intense sexual arousal you can get into trouble.

Next we turn to sexual coercion, which is a huge hot-button topic right now.

CHAPTER 11
SEXUAL COERCION

This chapter deals with sex by force rather than consent. Forms of sexual coercion include rape and sexual assault, incest, child sexual abuse, and sexual harassment. I also include domestic violence. First I'll deal with how to protect yourself from being raped, assaulted, or sexually harassed as an adult. The second half of the chapter will deal with the consequences of incest and child sexual abuse. Being a sexually aware and informed person whether you are currently sexually active or not means keeping yourself safe from sexual coercion. Again, this whole chapter is pretty much one long safe sex rule.

RAPE

The most common form of rape is a male perpetrator forcing his penis into the vagina of a female victim. It can more broadly be defined as nonconsensual penetration of the body and this could include forced oral or anal sex also. The actual legal terms may vary from venue to venue. Rape by instrumentation involves a perpetrator forcing a penis-shaped object into a victim's body.

Rape is a highly unreported and underreported crime. Statistics state that fourteen to twenty-five percent of women report that they have been raped. It's probably at least twice that or more, especially on college campuses.

One of the categories used to define rape is forcible versus statutory rape. Statutory rape is defined by the age of consent in your area. In California it's eighteen but that's not true in every state. That means in California it is illegal to have sex with someone under the age of eighteen, even if the person says yes, because by law, someone under the age of eighteen cannot legally consent.

This arbitrary age of consent creates all kinds of problems. By definition, kids who have gone through puberty and are capable of reproducing are biologically able to have sex, yet they can't legally consent to it in many states. I personally believe that there are some sixteen-year-olds who are capable of making the decision to have sexual intercourse. (I also believe that there are some fifty-year-olds who aren't emotionally mature enough to make that decision).

SAFE SEX RULE
Check out the laws about age of consent in your area and make sure you understand them. Unless the laws change, be aware that "sixteen may get you twenty".

Rapes are also divided into two categories reflecting who the perpetrator is. Perpetrators could either be a stranger or someone the victim knows (acquaintance rape). As women, we have all been socialized to fear the scary stranger who leaps out of the bushes and attacks us. But a woman is far more likely to be raped by someone she knows than by a stranger. In fact a woman is more likely to be raped by someone she previously had a consensual sexual relationship with.

There are other forms of rape. In marital rape, a man forces his wife to have sex with him against her will. Because our laws evolved from English common law in which a man's wife was considered his property, this didn't used to be against the law. Now all fifty states in the U. S. provide for a possible rape charge for a husband with his wife as the victim.

In gang rape, there is more than one perpetrator and they take turns raping a victim. An extremely sad and horrifying trend involves teenagers raping or assaulting a victim and recording it on their cell phones.

A woman can be arrested for rape if she helps a man rape another woman. In theory, a woman could incapacitate a man using drugs, restrain him, give him erection-enhancing medication, and force him to have sex. I've never heard of a case like this but it could happen.

Men rape other men by forcing their penis into another man's anus. This occurs a lot in prison but is less common in other settings because it is usually much more difficult for a man to physically restrain another man than it is for a man to physically restrain a woman.

Why do men rape? Understanding possible motives could help us protect ourselves. According to a well-known survey which is cited in almost every human sexuality textbook, about forty percent of rapes are motivated by anger, fifty-five percent are motivated by control, and the remaining five percent are the work of psychopathic serial sexual sadists who get turned on by torturing, raping, and possibly killing their victims.

Here's how I see this. I picture anger rapes happening in the context of a consensual sexual session that goes bad. A man and a woman are in a sexually intimate situation and she consents to intimate sexual behavior up to a certain point. When the man tries to insert his penis, she tells him no. There is a huge miscommunication here. Because she consented to previous levels of intimate behavior such as kissing, fondling, or oral sex, he was led to believe she would consent to intercourse because she didn't say no to that at the outset. So he is feeling very frustrated, because his progress toward a goal (intercourse) has been blocked. Social psychologists tell us that frustration leads to a state of heightened arousal, which then fuels aggressive behavior. He is frustrated, he gets angry, and he shoves his penis into her vagina. He literally doesn't believe that he has committed rape.

I see the control-motivated rapist as somebody who chooses unusual victims to assert his power. Most rape victims are young women, but control rapists often target really helpless victims such as kids, old women, hospital or rest home patients, or developmentally handicapped individuals.

Psychopathic serial rapists become sexually aroused by humiliating, raping, torturing, and even killing their victims. The psychopathic aspect implies they have no conscience or do not understand right and wrong the way most people do. Examples of sexually sadistic psychopathic serial rapists include Ted Bundy and the Hillside Stranglers, serial killers from back in the 1970's.

The aftermath of rape may include physical injury, a sexually transmitted infection, or pregnancy. Psychological consequences may include post-traumatic stress disorder (also called rape trauma syndrome), denial, withdrawal, anxiety, depression, sexual dysfunctions, insomnia, anger, and relationship problems. Some victims of acquaintance rape may initially feel guilty for allowing themselves to be in an intimate situation when they did not intend to have sex. Many women who have been raped often feel dirty or tainted.

What should you do if you have been raped? As much as you might want to, don't bathe or change your clothes. Call 911 or a rape crisis hotline. The police or a rape crisis counselor can take you to a hospital.

Many women don't report a rape because they have heard about the experiences of other women with the police or at the hospital. Unfortunately, many of these stories are true. Women who undergo a rape exam often feel like they were raped all over again. Your body will be photographed and swabs will be taken from your body orifices. The police may ask you the same questions over and over again, making you feel like they think you are lying. All in all it can be a very humiliating experience.

How do you protect yourself from being the victim of rape? It depends which type of rape you are trying to prevent—stranger rape or acquaintance rape. To prevent stranger rape, you would take the same precautions you would take to prevent being the victim of any violent crime. Keep your doors and windows locked. Avoid deserted or dark areas. Vary your routine and be vigilant about your surroundings. Have an alarm on your keychain and know the locations of alarms in your area. (Every week when I leave my class and walk through the dark parking lot at 9:45 p.m., I see female students staring at their phones and paying absolutely no attention to what is going on around them). Take a self-defense course. Don't answer your door unless you're expecting someone.

In order to protect yourself from acquaintance rape, or rape in the context of a date, if you meet someone online, agree to meet in a public place. Go out in groups rather than a one-on-one date. Watch your alcohol consumption. Don't be in an intimate setting with someone you don't intend to be intimate with. If you do find yourself in a situation like this, communicate your limits and refuse assertively.

Rape prevention experts disagree about whether a woman should resist if she is being raped. Some women have managed to talk a potential rapist out of it by saying something unexpected such as, "I have HIV" or, "I have children". There is no firm rule about this because resistance such as arguing or fighting might make a rapist even angrier. I would say if there is anyone in the vicinity who could possible help you, resist. If there is no one around who could possibly come to your aid, it might be best to just give in with no resistance. Sad but true.

In order to protect yourself from rape and sexual assault, you need to be aware that some perpetrators use drugs to incapacitate their victims. It's bad enough that a large percentage of acquaintance rapes involve alcohol use on the part of the perpetrator, the victim, or both. Perpetrators use other drugs called date rape drugs to render their victims pliable or unconscious and to make sure the victim doesn't remember the assault in enough detail to make a police report.

The three main date rape drugs are rohypnol (roofies), gamma hydroxybutyrate (GHB), and ketamine (Special K). These drugs can come in liquid or powder form. They can be colorless and odorless and can be slipped into a victim's drink. Being sedatives that also cause amnesia, they interact with alcohol. A victim feels as if she has had ten alcoholic drinks rather than two. Other drugs can be used as date rape drugs. Any sedative or sleeping medication will interact with alcohol and may cause a victim to pass out and have amnesia.

How are these drugs used? In private settings they are slipped into an already mixed drink. In bars, the perpetrator slips the drug into a drink when the victim goes to the bathroom or stands up to dance. Sometimes the perpetrator is in league with a bartender or waiter who slips the drug into a woman's drink. The perpetrator may pretend to be the hero who offers to drive a woman home when she appears to be severely intoxicated. Victims will pass out and not even realize that they have been raped or assaulted.

To protect yourself from being drugged, do the following. Go out together in pairs and promise to stay with each other all night. Many women are victims of date rape drugs because their female companion went off with a guy and left them alone. Don't order a mixed drink. Order a beer in a bottle or a can and watch the bartender open it at your seat. Don't let that drink leave your sight at any time. Don't go to parties in settings where it is rumored that girls have been given date rape drugs.

If you wake up the next morning and don't remember what happened but think you might have been raped or assaulted, follow the instructions for reporting any rape the same as you would if you remembered it. Call 911 or a rape crisis hotline. Don't clean up or change clothes.

People use alcohol regularly in social settings. You do not deserve to be raped because you were drinking in a social situation. Someone who is drunk, stoned, or passed out cannot legally consent to sex, and if you continue to have sex with a person you know is impaired, you are committing a crime.

It's difficult to protect yourself because we don't know who will rape. Rape is especially prevalent on college campuses and in the military. That's why it's important to report it if you are raped. It's one of the few ways we can bring attention to this all-too-common crime. Other recent rape prevention strategies have targeted men, who are encouraged to stop other men from raping women.

WHEN CONSENSUAL BECOMES NONCONSENSUAL

Most states have laws that allow a sexual partner to change her/his mind at any point during a sexual encounter, even after intercourse has started. If you continue to have sex when your partner has asked you to stop, you must stop, or you are committing rape.

Consensual S and M encounters can often sound like rapes-in-progress. People who are into SM practices such as bondage and discipline often yell at each other, hit each other, or loudly verbally resist sex. If you're into this kind of thing, make sure you have enough privacy so that no one will overhear you and call the police.

Here's a weird situation that could involve lack of consent. Picture yourself in this scenario. You're having sex with a new partner and all of a sudden, the person freaks out or even starts having a psychotic episode or threatens suicide. It's happened. What do you do? Well, obviously, stop having sex. You may actually have to call 911 or a suicide hotline, because this constitutes a real emergency. It could be a drug issue or a mental health problem.

SEXUAL HARASSMENT

Sexual harassment is deliberate or repeated unsolicited verbal comments, gestures, or physical contact of a sexual nature that is unwelcome by the recipient. There are two forms of sexual harassment—quid pro quo and the creation and maintenance of a hostile or abusive environment. Quid pro quo harassment means offering to trade favors for sexual acts. An example would be a male professor telling a female student that if she has sex with him he will give her an A in his class. An example of creation of a hostile environment would be a male English professor who requires female students to read sexual passages from assigned books aloud in class.

Sexual harassment is likely to occur in contexts where there is a power differential between the sexes. The most common settings for sexual harassment are educational institutions, the workplace, clergy offices, and medical offices.

In most cases of sexual harassment, the perpetrator is male and the victim is female. However, there have been many cases of women harassing men, men harassing men, and women harassing women.

One of the most troubling aspects in defining sexual harassment and proving it is that not everyone agrees on what is meant by the phrase "of a sexual nature". Some people might interpret a particular remark as sexual whereas others may not. For example, the remark, "You look nice today" when spoken by a man to a woman has been the focus of many sexual harassment complaints.

Gestures are hard to prove. For example, in the Psychology department in which I teach, we had a male professor who was a notorious boob watcher. He couldn't talk to a woman without staring at her tits. I had students come to me in tears because they were failing his class. They couldn't stand to go to class because it was so uncomfortable. I could relate. Every time I had to talk to this guy, he stared at my boobs too. He's since retired. I don't know how many if any students made complaints about him but eye gaze is hard to prove. I'm thinking now that with cameras in cell phones, it could get a little easier. It might be possible to record problematic interactions or in the case of gestures, have a friend do it.

Cell phones and computers aren't always a positive for dealing with sexual harassment. Their existence has spawned a whole new kind of sexual harassment—cyberharassment. People can go on social media and say anything they want to about you. Disgruntled ex-partners can post sexual pictures of you online, or tell lies about your sex life. It's becoming more and more common for people to seek legal recourse because of this.

A very serious form of sexual harassment is unwanted physical contact of a sexual nature. This could involve anything from groping to outright rape. Many of these actions could constitute sexual assault and could qualify as the basis for not only a complaint or lawsuit, but arrest of the perpetrator. I think it's very disturbing when women feel they must put up with being fondled or physically assaulted in order to get jobs or keep their jobs. The recent sexual harassment scandals in the movie business illustrate this.

I'm not going to name names here, as in most cases nothing has been proven. The sexual harassment scandals in all areas are expanding every day. Hopefully, several authors are at work on entire books about this important subject.

If you are the victim of sexual harassment it's important to keep records of when the incidents occurred. It's also a good idea to try to find other victims who have experienced the same thing with the same perpetrator to make a stronger case to whomever you are going to report it.

Sexual harassment can take many forms. This list comes from a brochure put out by the university where I work.

- Demeaning references to one's gender
- Comments about one's body or clothing
- Staring, comments, or propositions of a sexual nature
- Jokes about sex or gender-specific traits
- Questions about one's sexual behavior
- Innuendoes or double meanings
- E-mail circulation of sexually explicit images or text
- Demands for sex

UNWANTED TOUCHING OR PHYSICAL ASSAULT

Sometimes it's difficult to differentiate sexual harassment from just plain rudeness. I remember one time I had a male student raise his hand in class and ask me if I used a vibrator. His frat brothers had obviously put him up to this. I replied, "Are you kidding? I have a whole gun rack of them next to my bed. When I plug in that mean machine, San Onofre nuclear plant goes into auxiliary power!" But not everybody is me. He totally deserved that.

I had a student wear a t-shirt to class that said "Fuck you" on it. Should I assume that was directed at me, since I was the only one in class who could see it? I gave him some grief about it. Another time I had an older male student call me "Honey" in class. Unbelievable. I said, "That's Doctor Honey to you." I try to deal with these situations with humor. Lord knows I've made more than enough inappropriate sexual remarks while teaching.

How do you protect yourself so sexual harassment doesn't happen in the first place? Perpetrators often seek out victims who come across as weak and helpless, so try to project an image that says, "I'm not somebody you can mess with." That being said, also realize that some people make sexual remarks and they really are not aware that others might be offended. If the remarks aren't deliberate or repeated, they don't qualify as sexual harassment.

Some recent court rulings about sexual harassment have made the issue even more murky. For example, say you worked at a company, and your female boss was having a sexual affair with a male colleague. Even though you're not the one having sex, if her behavior affects your work environment and your ability to do your job (for example, if she asks you to cover for her while she's out screwing around), that could be construed as sexual harassment.

The social view of sexual harassment has radically changed over the past four decades. In the 1970's, no one thought about sexual harassment. Now workplaces and educational institutions regularly require employees to attend workshops on the topic. Organizations are now doing their best to not put up with this type of behavior. They are starting to recognize that sexual harassment ends up costing more money in the long run.

The line between sexual harassment and sex discrimination can be a fine one. Sex discrimination is when members of different genders are treated differently. An example would be a manager having to choose between hiring a man or a woman with the same educational and occupational backgrounds and level of experience. If he chooses the man because he believes that women are difficult to work with (a stereotype) he would be discriminating on the basis of sex. The same could be said if a male employer refused to hire a woman for a position because he thought she might get pregnant and miss work.

If you can't figure out the exact difference between sexual harassment and sex discrimination, you are not alone. Recent decisions/opinions by members of the Supreme Court indicate many of them don't understand the nuances either.

What about relationships at work? Years ago, many people began intimate relationships or met their future spouses at work or in school. That's understandable, because people who go to the same college or work in the same industry often have a lot in common. However, that situation is becoming increasingly not okay. Many employers as well as educational institutions now have strict rules about co-workers and students having relationships with each other. If you begin work in a new place or start attending a new school, be sure to find out the rules that will apply to you in this area.

You have many more options than people in the past did for meeting potential romantic partners, including online sites. It's not as if the people you go to school with or work with are the only people you will have access to. Avoid intimate relationships that could interfere with your educational or occupational functioning.

SAFE SEX RULE
Don't shit where you eat. I guess I could have some class and say don't foul your own nest.

DOMESTIC VIOLENCE

Sexual violence including rape often occurs in intimate relationships such as marriage. The impact of rape and sexual assault in the context of an intimate relationship can be just as devastating (if not more so) as it can be if perpetrated by a stranger. I want to take a look at domestic violence and abuse in this context. Sexual violence is often only one part of an abusive relationship.

What are the signs that a person you are involved with is abusive or could become an abuser? The signs are often quite clear and yet many people ignore them. Warning signs of abuse have been published in many venues but I want to repeat them here.

The best predictor of future violence is past behavior. Therefore, the biggest warning sign that you may be involved with someone who is abusive is a history of violence, especially battery, in the context of an intimate relationship. Other signs include hitting or breaking inanimate objects, cruelty to animals and children, using force during sex and claiming it was just for fun, and forcing you to have sex when you're sick or upset.

This is different from sadism as described in the chapter on the paraphilias. Sexual sadists harm or humiliate others because it turns them on sexually. Abusers have different motivations. I think the main one is to establish a sense of power or control over the victim.

Other signs that you may be involved with an abuser include mood swings, jealousy, blaming others, not taking responsibility for actions, isolating their partners from friends or relatives, checking up on their partner by phone or other means several times a day, pressuring a partner for commitment too early in a relationship, being verbally abusive, and having rigid traditional gender roles.

Does your partner scare you? Have your friends questioned what you see in him? (I use language here to indicate that the woman will most likely be the victim, but women can be abusers too). Do you find yourself apologizing for your partner's behavior or making excuses for him? Finally, are you afraid to leave the relationship because of what he might do?

If you recognize or have experienced any of the above, please call an abuse hotline and describe your circumstances. There are people and organizations out there who can help you.

There are several types of abuse that can occur in a relationship. There are sexual abuse, verbal abuse, physical abuse, emotional abuse, and economic abuse. The abuse usually escalates and goes in cycles between abuse, apology, and promises never to do it again.

The only way to stop relationship abuse including sexual abuse is for the victim to leave. Even this is dangerous because the abuser is most likely to assault the victim during the separation process. In my opinion, the best way to avoid getting into or staying in an abusive relationship, in addition to paying attention to the warning signs, is to have options. The best way to have options is to achieve and maintain financial/economic independence. Remember that the main motive of abusers is control. You are less likely to be in a position to be controlled if you have your own separate job, house, car, and money.

CHILD SEXUAL ABUSE

It might surprise you to know that there is no hard experimental evidence that being sexually abused (also called molested) as a child is bad for you. That's shocking, isn't it? The reason we don't have this evidence is we can't randomly assign some kids to be abused and others to be left alone. Nevertheless, there is a strong belief in society that it's not good for kids to be forced to have sex with adults.

That wasn't always the case. In the 1800's in Europe that was how most kids were initiated into sex—they were forced to have sex with parents, older siblings, other relatives, or servants. Ironically, Sigmund Freud was the first to point out that this might not be a good idea. I say ironically because there is some evidence that Freud's father sexually molested him and that Freud himself had a sexual relationship with his oldest daughter Anna.

I say ironically also because Freud presented this theory, called seduction theory, to the top psychoanalysts in Europe at a conference. The theory was based on Freud's experience of hearing female patients on his couch go back to childhood under hypnosis and remember sexual acts perpetrated on them by adults. Many of Freud's theories strike us as weird or unbelievable today. (The Oedipus complex? Where's the evidence for that?) Of all of his theories, seduction theory seems the most reasonable to us today—adults have sex with kids and it messes the kids up. His theory was met with disdain from the professionals and he was forced to recant it.

You know what I think? I don't think his colleagues were reacting to his theory because the idea of adult-child sexuality was distasteful or offensive. I think they reacted negatively to his theory because they were all having sex with their kids and Freud was essentially saying, "Maybe this isn't a good idea. Maybe we need to stop doing this."

One hundred-plus-year old paternalistic obscure Eurocentric theories aside, we have anecdotal evidence that it's not good for adults to have sex with kids. If we survey people in therapy for various psychiatric ailments, we will find a large percentage of them were forced into adult/child sexual relationships.

Here are some of the possible consequences of child sexual abuse—post-traumatic stress disorder, anxiety, depression, suicide, drug and alcohol addiction, sexual dysfunctions, and problems with intimacy. Emotional problems may include guilt, shame, anger, powerlessness, low self-esteem, and isolation. People who were sexually abused as children often have long-lasting medical problems such as obesity, asthma, insomnia, headaches, eating disorders, and chronic pain. Relationship problems may include trust issues, revictimization, or victimizing others.

People who were sexually abused as children often somatize their emotional pain. That means they convert their emotional pain to physical symptoms. A mild example would be if you're anxious and you get a headache or stomachache.

This not to say that child sexual abuse causes the above problems. We just know that child sexual abuse is related to the above problems.

Here's an example. When I was a teenager, I had a boyfriend who had an older sister who was around twenty-one. Every time I went over to their house, his sister would be lying on the couch wrapped in a blanket watching television. She never dated or went out with friends. I asked my boyfriend what was wrong with her and he said she had a lot of medical problems. I somehow knew there was more to the story. It turns out when she was thirteen, her uncle raped her and her aunt and parents didn't believe her. She wasn't getting any kind of psychological help at all. I wasn't supposed to know this. I wormed it out of him when he was drunk. Can you imagine the degree of psychological damage that was done here? Fortunately in her later life she did get help.

The consequences of child sexual abuse depend on a number of contextual factors. One is the age and developmental level of the victim, as younger children will deal with sexual abuse in a much different way than older children will. Another factor is how long the abuse went on. Abuse that is longer-lasting tends to leave more serious consequences. Who the perpetrator was is also important. Children who are abused by relatives and trusted adults tend to be worse off than those who are abused by strangers. What sexual behaviors were involved? Actual penetration is more harmful than exhibitionism or fondling. Another factor is how the abuse is dealt with by the family and others. Was it dealt with appropriately or was there no reaction, underreaction, or overreaction?

For example, an extreme case of child sexual abuse could involve a child under the age of about six who is systematically physically and sexually abused by his mother who is an alcoholic paranoid schizophrenic. What if the abuse goes on several times a week for years? This is really a worst case scenario. Because the child is abused before he can think or process information in anything like an adult manner, he can't tell anyone about the abuse. Cases such as these often result in dissociative identity disorder (formerly called multiple personality disorder). The abuse is so frequent and so extreme that the child does not have any defense except to split off a complete new personality so as not to remember the abuse.

A two-year-old child will deal with sexual abuse in a much different way than an eight-year-old child will, and an eight-year-old child will deal with sexual abuse in a much different way than somebody who is thirteen or fourteen and is already at least partially through puberty. Sexual abuse that goes on for years has potentially more lasting harm than abuse that occurs once or twice. Abuse by a trusted person such as a parent or relative has the potential to be more harmful in the long run than abuse by a stranger. Forcing a young child before the age of puberty to have intercourse has more potential for lasting harm than a pedophile forcing a child to look at pornography or at his genitals.

Pedophiles are individuals (mostly men) who have recurrent, persistent, and uncontrollable urges to have sex with children who are below the age of puberty. Not all people who sexually molest children are pedophiles, and not all pedophiles act on their desires. Fondling a kid because of an alcohol-fueled error of judgment is one thing, and being a sexually sadistic psychopathic serial pedophile is something quite different. Pedophiles and others who abuse children tend to be in their thirties and forties, have no peer relationships, are sexually immature, and were abused themselves.

Let's look at some cases of child sexual abuse to see how the different contextual factors could affect the outcome for the child. We've already seen that systematic sexual and physical abuse of a very young child by a trusted but mentally ill adult could result in the development of multiple personalities. Here's a contrasting case that illustrates the importance of the victim's age.

Years ago a teenage runaway named Mary Vincent was hitchhiking and had the misfortune to be picked up by a sexually sadistic serial psychopath named Lawrence Singleton. He tortured and sexually assaulted her. He cut off her forearms and threw her in a ditch. He thought she was dead but she wasn't. She survived the attack and summoned help.

This is a horrible story. However, because Mary Vincent was past puberty, she was old enough to think and process information the way an adult would. She was in a better position than a really young kid would have been. She could talk about her experience, see a therapist, write about her experience, and seek out social support. All of these factors allowed her to adapt as best she could to this awful attack.

(Singleton served prison time for the attack. After his release he was arrested for murder in Florida and died in prison.)

Let's look at a hypothetical case that illustrates some of the other factors in child sexual abuse. Say a mother wants to go shopping and her ten-year-old son doesn't want to go. She drops him off at the movies to see the latest action flick. After the movie starts, a man sits next to the kid and tries to grope the kid's genitals. The kid screams, runs into the lobby, and the police are called. The man is arrested. Would this experience necessarily scar a kid for life? Probably not, for the following reasons. The kid was old enough to have been educated that this behavior was not okay. It only happened once, and while the behavior was intrusive it was not invasive or painful. It was committed by a stranger, not somebody the kid trusted. The potential outcome is even better if when the mother was called and informed, she reacted appropriately. The truth is that this type of thing happens once to a lot of kids and many of them either forget it or recall it as, "Remember the time the pervert tried to molest me in the show?"

When we change some of the variables, the possible outcome may change. Let's say we have an eight-year-old boy who generally likes school and seems to get along with his peers.

One day he tells his mom he can't go to school because he has a stomach ache and then he throws up. His mom allows him to stay home but several days later he's still refusing to go to school, and worse, his behavior has started regressing. He's wetting the bed and throwing tantrums that would be characteristic of a much younger child. Now the mom knows something is really wrong and she takes the kid to a child psychologist.

Therapy with children is quite different from therapy with adult clients. Therapists who work with children have many techniques including play therapy that help children open up. It turns out the reason this kid didn't want to go to school was that on three occasions the school janitor lured the kid into a closet and forced the kid to look at and touch the janitor's penis.

What will be the outcome of this case? The kid's age is iffy—he's kind of young, young enough to be really scared. On the plus side, the fact that he regressed and acted out is in his favor. It got him attention. A lot of kids, especially boys, who have similar experiences don't tell anybody. They may actually have enjoyed the contact on some level and may go on to act it out with younger kids. This is the root of the behavior of a lot of men who grow up to be child molesters.

Another factor is the nature of the abusive contact. It involved being forced to look at and touch an adult's penis. It did not involve forced oral sex or actual penetration. This is in the kid's favor. Another thing in the kid's favor is the abuse only happened three times, versus, say, every week for a year. Also, the perpetrator was an adult who had some level of authority but not the ongoing type of authority of a more trusted adult such as a teacher.

One of the real keys here is the reaction of the adults. The mother did the right thing by taking him to a therapist and reporting the abuse to school authorities. Unfortunately, this does not always occur. Recall that in the sex scandals in the Catholic Church, authorities often knew that certain teachers or priests were multiple offenders and reassigned them rather than firing them and/or having them arrested and prosecuted.

The fact that parents and school authorities believed the kid's account is also huge. Can you imagine how you would feel if this happened to you and nobody believed you and you had to look at the perpetrator every day? It happens all the time.

The flip side of believing young kids' reports of abuse was illustrated by the McMartin preschool case. It is very easy for kids to be influenced to report false memories, and the younger the kid is, the easier it is. Research on repressed memories indicates that even adults can be influenced to supposedly "remember" stuff that happened to them in childhood.

One of the most damaging forms of child sexual abuse is incest involving young children. Incest is having sex with someone who is a close enough blood relative that you would not be legally able to marry that person. The form of incest we know the most about is father-daughter incest, because these are the perpetrators who are likely to get caught. There have been many first-person accounts of this type of incest written by the victims which describe the extremely negative consequences.

Here's a typical scenario. A woman decides she no longer wants to have sex with her husband so she makes herself unavailable. The husband starts going into his daughter's room at night when she is between about six and eight years old. He starts with exposing himself and mutual fondling. As she gets older, the abuse may involve oral sex or penetration. The most damaging fact is that this abuse can go on for years and the mother looks the other way.

How does this guy get away with this for so long? Remember that sexual predators are superb manipulators. The father will say something like, "Don't tell anybody what we're doing. It's something that all fathers do with their daughter" or, "If you tell anybody what we're doing, the police will take me away and you won't have a family anymore and it will be all your fault." A six-year-old would buy that. A twelve-year-old wouldn't. As the girl gets older and threatens to tell, the father tells her that unless she keeps having sex with him, he will start doing the same thing with her younger siblings. In most cases, eventually she does tell somebody and the father is caught.

You can see how this type of abuse would be devastating. This girl has all the factors going against her. Her innocence was stolen by someone she should have been able to trust.

Interestingly, this perpetrator was probably not a pedophile. The root of that form of incest is in family dysfunction, not an uncontrollable urge to have sex with children.

Mother-son incest occurs too but the dynamic is usually different. It's usually a single mother with a teenage son. The mother usually has a problem with alcohol or drugs. We don't know much about the consequences of this form of incest because it is highly unreported.

The purpose of this chapter is not to shock you by relating the worst cases of child abuse I have ever heard of. I have them, and believe me, I could do that. I'd rather encourage you to get help if you were a victim of child sexual abuse.

Protecting children from sexual abuse is another safe sex issue. Because of recent changes in laws, it is easier to protect kids than it used to be, especially from abuse by strangers.

The first line of defense in protecting kids is sex education, including the concept of "private" body parts. The second line of defense is to realize that children are more likely to be sexually abused by someone they know rather than a stranger. It's not the creepy old guy in a raincoat standing outside the schoolyard with a bag of candy in his hand that we need to be worried about. It's relatives, step-relatives, members of the clergy, scoutmasters, choir directors, and other men who hold trusted positions of authority over children. I say men, because most people who sexually abuse children are men. In every case I've known about or read about in which a woman sexually abused children, the woman had major psychiatric problems including alcoholism or drug abuse, bipolar disorder, borderline personality disorder, schizophrenia, or anti-social personality disorder.

I want to make a comparison here between a hard-core psychopathic sadistic pedophile versus a pathetic guy who could never get laid and has the same sexual maturity level of an eight-or ten- or twelve-year old. As an example, let's look at Michael Jackson. In 1993 he was accused of molesting a thirteen-year –old boy at a sleepover. Apparently he paid off the parents and the case never went to trial. In 2003 the same thing happened, but the case did go to trial and he was found not guilty. I know I'm going out on a limb here and I want to state clearly—anything in this paragraph is my own opinion because I didn't know him, never talked with him, and never clinically interviewed him. But does anybody reading this think that in any way he had a normal childhood and adolescent sexual upbringing? Raise your hand. I thought not. In my opinion, if he wanted to play around sexually with kids, it was probably because he was at their same developmental level of sexual maturity.

I was not sexually molested as a child, but I know many people who were, both friends and clients. When I was a kid, awareness of child molestation was very high. I don't know if that's just the area in which I grew up, but we were warned to be on the lookout for possible child molesters all the time. Again, the belief was that it was the stranger in the schoolyard with a bag of candy stereotype, when the reality is we were more likely to be molested by an authority figure we knew or a relative.

I'm going to tell you an anecdote about the totally dysfunctional nature of my childhood. People were so aware of child molestation that every year when I was in elementary school, we would have a day designated as "Child Molester Day". The parents and teachers would attend workshops on how to prevent child molestation and we would have substitute teachers. To keep the younger kids busy, we would have a child molester coloring contest. We would all color pictures of kids playing in a schoolyard with a creepy guy watching. Seriously, I am not making this up.

One way to prevent child molestation is to do something to the abusers themselves. Pedophilia is not considered curable. It can be treated using forms of psychological therapy but they are generally not successful. Chemical castration can work. This involves giving a man female hormones to shut down his sex drive.

We can also try to prevent child sexual abuse by making it difficult or impossible for offenders to have contact with children. Unfortunately we can only do this with people who have already offended.

Megan's Law has made it so that residents of local communities can find out if convicted and released sex offenders are living in their area through the use of websites.

In some states, offenders have to wear an anklet with a GPS, and are not allowed to live near areas where children are likely to congregate. Unfortunately, an unintended consequence of this is that many landlords will not rent to sex offenders and so they end up homeless or end up all living together in the same building. This is definitely not a good idea, since the behavior of sex offenders tends to be fueled by fantasies that occur due to stories they hear from other offenders.

There is a movement (in California at least) to stop giving all sex offenders that label for life. A three-tier system has been recommended. A sex offender classification would apply for ten years to people convicted of indecent exposure, possessing child pornography, or masturbating in public. A twenty-year classification would apply for rape, sodomy, or lewd conduct with a child. Only sexually violent predators would receive the lifetime classification.

TWO PREDATORS

In addition to knowing many people who were sexually abused as children, I've also know several sexual predators. In this final section I want to tell you in detail about two of them in order to illustrate how manipulative they may be.

Most people who sexually molest kids are men. When women molest children, the women usually show evidence of having a fairly serious mental disorder.

I've known two women who molested their own children. In one case, the mother forced her young son to watch her take a bath and she also forced him to wash her vagina. She was an alcoholic and had narcissistic personality disorder.

In another case, the mother forced her young teenage daughter to sit on her lap and meticulously cleaned the daughter's inner and outer vaginal lips with Q-tips. This mother suffered from paranoid schizophrenia.

The first detailed case I will tell you about involves a form of sexual harassment. The second one involves a priest who was an ephebophile—someone who has a compulsion to have sex with teenage boys.

When I was in graduate school in the 1980's, there was a professor in our department who was probably in his mid-to-late fifties. We'll call him Dr. Mark. He was an internationally known scholar in his field.

When I started my graduate program, all of the experienced students were talking about a second-year female student who quit the program under mysterious circumstances.

"What happened to her?"

"She's gone."

"Wasn't she dating Dr. Mark?"

As I became more experienced in the program and asked questions, a pattern became clear. Every year for the past I-don't-know-how-many years, Dr. Mark had singled out a beginning female graduate student and asked her out. It was always the student who was doing the worst in the program as well as someone who was physically somewhat mousy. These were never his own graduate students. He never had female graduate students.

So he would pick out a woman, wine her and dine her, and generally treat her like a queen. He would start a sexual relationship with her. He would promise she could do research with him and co-author papers with him. In every case the woman would fall for it.

And then after a few months he would dump her. In every case, the woman was so demoralized that she quit the program. As I said, he had been doing this for years.

The final year I was there I happened to be alone in the restroom with his latest pick. I said to her, "You know this is none of my business, but he does this every year. I don't think you should get involved with him." Of course she replied, "You're right. It's none of your business." And of course she was gone within a few months.

Was this sexual harassment? It would be difficult to prove that, as he never forced anyone to have sex with him that I know of. All of these women entered into consensual sexual relationships with him. Who wouldn't be flattered by the attention from one of the most respected members of our department? As far as I know, he never directly offered to trade grades or opportunities for sexual services.

It's sexual harassment, but it's a bit more subtle than most cases. He used his position of power to seduce these women. Notice how he always picked a weak woman, sort of like a lion attacking the weakest antelope in the herd?

What should these women have done? I don't know, but I do know it's awfully difficult to turn down any kind of request from an authority figure. Under today's sexual harassment standards, the women should have gone to the university counseling center and asked for advice.

I also blame the culture in our department at the time. It was completely acceptable for graduate students to date or have relationships with professors at the time. It's kind of like the Harvey Weinstein thing today. Nobody talked about it. If the women whom Dr. Mark victimized had gotten together and complained, there could have been lawsuits that stopped this type of thing.

I'm not trying to come across as some kind of Goody Two Shoes. People have accused me of sleeping my way to a degree. This isn't true, because if it was true, I would have twelve doctorates now instead of one.

This next case achieved national prominence. In 1982 I was teaching at a Catholic high school in Southern California. The principal, a priest, was an extremely good-looking and charismatic man. Nevertheless, I started to get a creepy vibe about the whole school in general.

For one thing, there was a very gay male vibe. Male teachers would walk through campus holding hands with each other. I didn't have a problem with that, as I went to Catholic high school myself and that was not unheard of.

My problem was that there appeared to be a lot of physical contact between male teachers and male students—more than I was comfortable with, and like I say, it was kind of creepy.

I talked to my boss about it. She was a sweet woman who never wanted to believe anything bad about anybody. I asked her, "Is it just me, or is there a really creepy pedophile vibe around this place?" (At this time I didn't know the difference between a pedophile and an ephebophile). She laughed and told me I was paranoid and that because I majored in Psychology in college, I thought everybody had some kind of mental problem.

After I stopped working there and went to graduate school, I met a woman who told me that the principal of that high school had a cabin up in the mountains and that he would invite some of the high school boys up there for the weekend. She told me that the principal had fondled her brother on one of those weekends.

Then, in the very early 1990's, the Los Angeles Times reported that the archdiocese was being sued for millions of dollars by several plaintiffs who alleged that they had attended this high school and were molested by the principal. The archdiocese paid out five point two million dollars in this case, which I believe also involved other defendants. This payout was the largest at this time for a similar suit but was quickly eclipsed by other multi-million dollar lawsuits in other geographical areas.

Keep in mind, the priest I'm talking about was never arrested, charged with a crime, tried, or convicted, and yet the court still settled in favor of the plaintiffs. The alleged abuse happened in the early 1980's. I was right! There was definitely something going on.

Some of the plaintiffs were interviewed and asked why they waited so long to sue. All of them said some version of, "I didn't want to sue at first because I felt so special that he had singled me out to have a relationship." It was not until they realized how many other kids had been victims that they decided to be a part of the lawsuit.

This is my point. This priest was so appealing that he was able to get away with this for years. Students felt honored to have sex with him.

His strategy seemed to be very similar to that of the professor described above. He would choose students who weren't necessarily physically attractive, who were struggling academically, or had family problems. Imagine what was going through their minds when this attractive, popular successful man came on to them. There are still a lot of people who were associated with this high school that don't think he did it. That's how convincing he was.

I have researched this case a number of times and the results are a bit confusing in terms of exactly how much money was paid out to victims of this particular priest. I do know that in 2012, a lawsuit was filed by another man who claimed that in 1986, this priest had invited him to a private meeting in his office and grabbed his penis and performed oral sex on him.

It was very difficult to write this section, as I personally knew the people who were involved. What's the solution? I'm not going to go into a whole thing about the reasons for the massive amounts of sexual abuse and subsequent cover ups that went on in the Catholic Church, although you can bet I have my opinions. Let's move on to sex for sale between adults.

CHAPTER 12
SEX FOR SALE

This chapter deals with prostitution and pornography as well as other forms of sex for sale. Prostitution has been called the world's oldest profession and it may well be. I'm sure women have been trading sexual favors since before money was even invented.

Psychologists call this Social Exchange Theory. This is a very crass view of human sexual behavior. It's the idea that the ability to consent to sex is an asset that women have and men are always trying to trade for.

Most prostitution involves women selling sex and men buying it. This will probably continue to be the case as long as men have the money and women have the vaginas.

Prostitutes are not the only types of sex workers. Other workers in the sex industry include adult film actors, peep show performers, people who perform in live sex shows, some exotic dancers and strippers who cross the line and touch their clients, people who work in adult product stores, people who work in pornography on the Internet, surrogate partners, sex therapists…the list goes on. I guess you could include authors of books on sexuality and people who teach Human Sexuality classes.

Some sexuality-related occupations are legal and some are not. Since the Sexual Revolution in the 1960's and 1970's, the incidence of prostitution decreased from what it was in the days of Alfred Kinsey, the famous sex researcher. Prostitution decreased further in the 1980's due to concern about the transmission of HIV/AIDS. I think the use of prostitutes is up again because of the Internet.

Prostitutes operate at different social levels. If I asked you to picture a prostitute, you would probably picture a streetwalker—a woman soliciting in public while dressed in a slutty manner. That's our stereotype, but there are different levels of prostitutes who differ in the following ways—the acts they are asked to perform, the amount they charge, their physical and mental health, the degree of danger they face in their job, their looks, their average age, and their potential for contact with law enforcement. Most importantly for the purposes of this book, they differ in relative safety for both the prostitute and the client.

The stereotype of prostitute equals streetwalker is pervasive. I remember once I was taking a career counseling class and I volunteered for a role play. I told the therapist I basically liked my job but it didn't pay nearly enough. She suggested a second job that paid the bills. I said, "What? Prostitution?", and she immediately said, "No, that's much too dangerous." As we'll see, it doesn't have to be.

Most descriptions of prostitutes in human sexuality textbooks start with the highest social levels and work their way down. I prefer to start in the gutter and work my way up.

I know I said that prostitutes have a social hierarchy. Please don't misinterpret this to mean that I think there is upward mobility here. I don't think anybody says when they're growing up, "I really want to be a call girl, so I'll start as a streetwalker and work my way up." Doesn't happen. Downward mobility may occur, however. Sometimes women who started as brothel or massage parlor workers end up as street prostitutes because they did not make any other career plans.

The lowest level of prostitution is street prostitution—women who solicit in public. The lowest of the low are crack whores, who perform a sexual act in return for a rock of crack cocaine, or even for enough money just to buy a meal.

Street prostitution is a horrible life. Many street prostitutes are homeless women. People are recruited into street prostitution because they are homeless or have run away from an abusive home environment and believe that life on the streets would be preferable to the place they left.

Street prostitutes are often under the control of a pimp, who acts as their agent. I don't know when the word "pimp" started getting a positive connotation, but in the context of street prostitution, there's nothing positive about it. A pimp makes sure his workers see as many clients as they can, protects their turf, takes the money they earn, keeps them addicted to drugs, and beats them up to keep them in line.

The most common act requested of a street prostitute is oral sex, usually performed in the client's car. They get paid the lowest fees of any prostitutes. Their mental and physical health is not good. Many of them are addicted to alcohol and drugs. Contact with law enforcement resulting in arrest is extremely likely, both for the prostitute and the client in a sting operation. Street prostitutes are extremely likely to have an STI (or several) or get one from a client. To me, the worst danger of street prostitution is the extremely high chance of being victimized not only by your pimp but by a client. The customers of street prostitutes are called "johns" or "tricks".

I've been mistaken for a street prostitute more times than I care to think about, mainly because of the area where I live. I live about two miles from the most popular street prostitution site in Orange County, which is an area that also has a lot of automobile dealerships. I went to pick up my car from getting repaired one time and these two burly car salesman physically threw me out of the car dealership. Might be time to re-think my wardrobe choices. Hey, it was a summer day, I had just come from the beach, and I was wearing shorts and a tank top. We got it straightened out, but still. I swear I was not soliciting anyone in that waiting room.

Another time I was in Arizona and I was walking down the street next to Arizona State University during spring break. There was nobody else around—I guess they were all in Cancun. A man pulled up next to me in one of those big cars (a Lincoln?) with the giant front end with a steer horn hood ornament. The door handles were pistols. I swear I am not making this up. The driver, wearing a Stetson hat, of course, opened his window and leaned out and said, "Hey there, little lady! How'bout you get in the car with me and you and me get to know each other a little bit better?" I was just standing there with my mouth open, especially about the "little lady" part, because I'm over six feet in medium heels.

Oh, the regrets. It could have been the beginning of a beautiful friendship. I just think it's kind of sad that a woman can't walk down a street by herself wearing a nice outfit without someone propositioning her for a sex act.

There's another type of prostitute called a bar prostitute. Technically she is not soliciting in public. She works out of a cocktail lounge and the bartender acts as her pimp. He'll say, "The guy down at the end of the bar wants to buy you a drink." If she thinks he looks okay, she'll have a drink with him and then have sex with him in a back room of the bar. Again, dangerous.

Other prostitutes work out of hotels. Here's how that might play out. A woman looking to solicit investigates what conventions are being held at large local hotels. She dresses in business attire with a briefcase and/or laptop. She is not young and is not in any way dressed in what could be considered a slutty manner. She sits in the hotel bar as convention sessions are getting out. The bar is full of men. Pretty soon a man approaches her and asks if he can buy her a drink. If he looks like a good mark, she agrees; if not, she doesn't.

They talk. She makes up a story about her presence at the hotel. Things progress to the point that he asks her to have dinner with him. If things are going according to her plan, he's from out of town, married with a family. It gets to the point where they go up to his room after dinner for more drinks. At this point, if he has anything on the ball, he probably knows she's going to ask for money. But if he's naïve, he may not even know she's a prostitute. When he suggests sex or makes a move, she says, "You seem like a really nice guy and I had a good time at dinner. Thank you. I would like to stay with you, but unfortunately I'm having some financial problems."

At this point his reply would be, "What kind of financial problems?" "The kind that X amount of money would take care of." Or more subtly, she could say something like, "I'd like to stay, but I'm kind of down right now. I just found out I have several hundred dollars in unexpected car repair bills."

Okay, now what? If he says, "Oh my God, I picked up a hooker and didn't realize it" and asks her to leave, he doesn't get laid. If he's still horny, he has to go back down to the cocktail lounge and start over! If he says, "No problem, I can help you out", he gets laid, she gets paid, and everybody's happy.

Sure, he could call the police and make a big stink. There would be the embarrassment of having to give his name so he probably won't do that. If the woman is working with a contact in the hotel and cutting him in financially, she'll be fine.

I know women who have been successful at this. Their secret is they minimize the risks. They aren't desperate. They can pick and choose their clients. They look for clients who are from out of town. They don't use the same hotel all the time. They change their appearance with clothing, wigs, and eyeglasses. And, most importantly, they don't look like hookers.

The risk involved here would be if the woman has sex with the customer without a condom. If he's married, she feels safer. The main risk is that she has to be a good judge of people— the danger would be getting hooked up with some psycho and getting hurt. The customer is safe, because she gets checked regularly for STI's. She doesn't want to jeopardize her ability to earn a living.

Women who do this often get into the danger aspect of it. For some of them, it's actually a sexual turn-on to be able to get away with it.

There are corporations that hire women to perform a similar function. Let's say a corporation wants to make a major deal with a male out-of-town client. They hire an attractive woman as a "consultant" to drive him around, or help him purchase gifts for his family. Whether or not he is attracted to her and they end up having sex, she is there to sweeten the deal. She is paid by her corporate employer, not the client. She may get a bonus if the deal goes through. Think I'm making this up or have read too many Jacqueline Susann novels? Maybe not.

Let's get back on track here. To recap, street prostitution is extremely dangerous. Bar prostitution, convention prostitution and corporate prostitution are less so, because the women have a choice about their occupation and whether they want to work with a particular client.

There are some organizations that bring their own prostitutes with them when they have a convention. This would be fraternal organizations such as the Shriners and their offshoots. They bring women with them and take up private floors in a hotel with security guards so the other guests aren't aware of what is going on.

The next level up from street prostitution is massage parlor prostitution. In this case, a man goes to an establishment and asks for a massage. He is led to a room with a woman and a massage table. She tells him that a massage will cost a certain amount. Notice that I don't give any specific numbers about how much prostitutes will charge or how much clients will pay. That's because the range varies so greatly according to geographical area, and rates are subject to inflation. At that point the man may negotiate for a "happy ending" at the end of the massage—a hand job. The massage person will probably not agree to it at this point. She may just ignore the request. She's in a much better position to negotiate at the end of the massage when the man is desperate to get off and willing to pay more. Some massage parlor workers may agree to other sex acts also.

Does anyone care if a random guy wants to pay for a hand job? Probably not. Giving or receiving a hand job is safe. The major legal problem with massage parlors is zoning. People don't want massage parlors next to their homes, their churches, or their kids' schools. Business owners do not want massage parlors that attract sleazy clientele in the same strip malls as their dry cleaners and donut shops. So the business owners complain and the police raid the massage parlors. That's why massage parlors are often relegated to unincorporated or industrial areas.

Many women who work in massage parlors are illegal immigrants and may not speak English and may not know the local prostitution laws. In many locales, women who intend to perform massage services have to get a license and show that they graduated from a legitimate massage school. In many locales, it's also illegal to perform massages for people in their home. Everybody pretty much ignores that.

There was a fairly recent case in Southern California of several people who were convicted of prostitution and pandering for running a series of massage parlors. They employed Chinese women who worked for them voluntarily. What was interesting about this case is how they got caught. They had one of their workers go to Costco and buy seven thousand five hundred square feet of sandwich wrap (to use as condoms) and two hundred ninety-four ounces of Vaseline. A Costco employee found this suspicious and turned them in! If they hadn't been so cheap, they might not have gotten caught. By the way, don't use sandwich wrap as a substitute for a condom. I forgot to mention that in Chapter 6.

Please don't misunderstand me and think that I'm saying that all massage parlors are fronts for prostitution. There are many legitimate massage places where you can get a therapeutic or relaxing massage from a trained person. I go to one once a month myself. The massage person never sees you naked. You are always draped. Plus they have cameras in every room to make sure nothing illegal is going on.

The next step up is brothel prostitution. A brothel is a house of prostitution. It sounds funny, like a word from the Wild West—a bordello or a house of ill repute.

The only place in the United States where brothel prostitution is legal is some of the rural counties in Nevada. Here's how it works. You walk into the establishment and the madam tells you which women are available. You make your choice and are taken to a private room. The woman tells you that the house charges X amount. You then negotiate another fee for what acts you would like her to perform. She will quote you a price based on how long she thinks she will need to be with you.

The Nevada brothels are highly regulated and the workers are required to use condoms. They are also required to get tested regularly for STI's.

Most Nevada brothel workers live at the brothel for days or weeks at a time and then return to their partners, husbands, and families. Often they are working at the brothel to save up for a particular financial goal—a down payment on a house, a new car, a kid's college education. I had a student in my class who told me he was a mortgage broker. One of his clients was a woman who worked in a Nevada brothel. In order to qualify her for a mortgage, he had to look at her tax return. She grossed over four hundred thousand dollars a year! And that's just what she claimed. Well, I have certainly been in the wrong line of work all these years!

That doesn't stop people from thinking I'm in this line of work. Years ago, I achieved a certain amount of notoriety as a surrogate partner and I appeared on many television and radio shows. Back in the 1990's, I appeared on the Montel Williams Show. I had to fly to New York, and I was very suspicious because the producer refused to tell me what the theme of the show was. I figured they were trying to set me up and I was correct.

I found myself onstage with several women and the theme of the show was announced—"Women who take money or goods from men in return for sex, but don't think they're prostitutes." I almost walked off the stage. Oh shit! Fortunately Montel interviewed all of the other women first. They all said that before they would have sex, the man had to give them a car, or a television set, or jewelry, etc.

After they were done, Montel asked me what I thought about this. Apparently he expected me to say that what they were doing was wrong. Instead I said, "Here I've been having sex for free all along. I'm an idiot. I could have been getting all this free stuff."

Of course the whole audience cracked up. Montel tried to salvage the situation by saying to the audience, "Well, would it surprise you to know that Dr. Keesling has sex for money?" and the whole audience went, "Wooooo…". And I said, "Shame on you, Montel. I know you have had surrogate partners on the show before and you have treated them with respect so I know that you know what surrogate partners do. Why are you pretending ignorance now?" And the whole audience went, "Wooooo…".

Score one for Dr. Barb! A friend of mine who was one of the top editors at Playboy magazine was home sick watching the show. She said she almost fell out of bed from laughing.

Remember the movie "Indecent Proposal" in which a millionaire played by Robert Redford offers Demi Moore's married character a million dollars for a night of sex and she and her husband can't decide whether she should do it or not? Maybe I have more in common with those women on the Montel show than I would like to think, because I can only think of about three people I wouldn't have sex with for a million dollars (and two of them are dead!).

In order to understand modern brothels, you have to look back at the history, not only of how the West was settled, but also the social movement of people from farms to cities to suburbs. Women who worked in brothels before statehood were often not disrespected. There just were not that many social positions open to women at that time in that place. Wife, schoolmarm, or brothel worker, that was about it. If you've ever read John Steinbeck's "East of Eden", "Cannery Row", or "Sweet Thursday", you will get a feel for how the towns' madams were respected members of society. They were performing a necessary function.

When people lived in small towns, most men's initiation into sex was by a prostitute in a brothel. Many times a father would take his son who had just turned sixteen or seventeen to the local red light district and pay for him to be with a woman that every man in town knew. For many men in the World War II era, their first initiation into sex was with a prostitute overseas. This resulted in quite a few cases of STI's. No matter how many disgusting pictures they were shown by military doctors, horny GI's were going to want to get laid. Fortunately by that time sulfa drugs and antibiotics had been invented.

As of this writing a new television show has come out. It's called Harlots. It deals with the life of brothel prostitutes in England in the 1700's. According to the press for that show, something like a third of women were working as prostitutes and the brothels were so much safer than street prostitution. (Recall that in the 1800's, Jack the Ripper preyed on street prostitutes.) The prostitutes took the precautions that were available. Clients could use lambskin condoms and the prostitutes could douche with alum or other substances to try to prevent pregnancy. Women often knew about herbal concoctions that could induce miscarriages.

There are two situations I know of in which you will find illegal brothels. One situation is what Jerry Springer would probably call "Housewife Hookers". A couple of women whose husbands work during the day and whose kids go to school get together and decide to use one of their homes for prostitution. They both have a number of extramarital affairs going on and they decide to start charging money and see if any of their current or former lovers can refer potential customers. Pretty soon they build up a big enough customer base that they can hire other women to work for them.

One of the potential problems here is that soliciting for prostitution in public as an individual and getting caught is a misdemeanor. A first offense may not even end up with a conviction. Using your house as a house of prostitution means you are technically selling other people into prostitution and that's a felony called pimping or pandering. Legally, this is much more serious, not to mention that you are operating a business in a residential area without a license.

Another problem is that if you are too successful and get too busy, your neighbors will get suspicious if they see a lot of men coming and going out of your house. The only way this can work is if you have a residence that has front and back entrances that go through garages.

I knew a woman who operated a business like this for decades. The clients would refer other men and the women who worked for her referred others. She did not advertise other than word of mouth, and she only hired women who were recommended by clients or by other women who worked for her. The referral system got a little complicated because people would get discounts for referrals. But she stayed in business for a long time because she kept a low profile and didn't see too many clients. The women who worked for her had a choice and were not forced to do anything. She made appointments on the phone. This was before cell phones.

When she felt the business was getting too busy, she's send some customers out to her workers' houses for a while or work at a different location.

What about the safety issues in terms of the actual sex? Workers decided whether condoms would be used, and were voluntarily tested frequently for STI's. Most of the clients were married. On the surface, it would seem as if there was a serious danger of spreading STI's in this situation, but to my knowledge, it never happened.

Another type of illegal brothel occurs in Asian enclaves. Asian businessmen from the United States go to countries such as Thailand and basically buy girls from their parents with the promise that they have jobs for them. The girls, many of whom are underage, are brought to America illegally and forced to work in houses of prostitution, often seeing thirty or forty clients a day. The girls have no papers, don't speak English, and can't escape. They are being held prisoner. This is sex slavery, or trafficking in humans, and is a crime with worldwide repercussions, not just a local law-breaking situation. This is a very hot-button issue right now involving not just importing girls from abroad but also pimps forcing underage girls from the U. S. into street or house prostitution.

Escort services, also called outcall, are businesses you can call and they will send a woman to your house, hotel room, or place of business. There is a huge divide between the lowest end and the highest end escort services. On the lowest end, some businesses claim to be escort services and are really fronts not for prostitution but for home invasion and burglary. High end escort services are similar to what Heidi Fliess was running in the 1990's. She sent very attractive escorts to Hollywood parties and charged high fees for them to spend several hours servicing the guests.

In theory, escorts could face a high level of danger because the woman is being sent to an unfamiliar location to a person she doesn't know. The higher-end services will vet clients over the phone and verify that they do indeed own a home or business or are renting a hotel room. Higher end escort services also send a bodyguard with the escort, which adds to the cost.

The woman shows up and tells the client that the agency charges X amount just for her to show up. She then negotiates with the client about what acts will be involved and she quotes an amount of money based on how much time she thinks she will have to spend with the client. Some clients just want a quick sex act and others want the girlfriend experience—they want to share a meal or watch a movie to get in the mood before having sex.

Having sex with a stranger carries the same risk whether you are getting paid for it or not. Many women who work for escort services are college students paying for their education. I've had some of them in my classes over the years. Often if they are sent to the same client's location more than once, if they like the client they will give him a card and start having the client contact them directly to avoid the agency fee. It's well known that escorts steal clients from agencies all the time.

Remember what I said about there being no upward mobility in prostitution? Here's the exception. If an escort can collect enough private clients from agencies, she can go off on her own and become a call girl. She can make appointments by phone directly with the clients and see them at her house or a rental space.

Escort services used to advertise in newspapers and the yellow pages. Now they advertise online. When they used to advertise in newspapers, it was under a section called "Business Personals" and you had to present a legitimate business license at the newspaper office in order to advertise. Ads would often state that the service would send a woman to your location to model lingerie or to dance. Sometimes the ads would say that the woman worked alone and not with an agency. This was a huge lie because, as I said, you had to have a business license to take out one of these ads.

There is a legitimate form of escort service that's more like a modeling agency. These services employ very attractive women such as former beauty contest winners. Clients hire them to accompany them to business functions, school reunions, or any other occasion when they want to show up with a good-looking woman.

You have to be a little careful even when using supposedly reputable dating services. I won't name them (unless they pay me for the advertising). Some women use these services as a way to try to earn money having sex. The reputable services will all warn people in their contracts not to have anything to do with anybody who asks you for money. But you know it's happening.

Some prostitutes have been clever about finding ways to make money from sex without it seeming illegal. Here's what happened to a friend of mine. He called a woman from an ad in some sleazy throwaway paper. She showed up and she was really hot looking. They had sex, and instead of having him pay her cash, she had him take her to a lingerie store owned by a friend of hers. He bought three hundred dollars' worth of lingerie and they parted company. Obviously she and her friend were using the lingerie business to launder the cash they made from prostitution.

Here's a story about an extremely unscrupulous escort service. This happened to a friend of mine. He used a regular masseuse who used to come to his house and didn't have a problem finishing him off. She was out of town and he threw his back out helping his neighbor move a dining room table.

So he made his first mistake. He called a massage service that advertised in the local weekly free alternative paper. A girl showed up at his house, which was in a very upscale neighborhood. She looked young and didn't have a massage table with her. His first clue that something was wrong, right? Then she asked for the money up front and it was something like three hundred dollars—way out of line, especially as this occurred twenty years ago. You should have seen the look on my face when he was telling me this. Then he gave her the money! Instead of telling her to get lost because he had changed his mind, which is what he should have done.

Then she said she had to go put the money in her car and she would be back. I don't think so. Suddenly a man ran into the house through the front door, grabbed the girl, and they both jumped into a car which was pointing the wrong way in the cul de sac. This gave my friend time to go to his garage and pick up a piece of a gun that he had disassembled on a table where he had been cleaning it. He ran up to their car and pointed the gun part at them and demanded his money back. They threw the money out the window at him and yelled that they were going to call the police because he had robbed them.

He went back into his house, shaking due to adrenaline. His heart was racing. He poured himself a drink to help him calm down. The phone rang and he picked it up. "This is the police. We're coming to arrest you." In the background he could hear people laughing like they were in a bar. He hung up. They called again. This time he told them he was going to call the police and hung up. The phone rang again and this time he said, "Goddamn it, I told you not to call me again." It wasn't them. It was his neighbor. She said, "I don't know what's going on, but I think you better go outside. The SWAT team is in your front yard with guns pointed at your house."

He went outside with his hands up. The SWAT team threw him on the ground (which presumably did nothing for his bad back). They took him to the local jail and then transferred him to the county jail where he sat for three days before he was allowed to make a phone call. Finally he reached a friend who bailed him out.

During the trial, he and his lawyer tried to explain everything and it turned out the two people who had robbed him had prior convictions and warrants in an adjacent county. Nevertheless, to get this episode behind him, he had to plead guilty to the "brandishing a fake gun" law and it cost him fifty thousand dollars in legal fees even though he was the victim.

This unbelievable yet true story illustrates the idea that when you are hiring an unknown person for a possible sexual act, you may be getting into much more than you bargained for. Obviously, he should have just taken a Vicodin and waited for his trusted person to get back to town. He was naïve about what could happen when hiring a person through a shady source. He was also naïve in thinking that the police would treat him well just because he was an upscale white guy.

SAFE SEX RULE
If you're paying a person you know one-on-one for sex, you're probably safe. In other cases, you have no idea who the person you're hiring could be connected to.

You could be getting yourself involved with organized crime or worse—disorganized crime. Catching a sexually transmitted infection would be small potatoes compared to what did happen and what could have happened to this guy.

As I was reading back over this, I wondered if I should have gone into this much detail. But admit it—you read it because you wanted to find out what happened, didn't you?

The highest level of the prostitution hierarchy is the call girl. This is a woman who works on her own and makes appointments by phone. It may take a number of years to build up a large enough clientele to make a living at this, so call girls often have other part-time jobs to stay on the tax rolls and not arouse suspicion. They often see clients not just to survive financially, but to raise their standard of living. They may get referrals from clients or from other call girls. They don't have to split their earnings with anyone else.

The safety of being with a call girl or being a call girl is questionable. Many of them use condoms with some clients not others.

The relationship between many call girls and their clients often evolves over time so that the client doesn't directly pay the woman for sex. Instead he may pay monthly or do direct deposit. At this point the woman achieves more of a mistress status and moves up out of the per-hour ghetto. If neighbors get suspicious, call girls can often successfully pass themselves off as young horny fun-loving women who have a lot of boyfriends.

Here's a weird story about one of the dangers of being a call girl that you might not think about. I had an acquaintance who worked at a newspaper and also saw clients on the side. She had a girlfriend who would drive down from Bakersfield to L.A. once a week for a couple of days to work out of her house.

The girlfriend was scheduled to see an elderly man she had never met before. He walked into the house and asked to use the bathroom. When he didn't come out for a few minutes she got worried and looked in on him and he was dead! What was she going to do?

She called her friend who rushed home from work and they decided to prop him up on the couch and pretend he had died there. They called the police and told them that the man was wandering around the apartment complex looking confused and they asked him if he wanted to come in and sit down. They went to get him a glass of water and when they came back he was dead.

Whether the police bought this story I have no idea. But it's something to consider if you are working as a call girl or even having an extramarital affair with someone who is older. What if they dropped dead during sex? How would you explain that?

A wealthy client may want to see a call girl exclusively and pay a fair price. This type of relationship is quite common in Europe among older upscale married men with families. In the United States this lifestyle is less well-accepted. I remember seeing a newspaper photo of the funeral of a man who had been president of France. I forget which one. The photo, taken at the cemetery, showed two tearful older women embracing each other. They were his wife and his mistress.

Some people understand the word "courtesan" to be synonymous with a prostitute but that's not the case. Courtesans, who existed in certain cultural enclaves such as Japan or seventeenth-century Venice, were women who were trained to please men in a number of ways, not just by having sex. For example, the geisha of Japan were trained to sing, dance, perform the tea ceremony, and tell entertaining stories in addition to having sex with select clients. There are no courtesan cultures in the United States today. If someone describes herself as a courtesan, you are most likely going to be paying for sex.

Specialty prostitution refers to women who work as S-M mistresses or dominatrices as described in the chapter on paraphilias. They do not consider themselves prostitutes because they don't have sex with their clients. They don't even touch their clients' genitals. They consider themselves to be entertainers or role-players who act out consensual S-M scenes with clients for money. The clients get sexually turned on for psychological, not physical, reasons because they are not being touched by the woman.

These women are able to charge the most money per hour –five hundred dollars-plus per session. But you have to remember that their overhead is quite high. They must either rent a dungeon or build one in their house. Their leather clothing is custom-made and quite expensive, especially to clean. Any possible physical danger from an S-M encounter comes from the S-M practices such as whipping, not from transmission of body fluids. Again, this was described in detail in a previous chapter.

MOTIVATION

What motivates prostitutes and their clients? From the point of view of the prostitute the motivation is obviously money, but at different levels. For street prostitutes and massage parlor workers the motivation may be subsistence income. Brothel workers and escorts may have higher economic motivations. Call girls may be attempting to raise their social status by eventually winding up with a wealthy sugar daddy.

I've read accounts of prostitutes at the higher levels who like their work. Their attitude is, "If you like money and you like sex, why not combine the two interests?" Some high-end escorts enjoy their work also—getting paid to go to lavish parties.

From the point of view of the customers, the motivation is sex, but it might be more complicated than you would think. There are some men who would never pay for sex. Their pride couldn't handle it. They probably think women should be paying them. On the other extreme, some guys are pretty much sex addicts and drive around in a frenzy picking up street prostitutes all night.

Other men have different motives for paying for sex. Some men only see one woman and pay her because they like that particular woman. Some men like a little variety and so go to a particular house to see if they have someone new working. Other men only see prostitutes when they are out of town, for example, at a convention.

Some men like prostitutes because the act can be anonymous and there is no commitment. Prostitutes will often perform sexual acts that their regular partners won't. Some men are pressured into having sex with prostitutes, for example in Las Vegas or at a bachelor party. A largely overlooked group of prostitution clients are men who can't find mates through what we would consider to be traditional channels. These men might be old, overweight, or have physical, medical, or sexual problems. When I worked as a surrogate partner, we often saw clients such as these, but sex therapy may be beyond the financial reach of many men.

MALE PROSTITUTION

Male prostitution certainly exists. It doesn't have exactly the same hierarchy as female prostitution. There are male street prostitutes and in areas where there are large gay male enclaves you will find gay male-oriented massage parlors and escort services. Customers of male prostitutes are other men, often men who are married and claim to be straight.

I heard this one from a former boyfriend. When I knew him he was sober, but prior to that he was a huge alcoholic and cocaine addict. He went to Las Vegas (add compulsive gambling to his other addictions) and got really drunk and picked up this good-looking woman and took her up to his room. He took his clothes off and she saw what kind of shape he was in and she said, "Listen, honey. I don't think you're going to be able to perform, so why don't you just relax and I'll give you a blow job."

Of course you can see where this is going, even if he couldn't. When he told me this story I was cracking up. "That was a man! You had sex with a man and didn't even know it!" "No it wasn't a man! It was a really good blow job!" "Well, I don't doubt it, but the reason "she" didn't take her clothes off was she was a man!"

Do women ever pay for sex with men? I hope so, because I'm probably going to need someone's services pretty soon! You know, I really don't know. I know a lot of people—a lot of people who have paid for sex and a lot of people who have been paid for sex. Yet the closest thing I've seen to a woman paying for sex was a wife paying a prostitute to have a three-way with her and her husband for his birthday.

The term "gigolo" means a man who is paid for sex by an older wealthy woman. Again, I'm doubtful about this. In economic terms I just don't think there is a demand. I had a discussion about this with a (young male good-looking) student in my class. His point of view was that a man wouldn't be able to perform sexually if the woman was old or unattractive. My point of view was that the woman might be happy with oral and massage. So I asked him, "Would you have sex with a really old woman for money?" and he replied, "How much money?" Ding, ding, ding! Right answer. Sounds like he was already there motivation-wise.

CROSS-CULTURAL VIEW
Finally, I want to say something about prostitution in other

cultures. In some European countries such as the Netherlands and Germany, some of the cities have red light districts and regulated prostitution is allowed. Some countries are basically lawless and using underage kids as sex slaves may be the norm. In some countries in the Caribbean, social structures exist to help local young women meet wealthy men from the U. S., Europe, and Canada. Luxury resorts exist specifically for this purpose. The goal is for the woman to establish a relationship so the man can start supporting the woman's family in these extremely poor countries.

My take on prostitution is that it's extremely dangerous at the lowest levels. As you move higher in social status, some women have been able to keep themselves physically safer by picking and choosing their clients and using condoms. Whether having sex for money is emotionally safe is another question which will be explored in the last chapter.

PORNOGRAPHY

Another form of sex for sale is the distribution of sexually explicit materials. The word "pornography" originally meant either writings about prostitutes or writings by prostitutes. Today it means sexually explicit material that is designed to excite the person who is exposed to it.

Two related concepts are erotica and obscenity. Erotica can also be sexually explicit. It is defined as material that is motivated by artistic impulses. The definition of obscenity is more broad. For something to be obscene it doesn't have to be sexual. Obscenity means that something is lewd, offensive, or disgusting.

Looking at sexually explicit material and getting turned on is one of the safest sexual behaviors you can do, but a lot of people believe it's bad for you. There is no experimental evidence to show that looking at sexually explicit material is harmful in itself. Yet many people believe that it is. That's not true about sexually explicit material that contains violence, especially towards women, or scenes of rape. There have been many studies that have shown negative effects from viewing this violent type of pornography.

When we look at sexually explicit material, there are a number of overarching considerations. The first is that sexually explicit material is protected by the First Amendment to the Constitution—free speech. Nevertheless, people who produce pornography may be prosecuted anyway, and even convicted. Every once in a while a right-wing group goes after a pornographer and that person is tried under federal obscenity laws.

A fairly recent case reported in the Los Angeles Times illustrates this. A federal judge named Alex Kozinski had to recuse himself in the trial of a pornographer, because it turned out the judge had his own personal website with pictures on it that could be construed as pornography. Among these pictures, which the judge described as humorous, were a picture of women on all fours painted like cows, a picture of a man carousing with an aroused farm animal, a picture of a man performing oral sex on himself, and a picture of women in a café with their dresses pulled up to reveal their pubic hair. The women were sitting in front of a poster that said "Bush for President."

So the first judge recused himself and took down his website. The case went to trial with a new judge. The man on trial, Ira Isaacs, who often acted in his own films, defended his work saying it was art. Jurors reviewed the movie in question, which was called "Japanese Doggie Three-Way". Obviously, the jurors weren't buying his defense, as he was found guilty on charges of obscenity. He appealed and was convicted in 2013 after three trials. He was sentenced to prison and was scheduled to be released in 2017.

He is supposedly writing a book about his experiences which is scheduled to be released in 2018, so watch for it.

There is an interesting recent twist to this case. In December of 2017, Judge Alex Kozinski was faced with many complaints of sexual harassment from former clerks. He resigned in the face of these complaints. I'm no legal scholar, but I'm thinking Ira Isaacs would been better off with Kozinski as the judge in his case.

I once got a phone call from an attorney who specialized in First Amendment cases. He was defending a client who made a film about lesbian vaginal fisting. He called me because one of my students worked for him, and the student told him that I had been talking about fisting in class. I told him I was shocked, not because of the vaginal fisting aspect, but because a student actually remembered something I said in class. One of my suggestions was that maybe instead of defending the film based on the First Amendment, he should try to defend it based on the Second Amendment—the right to bear arms. No wonder I don't get called into court as an expert witness and get paid a bunch of money. Be that as it may, whether we like it or not, sexually explicit material is currently protected, with one exception—child pornography.

Child pornography is a special case. Sexually explicit materials containing pictures of real children is illegal and not protected under the First Amendment. It is illegal to make it, sell it, buy it, have it, or store it. Sexually explicit material using computer-generated images of children is protected.

When it comes to talking about pornography, there's also something called the "notion of harm". This is kind of a complicated concept that has to do with the philosophy of criminal justice. At least, I hope I understood this. It's been a long time since I've had to think. The theory is something is bad if it hurts people. This is the general belief that pornography is bad for you, or that it is indirectly harmful. This is true to a certain extent. The people who could be harmed by pornography are adults who are forced into making it through coercion without their consent, children who are forced to make it, or children who are forced to view it in the context of child sexual abuse. In these cases, it's not watching the pornography that is harmful. The harm has to do with the conditions under which the pornography was created or viewed that involved the violation of sexual coercion laws.

Another view of sexually explicit material is a feminist view. Some feminists like sexually explicit material and just wish there was more of it made for the female viewer. However, there is a group of very radical feminists who believe that even if pornography shows consensual sex, it is still degrading to women. Their belief is that women cannot consent to sex and that all heterosexual intercourse is basically rape.

Sexual explicitness and offensiveness are all in the eye of the beholder. There are some conservative individuals who find paintings or statues of nudes to be offensive. (Good thing they haven't seen the plaster cast of my vagina described in a previous chapter). There are some people who would no doubt find the textbook I use in my Human Sexuality class offensive, as it does contain photographic images that are sexually explicit. I used to use a book in my class called "The Guide to Getting It On" by Paul Joannides. One of the reasons a lot of students liked it was it had these graphic cartoon illustrations. I like the book a lot, but I had a couple of students complain about it, ostensibly because they had young children and couldn't have the book lying around their house.

I understand the point of view of parents who want to prevent their kids from viewing sexually explicit images. I mean, I get it. Research shows that if children are going to be exposed to fairly hard-core sexual images, it usually happens between the ages of six and twelve. Unfortunately, research also shows that if children are exposed to sexually explicit material, it's usually by a relative or other acquaintance of the child, and it's usually in the context of a sexual abuse situation. It's quite common for pedophiles to show child porn to potential victims and say, "Wouldn't you like to do this with me?"

I appreciate the desire to protect children, but it's pretty difficult with the increasing trashiness and vulgarity of society. The stuff they say and show on television now is extremely graphic compared to what it was like when I was a kid. And with satellite radio, you could be carpooling the kids to school, turn on the radio, and hear Howard Stern discussing his masturbation habits in detail.

I was staying in a hotel in San Diego and I could hear kids playing in the next room. I had the TV off, but I must have rolled over on the remote, because suddenly the TV came on and I was looking at a scene of a man on his knees in an alley giving a blow job to another man. One remote click! Sure hope the kids in the next room were watching the same thing! I didn't hear any adults in there. Then the scene switched to two guys in bed having anal sex. Good luck protecting your kids, especially since most of them are better at using the Internet than adults are.

A serious issue with pornography is where it is available and especially where it might be available to children. This was addressed in a court ruling in the 1970's that said that obscene material violated community standards. In other words, something was obscene if it would be found to be offensive by the average member of a community.

What constitutes a "community" or an "average member" is

open to discussion. For example, I live near the city of Newport Beach, where residents run the gamut from ultra-wealthy to rowdy all night partying surfers, to homeless people. I don't think these groups have the same taste in sexually explicit material.

I have a funny story about something that happened to me that illustrates the changing nature of community standards. In the 1980's I was in graduate school and we had a seminar on sexuality in which students had to present the material. My topic was a combination of paraphilias and pornography.

At the time, I had an acquaintance whom I've described in a previous chapter—the guy who used to stick sharp objects into his scrotum. I decided to get some magazines to illustrate my talk and I tried to think of the sleaziest adult bookstore in my area (not a problem). I walked in and started looking at the magazines and found a few things I could use—some fetish mags and basic heterosexual porn—but I wasn't finding what I was looking for. So I went up to the counter and said to the cashier, "What I'm really looking for is magazines that show pictures of people piercing their genitals."

The cashier replied, loud enough to be heard in the next city, "Are you kidding? We don't sell any of that disgusting shit in here!" Of course everyone in the store (all men) had to turn around to see what kind of freak asked for something so disgusting they didn't sell it at the sleaziest bookstore in town.

"Well, excuse me! I thought I was in an adult bookstore, but I seem to have stumbled into the Christian Science Reading Room by mistake!'

The point here is not that I'm a schmuck. The point here is that nowadays kids can find "that disgusting shit" in coffee table books or on the Internet with a few clicks. That's how much community standards have changed in thirty-plus years.

Sexually explicit material can be conveyed through several different media. I think that a rule of thumb is that as soon as a new communication medium is invented, the first thing that is produced is something religious and the next thing that is produced is something sexual. Media include the written word, audio materials, for example, recordings of obscene phone calls or recordings of comedians' raunchy performances, still photographs in magazines, and streaming content such as videos and DVD's. All these are available on the Internet, including specialized porn that caters to paraphiliacs.

There have been many attempts to stifle pornography through censorship. In the 1870's Anthony Comstock, a postal inspector, started the New York Society for the Suppression of Vice. He attempted to prevent family planning activist Margaret Sanger and others from sending condoms through the U. S. mail. He was a government agent and right-wing radical. It's still illegal to send sexually explicit materials through the mail if the content is on the outside and can be seen without opening the mail. But it's okay to send sexually explicit material it it's packaged in such a way that the content can't be seen unless the package is opened.

The Hays office, which began enforcement in 1934, was the organization that censored motion pictures. The Hays office got so powerful that at one point movies couldn't show married people going to bed together in the same bed. The successor of the Hays office is the Motion Picture Association of America (MPAA), the organization responsible for rating mainstream movies. They are also quite powerful. Keep in mind that when you see a mainstream movie that has some sex in it and is rated R, this may not be the cut of the movie the director wanted you to see. The MPAA forces movie directors to take out sex scenes or modify them in order to get an R rating.

Even though there is no proof that pornography is harmful, not one but two presidential commissions have been formed to try to show the opposite. In the 1960's, when Johnson was president, he formed the Commission on Obscenity and Pornography. Social scientists were gathered from around the country to look at the possible negative influences of pornography. Here's what they found. The commission could find no association between the use of pornography and sex crimes or anti-social behavior even in convicted and incarcerated sex criminals.

You have to keep in mind that the pornography of the mid-1960's—before the Sexual Revolution—was quite different from the stuff available today and much tamer. What was considered porn back in the day was cheesy eight millimeter movies that showed people having sex with their clothes on, or anthropology documentaries that showed natives dancing around naked. The only thing that was available at the time that even approximates today's porn was pictures of people having sex with animals (bestiality porn). This is probably the oldest form of pornography. As we saw in a previous chapter, bestiality is probably the oldest paraphilia, and is a cultural universal.

As kind of an interesting aside, there were other members of the Commission on Obscenity and Pornography who were appointed by the president but were not social scientists. Two of them were Charles Keating, founder of Lincoln Savings and Loan and architect of a major financial scandal in the 1980's, and Father Bruce Ritter. Charles Keating's original savings and loan building was in Santa Ana and he was incensed that he had to look out his window every day and see the Mitchell Brothers X-rated theater. The only reason I know this is I went to Santa Ana College right across the street.

Bruce Ritter was a priest who founded a charity called Covenant House to help homeless teenagers. In 1996 he was accused of having sexual relations with kids and there were also allegations of illegal financial dealings. He resigned.

In the 1980's another commission to study pornography was formed under President Ronald Reagan. It was called the Meese Commission after Attorney General Edwin Meese. One of the findings of this commission was that in the previous twenty years there was a huge increase in the amount of violent porn. Well, duh. The Sexual Revolution happened. There was a huge increase in every kind of porn. The finding of this commission was that pornography causes sex crimes. Unfortunately this commission failed to differentiate between violent porn and porn with no violence or sexual coercion in it. This conclusion was based on political ideology and not on scientific research. Later research has shown a causal relationship between viewing sexually violent material and aggression. It has not shown a relationship between viewing sexually explicit material with no violence and sexually violent outcomes.

I may have come across as sounding like I think porn is totally harmless. From a physical standpoint it's safe. That may not be the case for emotional safety as we'll see in a future chapter. There are a number of negative things that can be said about porn.

One is that the relationship among porn, fantasy, masturbation, and sexual behavior is different for sexually sadistic serial psychopathic pedophiles than it is for other people. These pedophiles use porn to fuel their fantasies and masturbation and then they molest children, which further fuels their fantasies. The rest of us can usually use porn with no harmful effects.

The use of porn can become addictive. Sometimes people

will spend hundreds or even thousands of dollars a month viewing porn online. This becomes a compulsion. People can't get enough and they keep looking for something new and better. If you're spending a lot of money on pornography, you might want to ask yourself who you are supporting. Distribution of pornography has historically had ties to organized crime. Are you sure the people performing in the movies you like were not coerced?

There are studies that have shown some negative effects of sexually explicit material that doesn't contain violence. Men who view a lot of this stuff tend to get a negative view of their own body and sexual performance, and a negative view of their partner's body and sexual performance. This is true now that many porn stars are quite physically attractive.

This was not always the case. Back in the 1970's, porn stars looked like average people, or worse, especially the men. Back then, the only qualification for being in a porno movie was that you could screw anything that moved (Ron Jeremy, anyone?). Also today the production standards for pornographic movies are much better than they were in the past, as they are for all movies. Plus, porn stars often take performance and endurance-enhancing drugs, making the rest of us feel inadequate.

Many feminists still object to porn. Men who use porn as role models for how to have sex usually learn to have sex in ways that women don't like. The message that is conveyed by most mainstream porn (and by that I mean heterosexual porn but not fetish) is that all women can get turned on by all kinds of sexual acts and this is definitely not true.

Everybody has their own personal tastes, but in general there are differences between male and female responses to porn. It's a cliché, but men do get more turned on in general by visual images. When men view porn they get turned on both physically and psychologically. Women can watch porn and their vaginas may lubricate, but they may state that they are not psychologically turned on or they may even say they find the material distasteful or disgusting and mean it.

Sexually explicit material does have benefits. As I said before, it is physically safe to use. It causes people to have a temporary increase in sexual desire, arousal, and behavior. (That's kind of the point). It is used in sex therapy to desensitize people who have sexual fears and anxiety, and also for sex education.

I've recently read a few opinion pieces that state that pornography is more harmful than previously thought and may be creating a new public health crisis that is fueling the rise in sexual harassment. Interestingly, these articles described research findings, but did not cite their sources, which always makes me suspicious. I'm guessing these authors are fueled by a political ideology as stated above. They may be conflating violent porn with erotica or non-violent sexually explicit material.

In conclusion, viewing violence creates imitation of violence. Viewing sexually explicit material does not appear to cause violent outcomes, although it may have other unintended consequences. Viewing sexually explicit material does make you temporarily horny.

The potential effects of sexually explicit material can be difficult to study. Most studies use college students who (believe it or not) may not have been exposed to porn before, and most studies are correlational, not causal. It's also really difficult to study the possible effects of child porn due to legal strictures.

My opinion is I'm not crazy about porn. To me, it's boring. At least some of the stuff from back in the 1970's had some humor to it. Nevertheless, you can't ignore the fact that you might find something disgusting when you're not aroused, and get turned on by it when you are aroused.

I will not tell any adult to refrain from watching sexually explicit material if they want to. You are an adult and your choice of entertainment is up to you.

In the next and final chapter, I'll talk about values and how to make sexual decisions. Some systems that we use to make sexual decisions turn out to be riskier than others, and some of our motivations for having sex may put us at risk.

CHAPTER 13
MAKING SEXUAL DECISIONS

Is it possible to have a lifestyle in which you have a lot of sex with different people, stay safe, be a good person, and feel good about yourself? I hope so, and I think so.

This chapter will illuminate the process you use to make sexual decisions. I'll cover motivations for having sex and the use of different ethical systems to help you make sexual decisions. This relates to safe sex because some motivations for having sex are more likely to put you at risk.

Sex is never completely safe. You can do your best to stay physically safe by preventing unwanted pregnancy and sexual assault, and protecting yourself from STI's. But emotional safety is another issue. Just because a sexual behavior is physically safe doesn't mean that it's emotionally safe—for you.

Here's an example. As a woman, there's a man to whom you are sexually attracted. You've determined that he does not have an STI and you are using birth control. There's nothing stopping you from having sex with him, but for some reason you are hesitant. You just don't feel safe with him, because you really don't know him. If you were to have sex with him at this point, you probably would not enjoy it as much as you could. This perception of lack of safety might prevent you from getting aroused or having an orgasm.

Does this mean there's something wrong with you? Absolutely not! You may be having conflicting feelings because you think that just because you can have sex with someone you should. This is kind of an unfortunate legacy of the Sexual Revolution that hasn't caught up to a lot of people yet. Your feelings are telling you to hold off but our cultural influences are whispering in your ear, "Why not?" So you are conflicted.

Here's another example. Let's say you're a man. You meet a woman to whom you are attracted. It turns out she's married, and if she started a sexual relationship with you she would lie to her husband about it. You don't feel okay about this situation. What do you do? You get the feeling that most guys would just go for it.

What's upsetting you is the conflict between your feelings of lust for the woman and the sexual ethic that says anything is okay between two consenting adults, plus the remnants of an outdated system that says that a wife is her husband's property. No wonder you're conflicted.

Some people would probably be okay with the situation and dive right in. For other people, having sex with a married person would go against their system of sexual values. In the two scenarios I just described, something about the situation made you feel emotionally unsafe, as if you would in some way feel bad if you chose to have sex.

That's the point. Everybody makes sexual decisions differently. In our culture we have a lot of sexual diversity. Everybody doesn't have sex in the same way. If everybody had sex in the same way, we wouldn't need this book, or for that matter, any books on sexuality, would we?

People make sexual decisions differently because they are using different value systems. That's why we often don't understand sexual decisions that other people make. So many factors go into our sexual decisions—the heat of the moment, hormones, cultural and family background, religious beliefs, education, morality, self-image, emotions, personality, physical and mental health, and so many other factors. Each of us has our unique personal history and experience.

Even people who choose to be celibate are making a sexual decision by default. You can't just say, "Okay, I'm going to shut sex out of my life for good." It's not going to happen. Fantasies will spring into your mind out of nowhere. You may experience orgasms in your sleep. Worst case scenario, the fact that you try to repress your sexuality may cause you to act it out in extreme, disturbing, or illegal situations.

Here are some possible sexual situations/dilemmas with which you might be faced at some point in your life.

- Do I have sex with a particular person, in a particular situation, right now?
- Do I have to be in love to have sex?
- What sexual behaviors am I okay with and what sexual behaviors am I not okay with?
- Which sexual behaviors might I be willing to do if I was really in love with the other person?
- Should I come out as homosexual or bisexual to my family and/or other people?
- Should I give in to sexual pressure?
- Should I be sexually faithful to one partner?
- Should I cover for another person who's having an affair?
- Should I have sex with an ex?
- Should I stay in a relationship with someone who has cheated on me?

Most of us (especially women) would probably not vote for a politician if we didn't like his or her sex life. But how far do you take that? With the current (2017) sexual harassment scandals in Hollywood, would we feel comfortable paying to see a movie that was directed by someone who was accused of sexually harassing multiple women?

There are no right answers to these questions for everybody. There are only the best answers for you. This is just a small number of sexual questions you could confront. One of the roles of sex educators is to help people clarify their value systems. Clients often consult with me because in addition to needing sexual information, they need permission to do certain sexual behaviors.

Sex educators abide by similar ethical codes to therapists and counselors. We don't have sex with our clients, or give them permission to do illegal acts. I recently had a client contact me. He was a man in his late fifties who was unsatisfied in his long-term marriage and wanted to discuss an attraction he had for a much-younger woman (obviously a very common scenario). It was like he was looking for my permission to go for it. Decades ago, I might have said, "Go for it." But instead we looked at the different ramifications of making that decision.

VALUE SYSTEMS

Here are some common value systems that are used to make sexual decisions. A person who uses a legalistic approach to values relies on laws from an external source such as the laws of your community or the rules set down in religious codes. Example—a man says, "I want to have sex with this woman so much that I would force her, but rape is against the law so I won't do it." (Sadly, research has shown that a large percentage of men have admitted they would rape a woman if it wasn't against the law and they knew they wouldn't get caught). The main deterrent here is fear of punishment. Making sexual decisions based on laws does not indicate a very mature or deep level of mental processing.

There's another problem with the legalistic view. People think up potentially problematic sexual behaviors to do before the laws can catch up with them. Take for example the issue of cyberstalking. I'm not even really sure that this is what it's called, but it's where, for example, a man and woman break up and one partner e-mails sexual pictures of the former partner, along with offensive comments about what a slut the person is, etc. I think there was a fairly recent (2017) story in the news about this involving one of the Kardashians (big surprise). This wasn't even against the law years ago because the technology outpaced the legal system. We didn't know whether we should class this under sexual harassment, hate crimes, or even terrorism. Legal steps are underway to clarify these issues. Meanwhile people are being subjected to this terrifying experience that can ruin their status in school and the workforce.

Another example—several years ago a man was arrested in a mall because a woman claimed he was following her around. He was carrying a shoulder bag with a long strap. It turned out he had a video camera in the shoulder bag and was filming up her short skirt.

At the time, this wasn't against the law! A court ruled that people have the right to privacy for the area under their clothes. That ruling didn't hold up. I'm not even sure of the status of this now because it keeps changing. That's why it's important to continually educate yourself about the laws in your area. In my personal value system, it's not okay to video up someone's dress without their consent. But that's me. There are a lot of people who would say, "Hey, if it's not against the law then it's okay."

The same goes for cameras placed in restrooms. You have to figure that if it's a public restroom, there could be cameras. But what about cameras in the restrooms of restaurants? Didn't the singer Chuck Berry get in trouble for that one?

Speaking of recording devices, and this is important with today's phone technology which is changing on a daily basis, do not let anyone take pictures of you naked or while you're having sex. I know it's a sexy idea—when you're in love with somebody it's a turn-on to see them naked or watch yourselves having sex. But you have no idea what the future of your relationship might be or where that footage may end up.

This is not just a problem that developed because of the invention of cell phones and smart phones. This has been a problem since movies were invented. By the way, there is some video footage of me taking a shower in my ex-boyfriend's house circa 1991 that I would really like to have back. If anyone happens to come across this, please return it to me via the post office box on my web site and I'll reimburse you for postage. I think I probably recorded "Pollyanna" or something over it, but I lost track of it.

People do dumb sexual things with phones and phone cameras all the time. Examples are accidentally sending a sexual message meant for your boyfriend to your boss, or accidentally sending a sexual message meant for your girlfriend to your whole office staff. Whoops!

SAFE SEX RULE
No naked or sexual pictures of you on phones, computers, or other electronic equipment ever, unless you're fully prepared for the possible consequences.

Public figures are certainly no exception here. How many of them have gotten caught in recent years sexting inappropriate people? I'm thinking of Anthony Weiner, the former congressman. In 2017 he was ordered to prison for sexting a teenage girl. This was the third time he was caught doing this.

I remember the second time because I was sitting in the gynecologist's office waiting for my appointment. There was a television in the waiting room but the sound was off. The caption read, "Weiner exposed again."

Here's another example of the law not catching up with all of the perverted things people can think of to do. In 2011, a Los Angeles elementary school teacher named Mark Berndt took some pictures to be printed at a photo-developing facility. The photo clerk became suspicious because the photos showed kids about seven or eight years old blindfolded and being fed cookies with a white shiny substance on them. He called the police.

It turned out Berndt had his students playing a "tasting game" in which he put his own semen on cookies and had kids eat the cookies while blindfolded, and took pictures of it! When I tell my students about this case they are appalled. Most of them have never heard of this case even though it happened in L. A.

The point about laws was that Berndt was charged with lewd conduct with children, and that's the best they could do! This behavior was not specifically against the law, because who would think that somebody would ever do this?

In 2013 Berndt pleaded no contest to the charges against him and was sentenced to twenty-five years in prison. He was sixty-two years old at the time. This case resulted in one hundred and forty million dollars' worth of lawsuits for the Los Angeles School District.

I'm sure there were a lot of people who would like to cheerfully kill this guy—pretty much everybody who was affected, which includes the kids, the parents and the other teachers. LAUSD had major financial problems before this happened. I'll say a little more about this case later as an example of another value system.

Another approach to values is situation ethics. This approach is more flexible and you are guided by the perceived greater good rather than the letter of the law. In this approach, sexual decisions depend on many contextual factors, not just the existence of laws.

Here's an example. I'm paraphrasing this from the work of psychologist Lawrence Kohlberg, who did pioneering work on moral dilemmas. What if you believed that selling your body for money was wrong? But what if prostitution was the only way to earn the money you would need to pay for expensive medical treatment for your child who would die without it?

Here's another example that is probably closer to home for most people. Many people believe that abortion is morally wrong. And yet if they found themselves with an unwanted pregnancy, they might choose an abortion even if it goes against some aspect of their personal moral sense. So the situation ethics approach is more of a lesser-of-the-two-evils approach.

The problem with the situation ethics approach is that everybody doesn't have the same well-developed moral sense based on teaching and experience. As Kohlberg pointed out many years ago, some people get stuck at a lower moral level and have trouble making complicated decisions that aren't dictated by an outside source.

Ethical and cultural relativism state that there is no single correct moral view. What to do is internally derived from your own conscience. This approach also implies that our own culture has a significant influence on our sexual decisions. What is okay in our own culture may not be okay in another. An example of this is that in some cultural groups female circumcision is not only okay but is accepted and/or required, whereas in other cultures these practices are considered abominable.

I think you can see the biggest problem with ethical relativism. Not everybody has a conscience, and not everybody's conscience or superego has developed to the same degree. Conscience usually develops in childhood as a result of teaching and/or punishment by parents and some kids don't get that. Also, some people called psychopaths or people with anti-social personality disorder don't seem to really have a conscience or any kind of internal ethical mechanism. They are incapable of feeling empathy for others.

Some people base their sexual decisions on the philosophy of hedonism—the pursuit of pleasure for its own sake. In other words, if it feels good, do it. And if it feels really good, do it more than once! This value system became very popular during the Sexual Revolution of the late 1960's and early 1970's as a reaction to the strict morality of the previous era, as well as the existence of social factors such as mistrust of authority, the women's rights movement, the civil rights movement, the development of the birth control pill, and sex research.

Conversely, if it doesn't feel good, don't do it. A hedonistic decision-making orientation can have a profound effect on safe sex practices or lack of them, because hedonists are likely to live in the moment and not be concerned about future consequences.

The danger of a lifetime of sexual hedonism in the past was incurable STI's. That's still a concern with herpes, HIV, HPV, and AIDS. Another more subtle danger of a long-term hedonistic lifestyle is you start to become compulsive about sex and end up seeming kind of pathetic (Hugh Hefner?).

I had a hedonistic orientation for many years. For hedonists sex is not a moral issue. I did things sexually that other people found questionable to say the least. It's not like I changed my attitude and behavior just because I got older (and more tired) and had trouble getting laid. That's part of it. But some things that worked for you in your twenties, thirties, forties and fifties and even beyond that, may not work for you now.

One of the most famous sexual hedonists in history was Giacomo Casanova. His name is synonymous with sexual hedonism, mainly because he wrote a ten-volume memoir in which he detailed many of his conquests. Most people think that his name is synonymous with having sex with a lot of people, but in fact his memoirs only describe one hundred and thirty two partners. (Only, right?) Of course that included men, nuns, and possibly his own daughter. That's fewer partners than have been claimed by many modern celebrities.

What made him a hedonist was his approach to sex, not the number of partners. He gloried in every aspect of the sensuality and seduction. He says something in his memoirs that is very telling. I'm paraphrasing. He says something like, "I know I've had sex with a lot of people and I was judged for that, but as far as I know no one got hurt and I never forced anyone to have sex." At the end of his life when he was through with sex, at least with other people, he became a writer and librarian. Hmmm.

Some people use feelings other than pleasure to make sexual decisions. This would be going with your gut. If the thought of a certain person or a certain sexual behavior makes you anxious or queasy, that's a sign that you should step back and take another look at what you're planning to do.

The opposite of hedonism is sexual asceticism, or celibacy or self-denial. Some people decide not to have sex at all for various reasons. In some cases people make this celibacy decision for religious reasons. I find this problematic because I grew up in the Catholic Church where priests take a vow not to have sex with women. Many of the men who take this vow have never had sex with a woman, so they don't really know what they are promising. They are making this promise from a position of weakness, not strength, and a position of ignorance, not knowledge. Many of the priests I knew when I was a kid in Catholic school had been in the seminary since they were about twelve years old. I know I wouldn't want to be held to a sexual decision I made when I was twelve. I don't think I'd want to be held to a sexual decision I made yesterday, for that matter. And we've seen that in many cases the promises of these priests along with other factors set the stage for the ongoing sex scandals in the Catholic Church.

Several years ago I met this interesting guy. I was teaching at the University of California, Irvine. I only taught there for one quarter because when I got the job, I didn't ask how much it paid (stupid), and it was the lousiest-paying job I ever had in my life. Anyway, I was walking around campus before my class, and they had a lot of tents with people selling stuff. I will say that their campus had the best shopping, but that really doesn't make up for the crummy salaries. There was this booth with really pretty sensual wall hangings from Tibet and I started talking to the guy who sold them. He was maybe in his thirties. He told me that from age fifteen to twenty-five he lived in Tibet and was celibate. Then he returned to the U. S. and started having sex. We had a really interesting conversation about his reasons for that temporary decision. I left thinking that I had probably been celibate from the fifteenth to the twenty-fifth of a month once, but I can't remember when that was. And that wall hanging looks awesome in my bedroom!

Another value system is utilitarianism. It's a little bit more complicated than some of the other systems. It's based on the philosophical approach of Jeremy Bentham.

Utilitarianism says that behavior is ethical when it does the greatest good and causes the least harm. This approach says that when you are making sexual decisions you have to look at possible third-party effects. You may think that the only people who are affected by your behavior are you and your partner but there might be others who are affected.

One way of saying this is asking who the stakeholders are. You might be surprised how your personal behavior has the potential to affect other people. Another way of saying this is, "Who's got a dog in this race?"

Here's an example. You and your partner decide to have a baby even though you both know that you are unable to support a family and that other family members or taxpayers will end up supporting you.

Or how about this one? If you and a co-worker are alone in the office at night and the two of you decide to have consensual sex, no one cares, right? You're probably correct—no one cares. However, if you are the President of the United States, and you have sex with someone who works for you after hours in a hallway in the White House, and people find out about it, look out! What happens? I think we all know the answer to that one. The country becomes a laughingstock, among other things. If you think there's any chance that you will become a public figure in the future, you need to be really careful about what you do sexually, as those actions could come back to haunt you.

Look at the above case in which the teacher fed semen-laced cookies to his students. The school district had to completely shut down the entire school and reopen it later with all new employees, disrupting the lives of literally thousands of people. All because one guy was a pervert and made poor sexual decisions.

The problem with utilitarianism is it's impossible to identify all of the potential ramifications of your sexual behavior. You would have to be trained as an ethicist to even begin to do it.

Another ethical system is rationalism. In this system you make decisions based on knowledge, logic, facts, and intellect rather than emotions or faith. The problem with this system is that at any given time the state of scientific knowledge is what it is.

Here are some examples.
- In the early 1900's, a treatment for impotence was to insert a heated or irradiated rod into the penis.
- In the 1960's, there was a case in Canada in which a doctor performed a circumcision on a sixteen-month-old boy named David Reimer which destroyed his penis. His parents consulted with Dr. John Money at Johns Hopkins University in Maryland, who at the time was the leading expert in gender roles. Dr. Money advised David's parents to raise him as a girl. The upshot of this is detailed in David's book "How Nature Made Him". He eventually committed suicide. I described this case in more detail in a previous chapter.
- In the 1960's and 1970's, sexual researchers including Masters and Johnson believed that you could change a person's sexual orientation.
- When HIV and AIDS were first identified in the early to mid-1980's, epidemiologists predicted that at the frequency with which it was spreading in the population, pretty much everybody in the U. S. would be infected by the year 2010. That didn't happen. Why not? Because new drugs were developed and people changed their behavior.

That's the point. Scientific discovery is going on all the time and so it is difficult for us to know the most rational course of action.

Part of a rationalistic decision-making system is using a cost/benefit analysis. To do this you put two possible choices at the top of columns. Then you list all the possible costs and benefits you can think of that would accrue to each decision.

When people make sexual decisions they often aren't using their heads. They're thinking with their genitals. Sometimes taking the time to do a cost/benefit analysis can be worth it to influence you to brainstorm and come up with new ideas.

Here's an example. Let's say you're trying to decide which type of contraceptive to use. You think, "Well, the pill is the best." That's what you heard from your friends. But it may not be the best for you. You may not be able to tolerate the side effects. Or, if you're having sex only once a month or less, condoms and spermicide may be a better option.

Factors that we use to make sexual decisions include experiential factors, biological/medical factors, financial factors, legal factor, and moral factors, among others. You can combine any of the above value systems. For example, you could use hedonism tempered by rationalism. See if you can state your sexual philosophy in one sentence. For some people, it's "If it feels good, do it", as we've seen. For others it might be that anything is okay as long as it's between consenting adults and doesn't draw blood. Or, anything is okay as long as it doesn't make so much noise that it wakes up the dogs and horses.

You will have to decide on your own limits, if any. No married people? No same sex people? No kinky stuff? It's okay to try anything once to see if I like it?

Are any of these systems inherently safer than others? I believe so. For example, I think that hedonism as a lifestyle choice is more dangerous than some of the other systems, whereas people who choose celibacy are safer during the period when they are celibate. People who adhere to the strict letter of the law may be safer, but may feel as if they are missing out on something.

MOTIVATIONS FOR SEX

People don't have the same motivations for sexual behavior including intercourse. Different motivations are not bad or wrong; however, certain motivations can result in sexual behavior that is safer.

Many of us have this sexual script that says we are attracted to a person, we fall in love with that person, and have sex. To put a heterosexual spin on it, it's boy meets girl, boy falls for girl, boy has sex with girl, and they live happily ever after. Where did we learn this? Let's face it, all of us saw this script in the movies when we were growing up. But it doesn't always work this way. This script is outdated, and people often have sex for reasons some of us might consider unusual to say the least.

Motivations for sex can be divided along gender lines. When asked about motivations for intercourse, many men will say, "I had sex with that woman because I was horny." Women are more likely than men to cite a motivation of being in love with the other person. You can easily see that these two motivations could conflict and result in the kind of "he said/she said" scenario that characterizes acquaintance rape.

Here are some other motivations for sex—
- curiosity
- to show how great I am sexually
- to assert control over my partner
- to affirm my attractiveness

- it's a compulsion—I can't help myself
- to make money

And the list goes on.

Some people are able to work as prostitutes and stay emotionally safe. They are able to compartmentalize to the point that they see their sexual encounters as business transactions rather than sexual acts. Not all of us are able to do this. It's natural to develop feelings for people you have sex with—this is especially true for women and especially true if you have orgasms with the partner. This has to do with the way our brains are set up.

Is it emotionally safe to use porn? Again, some people can successfully compartmentalize and the use of porn does not have an impact on their intimate relationships. However, in most cases, compulsive use of pornography by one person in a relationship ruins intimacy. It's kind of a cliché that most guys use porn and either view it secretly online or keep a private stash of it. As a woman, I would feel a bit uncomfortable knowing that my partner had a stash of, for example, anal-themed porn and was keeping it a secret from me. I'd wonder whether he was having fantasies about anal while we were having vaginal intercourse and that would distract me and prevent me from being in the moment.

Sometimes people engage in very off-script sexual interactions guided by unusual sexual motivations. People sometimes agree to have sex even when they don't want to. And that's not just women; men do it too. The thinking here is reciprocity in a long term relationship—"If I agree to this now the next time I want it and he doesn't he'll owe me one." Sometimes you just have to take one for the team. But that's only in long-term relationships where a sense of equity has been worked out. Sometimes people say no to sex when they really want it. What's up with that? Game-playing? Playing hard to get? Maybe.

Ever heard of a mercy fuck or a revenge fuck? Those are certainly some questionable motives for having sex.

Teenagers especially are likely to give in to the type of pressure of—"If I don't agree to have sex with him, he'll end the relationship and find someone who will have sex." This leads teenage girls to have sex without protection. Please recognize this for the sexual coercion that it is.

Have you ever heard of the Greek play "Lysistrata"? In this play the Athenian women are so upset about the war with Sparta that they agree to stop having sex with their husbands until the men put an end to the war.

There's another motivation for sex. I'm not sure what to call it. It's having sex to get the other person to leave you alone and stop pestering you for sex. The thinking is, "I could keep saying no and this guy will never leave me alone. But if I go along with it once, I'll never hear from him again." This is also problematic because it guarantees that the person who is pressuring you will go on to pressure other women. I think that's what happened in the Hollywood sexual harassment scandals. Everybody was afraid to lose their job so no one came forward and perpetrators continued to harass hundreds of women over decades.

Another way to look at the motivations for having sex is from the perspective of intrinsic versus extrinsic motivation. Intrinsic motivation means the person is motivated by something inside the self, most likely your personality. Extrinsic motivation means you do something because of factors outside yourself, such as external rewards.

I don't know whether sex resulting from intrinsic versus extrinsic motivation is essentially safer. I think you could make a case for either one. For example, people who are intrinsically motivated by sex are called erotophiles—they like everything about sex. This could cause you to make poor sexual decisions.

On the other hand, people who are extrinsically motivated might be more likely to give in to sexual pressure from sources outside the self. This also could result in unsafe sex.

It's also important to consider motivation when trying to decide whether to label something as sexual coercion or as a paraphilia. The recent sexual harassment scandals in the entertainment industry illustrate this. If a powerful man exposes his genitals to an aspiring actress, what is his motivation? Is it to get power or control over the victim? In that case, it's sexual coercion. Or is he a frotteurist—someone who gets sexually turned on by rubbing up against or groping an unwilling victim? In that case, he would be considered to have a paraphilia and we would believe that he has a compulsion and can't control himself. The importance here is the implication for how this offender might be treated in a clinical and legal sense.

A lot of people put off making active sexual decisions. Instead, they go along with the path of least resistance—staying with partners or spouses when they really don't want to rather than rocking the boat.

INDIVIDUAL VALUES

Analysis of whether a sexual motivation is healthy requires us to look at individual values such as respect, trust, and honesty. Someone who tries to sexually coerce you does not respect you. Many people, especially women, find it difficult or impossible to agree to sex and enjoy it if they don't fully trust the other person, and achieving that level of trust may require experience.

I consider honesty a core value when it comes to sex. I've got no use for people who lie to me about their sex life. Lying about anything (previous partners, STI's, extramarital sex) does not give your partner a chance to make an informed decision about whether to stay with you or not.

Some of the biggest offenders in this dishonesty category are men who are married to women or are in supposedly monogamous relationships with women. The men then go out and have sex with other men, sometimes in a semi-private situation such as a gay sex club, or sometimes in a public situation such as a restroom. These men don't consider themselves gay. Yet they are placing their partners and their families at risk.

This situation actually happened to a close friend of mine. She met her future husband in college but after several years of marriage and two kids they broke up. She hacked into his e-mail and phone accounts and found out he had been having sex with men since before they were married. Here's the point—she had no clue! Absolutely none.

It's one thing if you tell a prospective partner, "Hey, there's something you should know. Once in a while I like to get a blow job from a guy I don't know in a public bathroom." At least you were honest and gave your partner a chance to make an informed decision.

When you start a sexual relationship with somebody that might turn out to be long-term and monogamous, it's important to have frequent discussions so everybody stays on the same page. Don't assume that your partner intends to be monogamous. Making sexual agreements with your partner is an extremely important aspect of safe sex. It's a whole lot more important than writing some vague wedding vows. How many times have I heard, "I just assumed he would never fuck around on me" or "I just assumed that she didn't have an STI" or "I just assumed my best friend was off limits."? Too many times, and that's just in my own extended family. I don't say honesty is the cure for all sexual problems or that being totally honest will guarantee that your sex will always be safe. But I think it's the best value that we have.

Part of sexual honesty is finding a medical doctor you can confide in. I have heard of many cases of patients who lied to their doctors about their sexual practices and therefore the doctors were not able to provide adequate treatment because they didn't know the whole truth.

NEW SEXUAL POSITIONS

There are a few new sexual positions I would like you to try. The first is a position of knowledge rather than ignorance. Learn all you can about sexuality, especially practices that might be risky. In addition to this you need to be legally and culturally aware. Find out the laws governing sexual expression in your geographical area. Many people who embark on a sexual relationship know very little about sexuality, which to me is scandalous in this day and age.

Another sexual position is a position of strength rather than weakness. Try as best you can to know your own values. Part of being strong sexually is to make sure your sexual choices don't harm another person. Another part of sexual strength is being strong enough to say no when a sexual invitation violates your values.

A third sexual position is a position of love rather than fear. People who are erotophilic love sex and everything about it. People who are erotophobes pretty much say no to everything sexual because they are afraid of sex. Most of us fall somewhere in between.

We can't always expect to find a sexual partner we love. If

you do, you're lucky. But even if you don't, you can still go into a sexual interaction with good intentions and caring for the other person.

An example of having sex out of fear is people who have sexual compulsions. They do sexual behaviors, whether they are considered normal such as masturbation, or unusual, such as sex with animals, because they become anxious if they don't do the behavior. Thus, they are operating out of a fear motive.

UNSAFE SEX

In this book, I've written about many sexual behaviors that are inherently unsafe, such as sticking foreign objects into your urethra, or drinking the contents of someone's intestines. You have to put this in a cross-cultural perspective. There are some countries and societies in which sexual behaviors we take for granted are forbidden. For example, in cultures in which Islam is the primary religion, pornography and alcohol are not allowed, and there may be extreme physical punishment including death for sexual transgressions. In some cultural enclaves, if a woman has premarital sex or is raped, male members of her family may be justified in killing her for bringing dishonor on the family.

In other cultural groups, women can be forced to marry a man who rapes them. In other groups, during tribal warfare young girls may be raped so brutally that they die or suffer so much damage to their internal organs that they can't get pregnant. Other girls who are raped and become pregnant may suffer fistulas during delivery. These are openings between the bladder or bowel and the vagina. In many cases health care is unavailable and the consequence is that these girls uncontrollably leak urine and/or feces from their vaginas, making them social pariahs.

These facts kind of put a whole different face on safe versus unsafe sex, don't they?

We've finally come to the end. Any one of these chapters could have been a book in itself. There are many topics that are normally taught in Human Sexuality classes that I did not include in this book. Some of these include attraction and love, sexual orientation, and gender issues. I did not include them because they had no direct bearing on safe sex. Maybe in the next book!

When I teach my class and I get to the end of the semester, I always think I should leave the class with a bang—some really important insights. And I can never figure out how to do it. My students usually feel like they have been left hanging. I'll leave you with one final thought.

I think the most basic safe sex rule is the following—Never have sex with someone crazier than yourself! Easier said than done!

Class dismissed!

AUTHOR BIOGRAPHY

Dr. Barbara Keesling has a Ph.D. in Health Psychology from the University of California. She has worked in the field of sexuality in various capacities since 1980. She has taught sexuality and other Psychology subjects at several California universities.

She is the author of thirteen books on sexuality, including *Sexual Healing, How to Make Love All Night*, and *The Good Girl's Guide to Bad Girl Sex*.

She has appeared on many television shows including Geraldo, Montel, and Real Personal. She has also been a guest on hundreds of radio shows. In 1998 she produced and hosted her own radio show—Sexual Healing, on KUCI-FM. Her work has appeared in *Cosmopolitan, Playboy, Psychology Today, Men's Health*, and *Marie Claire*, among many other publications.

Currently, Dr. Keesling is semi-retired and teaches Human Sexuality and Abnormal Psychology at California State University, Fullerton. She is a member of the American Association of Sex Educators, Counselors, and Therapists (AASECT). She has thousands of hours of education and teaching experience in sexuality. She currently has a private practice as a sex educator and can be reached through her website at www. masteryourjohnson.com.

Dr. Keesling lives in Southern California, where she enjoys cycling, kayaking, and stand-up paddling.

SELECTED REFERENCES

NOTE ABOUT REFERENCES:
I have tried my best to list these references according to the style of American Psychological Association standards. In some cases this was not possible because not enough information was available. Most journal articles now have a doi—a digital object identifier. I have not included those. I find it easier to access articles by author's name or subject. In many cases I include only one reference on a particular subject, for example, "Objects removed from the rectums of emergency room patients". You can research this stuff as easily as I can. If there is a subject you would like to learn more about, no doubt you will find tons of articles on it. Just Google "Penis accidents" or "Foreign objects in urethra" or whatever. This is such an improvement over when I went to graduate school thirty years ago. We had to look this stuff up in giant index books. Then, only librarians had access to the data bases. Now, you can do all this yourself! The Internet is updated constantly. If you are interested in any of the more obscure books that are listed below, you could look them up through the publisher.

Aerts, L., Rubin, R. S., Winter, A. G., & Goldstein, I. (2017). Prevalence of clitoral adhesions in a sexual medicine practice: Retrospective vulvoscopy review. *The journal of sexual medicine 14*(6), 360-361.

Agnew, J. (1986). Hazards associated with anal erotic activity. *Archives of sexual behavior 15*(4), 307-314.

Annon, J. (1976). *Behavioral treatment of sexual problems: Brief therapy*. Hagerstown, MD: Harper& Row, Publishers.

Anonymous. (1989). *Modern primitives*. San Francisco, CA: Re-Search Publications.

Brame, G. G., Brame, W. D., & Jacobs, J. (1993). *Different loving: An exploration of the world of sexual dominance and submission*. New York, NY: Villard Books.

Chan, G., Mamut, A., Tatzel, S., & Welk, B. (2016). An unusual case of polyembolokoilamania: Urethral avulsion from foreign object use during sexual gratification. *Canadian urological association 10*(5-6), E181-E183.

Colapinto, J. (2000). *As nature made him: The boy who was raised as a girl*. New York, NY: HarperCollins Publishers.

Dean, K., & Malamuth, N. (1997). Characteristics of men who aggress sexually: Risk and moderating factors. *Journal of personality and social psychology 72*(2), 449-455.

DeMaria, L., Flores, M., Hirth, J., & Berenson, A. (2014). Complications related to pubic hair removal. *American journal of obstetrics and gynecology, 210*(6), 528-534.

Dzokoto, V. A., & Adams, G. (2005). Understanding genital-shrinking epidemics in West Africa: Koro, juju, or mass psychogenic illness? *Culture, medicine, and psychiatry 29*, 53-78.

Easton, D., & Liszt, C. A. (1997). *The ethical slut: A guide to infinite sexual possibilities*. San Francisco, CA: Greenery Press.

Elias, J. E., Bullough, V. L., Elias, V., & Brewer, G. (Eds.). (1998). *Prostitution: On whores, hustlers, and johns*. Amherst, NY: Prometheus Books.

Elias, J., Elias, V. D., Bullough, V. L., Brewer, G., Douglas, J. J., & Jarvis, W. (Eds.). (1999). *Porn 101: Eroticism, pornography, and the first amendment*. Amherst, NY: Prometheus Books.

Ford, C. S., & Beach, F. A. (1951). *Patterns of sexual behavior*. Harper & Brothers, Publishers.

Gates, K. (2000). *Deviant desires: Incredibly strange sex*. New York, NY: Juno Books.

Graber, B., & Kline-Graber, G. (1979). Clitoral foreskin adhesions and female sexual function. *Journal of sex research 15*(3), 205-212.

Hartsuiker, D. (1993). *Sadhus: India's mystic holy men*. Rochester, VT: Inner Traditions International.

Herrman, B. (1991). *Trust: The hand book*. San Francisco, CA: Alamo Square Press.

Hock, R. (2016). *Human sexuality*. Boston: Pearson Education, Inc.

Joannides, P. (2017). *Guide to getting it on unzipped!* OR: Goofy Foot Press.

Kaysen, S. (2001). *The camera my mother gave me*. New York, NY: Alfred A. Knopf.

Kinsey, A. C., Pomeroy, W. B., & Martin, C. E. (1948). *Sexual behavior in the human male*. Philadelphia: Saunders.

Kinsey, A. C., Pomeroy, W., Martin, C., & Gebhard, P. (1953). *Sexual behavior in the human female*. Philadelphia: Saunders.

Koops, E., Janssen, W. Anders, S., & Puschel, K. (2005). Unusual phenomenology of autoerotic fatalities. *Forensic science international, 147S*, S65-S67.

Krafft-Ebing, R. (1965). *Psychopathia sexualis: A medico-forensic study.* New York, NY: G. P. Putnam's Sons. (Originally published in 1886).

Love, B. (1992). *The encyclopedia of unusual sex practices.* Fort Lee, NJ: Barricade Books.

Masters, W. H., & Johnson, V. E. (1966). *Human sexual response.* Boston: Little, Brown.

Messineo, A., Innocenti, M., Gelli, R., Pancani, S., Lo Piccolo, R., & Martin, A. (2006). Multidisciplinary surgical approach to a surviving infant with sirenomelia. *American academy of pediatrics* (no page numbers given).

Miletski, H. (2002). *Understanding bestiality and zoophilia.* Bethesda, MD: Hani Miletski.

Mire, S. (2011). *The girl with three legs.* Chicago, IL: Lawrence Hill Books.

Morin, J. (1998). *Anal pleasure & health: A guide for men and women.* San Francisco, CA: Down There Press.

Moser. C. (1999). *Health care without shame: A handbook for the sexually diverse and their caregivers.* San Francisco, CA: Greenery Press.

Moulton, L., & Jernigan, A. (2017). Management of retained genital piercings: A case report and review. *Case reports in obstetrics and gynecology* (no page numbers given).

Nugteren, H. M., Balkema, G. T., Pascal, A. L., Weijmar Schultz, W. C. M., Nijman, J. M., & Van Driel, M. F. (2010). Penile enlargement: From medication to surgery. *Journal of sex and marital therapy 36,* 118-123.

Romics, M., Romics, I., Kopa, Z., & Nyirady, P. (2016). Self-inflicted foreign objects in the urethra: Case collection and review. *Journal of sexual medicine 13*, 5163.

Reuben D. (1999). *Everything you always wanted to know about sex but were afraid to ask.* New York, NY: HarperCollins Publishers.

Sauvageau, A. (2014). Current reports on autoerotic deaths: Five persistent myths. *Current psychiatry reports, 16* (no page numbers given).

Sauvageau, A., & Racette, S. (2006). Autoerotic deaths in the literature from 1954 to 2004: A review. *Journal of forensic sciences 51*(1), 140-146.

Savage, D. (2013). *American savage.* New York, NY: Penguin.

Schwartz, P. (2007). *Prime: Adventures and advice on sex, love, and the sensual years.* New York, NY: HarperCollinsPublishers.

Spitznagel, E. (2016). How not to snap, crush, or otherwise mangle your privates. *Men's health, 31* (9), 130-133.

Stewart, E. G. (2002). *The V book: A Doctor's guide to complete vulvovaginal health.* New York, NY: Bantam Books.

Wallace, I., Wallace, A., Wallechinsky, D., & Wallace, S. (1981). *The intimate sex lives of famous people.* New York, NY: Delacorte Press.

Winchester, S. (1998). *The professor and the madman.* New York, NY: HarperCollins Publishers.

Zacks, R. (1994). *History laid bare.* New York, NY: HarperCollins Publishers.

www.ingramcontent.com/pod-product-compliance
Lightning Source LLC
LaVergne TN
LVHW041248080426
835510LV00009B/633